Anne Llewellyn Barstow's *Witchcraze*

"Serious scholarship and accessible style combine here for fascinating reading and for an important contribution to the history of women (and men). This may well be the first—and best—work to dare view The Burning Time through unashamedly feminist, and truthful, eyes."

—Robin Morgan

"[Barstow's] writing is elegant, even when unsettling. . . . *Witchcraze* zeros in on a profound tragedy, not just of women who were murdered senselessly, but also of the gradual eradication of a vital female culture over these two centuries."

—*San Francisco Chronicle Review*

"Anne Llewellyn Barstow has thought long and hard about witchcraft. To *Witchcraze* she brings a rich historical understanding of Europe during the period of the persecution of witches. . . . The book is a goldmine of information."

—*Ms.*

"Barstow's careful and committed scholarship gives us a new and important geography of this woman-hating persecution. She recognizes the sadism and terror of the witch hunts while scrutinizing the economic and sociological dynamics that may have been crucial factors in the murders. Surely we must know what happened to these women and why. *Witchcraze* brings us closer to the truth."

—Andrea Dworkin, author of *Intercourse*

"This is a powerful book. . . . Focusing on gender and the power relations of the accusers and accused, Barstow reveals the horrifying violence against women committed in the name of religion and social order. . . . She contributes a crucial perspective to awareness of the male fear and hatred of women in early modern societies. In our own time, in which violence against women is epidemic, Barstow's book encourages unblinking investigation of the roots of sexual violence wherever it occurs."

—Margaret R. Miles, Harvard University;
author of *Carnal Knowing*

"Thought-provoking. . . . Barstow describes in gripping detail the sexual torture and psychological abuse these women endured."

—*New York Times Book Review*

"*Witchcraze* is a landmark work of feminist scholarship, exactly the sound, dispassionate, and thorough research which has been so needed on this subject of so much importance to women. Every Witch and every woman should read this book!"

—Starhawk, author of *The Spiral Dance*
and *The Fifth Sacred Thing*

"To me, witches have always been uppity women who had to be got rid of. What I, not a historian, have learned here is what none of the studies of witches prior to this one has demonstrated: the gendered nature of the historical witch hunts, and the unchanging urgency to find women who threatened patriarchal hegemony punishable by death, so that all women can be kept securely within the patriarchal order."

—Carolyn G. Heilbrun, author of *Writing a Woman's Life* and *Reinventing Womanhood*

"This monumental work on the European witch hunts is the most comprehensive history to date. The legacy of the witchburnings and torture documented by Barstow sheds much light on the gender-based violence and sexual exploitation of women that continues today."

—Janice G. Raymond, University of Massachusetts, Amherst; author of *Women As Wombs*

"Anne Barstow's measured indictment of appalling violence against women in the medieval and early modern period sets off alarm bells about its continuance into our times. Her remarkable book should be read by all those concerned with civil rights and the history of oppression."

—Jocelyn Harris, University of Otago, New Zealand; author of *Jane Austen's Art of Memory*

Witchcraze

Witchcraze

A New History of the European Witch Hunts

Anne Llewellyn Barstow

HarperOne
An Imprint of HarperCollins*Publishers*

HarperOne

Illustration for chapters 1, 4, 5, 6, and 8 courtesy of Dover Pictorial Archive Series. From Ernst and Johanna Lehner, eds. *Picture Book of Devils, Demons, and Witchcraft* (New York: Dover Publications, Inc., 1971).

FIRST HARPERCOLLINS PAPERBACK EDITION PUBLISHED IN 1995

Library of Congress Cataloging-in-Publication Data:
Barstow, Anne Llewellyn.
Witchcraze : a new history of the European witch hunts / Anne Llewellyn Barstow
p. cm.
Includes bibliographical references and index.
ISBN 978–0–06–251036–5
1. Witchcraft—Europe—History. I. Title.
BF1584.E9B27 1994
133.4'.3'094—dc20 92–56410

HB 02.07.2023

For those who did not survive

Contents

Acknowledgments

FIRST I MUST THANK the staffs of the libraries and rare book collections that enabled me to complete this research: the staffs of the Witchcraft Collection at Cornell University, the Henry C. Lea Collection at the University of Pennsylvania, the New York Public Library, the Library of Union Theological Seminary, and the Houghton Library of Harvard University. Special thanks go to Seth Kasten, Reference Librarian at Union Theological Seminary, and to the Inter-Library Loan staff of SUNY College at Old Westbury.

The following scholars have generously shared information and ideas with me: Walter Wink, Jape Spaanes, Dorothee Sölle, Dana Greene, Ann Hill Boeuf, Jeffrey Merrick, Brian P. Levack, Allison Coudert, Sigrid Brauner, and John Russell-Wood. The Feminist Scholars in Religion group of New York City discussed an early draft of the Introduction and gave me welcome encouragement. Sumi Ishvarwaren, Corinne Scott, and the New Dawn Collective of Bangalore, India, provided important comparative material on witchcraft in India. And Elisabeth Schüssler Fiorenza provided hospitality while I used the Harvard Library.

In the early stages of this work I was much helped by Anita Berkowitz, my research assistant. At the finish, Hilah Thomas gave the manuscript a careful, critical reading. At Harper, Karen Levine, Rosana Francescato, and Georgia Hughes earned my gratitude by their painstaking work. Throughout my work Tom Driver helped me to see the forest again after so many trees; he also solved a hundred tangles at the computer. His patient work was a labor of love, for which I am deeply grateful.

Prologue

ALTHOUGH HISTORIANS customarily avoid discussing their own times, I choose to begin this historical account in the present. The longer I have worked on these sixteenth- and seventeenth-century events, the more I have found them relevant to problems of violence and discrimination against women today. So let me begin there.

We seldom question today that there is widespread violence against women because they are women, but few acknowledge that it is increasing. In the United States, one out of two women is a victim of sexual assault or domestic violence in her lifetime, and assaults against young women have risen 50 percent since 1974.[1] Canadians continue to ponder the 1989 tragedy at the University of Montreal, when a man massacred fourteen female students, screaming that he hated women. Carole Sheffield reported that in the United States "acts of sexual violence are more severe and brutal than ever before. There is an apparent increase in gang rapes, serial rapes, and murders (which often involve dismemberment of women's bodies)."[2] Violent pornographic films can be purchased at the shopping mall. On a more subtle level, as women grow more assertive, some men resort to other forms of abuse and control, such as verbal put-downs at home and harassment on the job.

We are witnessing a worldwide rise in the level of violence against women. A newspaper reports that "Kenyans Do Some Soul-Searching After the Rape of 71 Schoolgirls" (an attack in which nineteen girls died trying to escape).[3] The status of *machismo* in Nicaragua is revealed by the following comment I heard in Managua in 1990: "It is all right now for a woman to work outside the home, because that is seen as supporting the revolution. But if she should work late and not cook dinner on time, she would have to wear dark glasses to the office next day." At the Fifth International Interdisciplinary Congress on Women, a conference open to the entire range of feminist research, an overwhelming forty-seven panels, workshops, and papers were devoted to violence against women.[4]

Material from India, however, most closely parallels the violence analyzed in this book. Reports in Indian media and governmental papers document the widespread and diverse nature of attacks on women.[5] From verbal abuse to murder, a tradition of oppressing women permits some Indian men to consider women fair game as objects of their scorn or rage. In many groups, wives are so routinely beaten that they *expect* to be battered. They may be tortured with electric shock and painful vaginal insertions. Girls as young as twelve are raped; mass rape occurs, sometimes aided by police, who take part.

All this can be documented in many countries, but the Indian atrocities surpass other instances of harassment and abuse by sheer volume. Because tradition allows husbands to consider marriage an economic investment, some families get rid of wives who are not profitable; it may be because they are barren or do not work hard enough or because their families did not provide a full dowry. They rid themselves of these unwanted women by murdering them—the current method of choice is to burn them alive. Most often these young women are killed at home, by having kerosene poured over them and then ignited. By this method there are no witnesses and the death is called accidental.

This custom is found most frequently not among the rural poor but among the urban middle class—upwardly mobile families who want to get ahead in any way they can. Thus, modern bride burning arises from a different motivation than the older custom of widow immolation, yet both practices raise the same image of women being burned to death in order to satisfy the honor of male family members.

The hatred of women that underlies these practices is made crystal-clear by two extreme Indian customs: neglect of female children and the amputation of women's breasts. The generally acknowledged practice of starving little girls, coupled with outright infanticide of girls and the aborting of female fetuses, proves the scorn of women that is accepted in much of the society. Likewise, the rarely reported cutting off of women's breasts can only be viewed as a supremely misogynist act (more about this practice in chapters 7 and 8).

As a study of the European witch hunts will show, acts like these expose other layers of a society's values. From India come reports of higher caste men tormenting lower caste women; in a village of Tamil Nadu, for example, a single family of *thevar* (high-caste) men regularly raped the women of the *harijan* (untouchable) community. Much of this behavior has ancient roots, but as political upheaval has swept over India in the last forty years, public tensions have triggered even more violence against women, especially poor low-caste females. When Indian men feel pressured, they often take it out on women, as did European men in the sixteenth century. The painful irony is that part of the increase in violence against women today comes as a reaction to Indian women's response to India's new democratic goals. As women have begun to assert themselves, they find themselves targets of increased male hatred and efforts at control. When faced with this new level of harassment, some women kill themselves; many more internalize the message that they are evil.

It should not surprise us that such a society is prey to outbreaks of witchcraft accusations. Among some Indian tribal groups—those who associate evil with women and who have a tradition of strong, even matriarchal roles for women—witch hunts are on the increase.[6] The women accused are mostly widows without children to support them. Because they have a life interest in lands that will pass at their death to their male relatives, they become targets of greed: by accusing them of witchcraft and having them stoned or beaten to death, those men inherit the land immediately. This persecution is part of a wide attack on women's traditional rights and part of a successful attempt to establish a patriarchal order, "an attempt to force women into a particular gender role."[7] It is also a way to discredit women who have an inside track with the *bongas* (household spirits). We will see a similar pattern in the development of witch hunts in Europe, which occurred at a time when women's traditional roles as healers, prophets, *and* producers were under attack.

We have seen that this situation is not essentially different in the Western world today, and again, we must not be surprised that independent women are being named witches. When Pat Robertson declared that supporting the Equal Rights Amendment was a "socialist, anti-family political movement that encourages women to leave their husbands, kill their children, *practice witchcraft,* destroy capitalism and become lesbians," he drew on an old combination of stereotypes hostile to women (emphasis added).

Any woman who challenges the patriarchal order may be suspect. Women exercising their right to have an abortion are a perfect example. When the liberal Catholic ethicist Daniel Maguire observed picketers shouting obscenities at women entering an abortion clinic, he was appalled to see the pregnant women treated "like witches," and he went on to describe the attackers as "the successors of the witch-hunters."[8] When British women organized to picket the U.S. missile base at Greenham Common, they were called "the screaming destructive witches of Greenham." The invectives hurled at them could have come from a witch trial—they were called "belligerent harpies . . . women who lived like dogs [and] smeared Newbury with their excrement." Furthermore, there were unpleasant sexual connotations: the "women smelt of fish paste and bad oysters"; they were "a bunch of smelly lesbians." Punishment was meted out by youths from Newbury, who "came down in the night and poured pigs' blood and maggots and excrement all over them."[9] Here we are not far from the kind of fury carried out three hundred years before by the youths of Hadley, Massachusetts, when they strung up the accused witch Mary Webster and then rolled her in the snow; hadn't a sickening smell of musk been attributed to her as well? Most of the "witches" of Greenham ended up in British jails, just as their predecessors had. Women who challenge patriarchal structures, whether compulsory pregnancy, harassment on the job, or nuclear war, will be made to pay.

Given the extent of women's oppression, we need to know our past and expose our minds to the shock of the experiences, three or four hundred years ago, of women in Europe and New England. Starhawk, a spiritual leader who calls herself a witch, maintains that the memory of the witch hunts "remains with us today as a wound in the collective psyche. . . . Like the trauma of [childhood] abuse, the trauma from the Witch-burning days cannot be healed unless it is named and brought to light."[10] This book is an effort to remember the names of those who died, to understand why it happened—and happens still.

Introduction

IN READING the archival studies of the European witch hunts that began to appear around 1965, I was impressed by three factors that have been practically ignored. First, the lack of gender analysis in most of these works stands out; all agreed that the overwhelming majority of the people accused and killed were female, but few took that pertinent statistic into account in their interpretations. Second was the high level of physical violence often used in the proceedings, a gratuitous use of torture that went beyond judicial limits. Finally, the sexual nature of that violence stood out. My reflections on these three aspects of the witch trials set the parameters of this study.

The recent archival works are to be welcomed for opening a new chapter in sixteenth- and seventeenth-century European studies. Documenting "the greatest [European] mass killing of people by people not caused by war,"[1] this research could establish a persecution by gender alongside the more familiar studies of religious upheaval, Renaissance achievement, world conquest, and the early stages of capitalism. As such, it is part of the history that challenges the idea of universal progress in early modern Europe. Yet none of this recent literature definitively explains the strange and tragic events that historians call the "witchcraft persecutions." Why they happened at all, why they occurred when and where they did, and why European society turned against certain groups of its own women remain unanswered questions.

Bearing in mind the complexity of these issues, I did not seek a single-factor solution. The gender of the victims no more explains the entire witch-craze phenomenon than the legal, religious, political, or social-functional arguments that have been put forward. All these factors, and the generally neglected economic changes as well, are part of a valid explanation. Nor have I carried out additional archival research—the problem in witchcraft studies at present is not a lack of primary material to work with (although more information will undoubtedly be uncovered) but an incomplete analysis of what is available. Instead, I attempt a synthesis of the work that has been done, subjecting this material to the three issues posed above: the meaning of the gender of the victims, the events closely related to gender, namely, the excessive use of violence inflicted primarily by men against women, and the sexual nature of much of that violence. For outbreaks involving more than six or eight killings, I use the terms *witchcraze* or *mass panic;* most of these took place in the German lands. Smaller persecutions I call *witch hunts.*

Because this work depends on research already published, a brief historiographical survey is in order. I will discuss here only the issue of how gender is or is not treated in these works. A methodological discussion of the need for gender as a category of historical analysis will conclude the Introduction.

SEVERAL CYCLES of interest in witchcraft research preceded the present one,[2] but the current generation of studies began with Julio Caro Baroja's 1965 book surveying European witchcraft, especially in the Basque lands. Although Caro Baroja's understanding of folk religion makes this study especially valuable, his typical view of witches as "slightly mad, weird" old women precludes any depth of gender analysis.[3] Seeing them as pathetic outsiders "with an overdeveloped sense of their own importance," he concluded that "a woman usually becomes a witch after the initial failure of her life as a woman, after frustrated or illegitimate love affairs have left her with a sense of impotence or disgrace," and he regretted that "those unfortunate sick people" were put to death because their type of neurosis was not understood.

The 1967 essay that inspired much of the recent witchcraft studies, H. R. Trevor-Roper's "European Witch-Craze of the Sixteenth and Seventeenth Centuries," though utterly deficient in gender analysis, sheds some light on how historians were missing the point.[4] While analyzing how social tension was generated "by unassimilable social groups," he had a logical opening to discuss women and why some of them were seen as unassimilable. But he could not seem to think of "women" as a group, as a societal category. Sixty pages later, at the end of the essay, he finally identified the victims, calling them "hysterical women in a harsh rural world or in artificial communities—in ill-regulated nunneries . . . or in special regions like the Pays de Labourd, where . . . the fishermen's wives were left deserted for months." Again, we find the theory of the sexually deprived female. But for most of his essay, the victims have no identity at all. These important works from the 1960s show that some historiographers of the witchcraze had not demythologized their own attitudes toward the women they wrote about.[5]

Trevor-Roper's controversial essay inspired a series of archival studies of witch trials, written in order to refute him but all showing their debt to him nonetheless. Alan Macfarlane's careful analysis of the Essex trials confirmed that 92 percent of the victims were women, an extraordinarily high percentage, but he concluded that "there is no evidence that hostility between the sexes lay behind their prosecutions."[6] Keith Thomas, in his influential study of English folk religion, concurred with Macfarlane. Though denying that either misogyny or psychological factors affected the female victims, he made the useful point that economic and social considerations were valid, because women "were the most dependent members of the community, and thus the most vulnerable to accusation." He also pointed out that charges of female sexual transgressions—illegitimacy, promiscuity, sexual voracity—figured in the trials, but he seemed not to realize that these accusations are the stuff of which misogyny is made.

Both Macfarlane and Thomas assert that the question of why women were singled out must be looked into—but neither of them did so. Succeeding works documented a vast amount of woman-hatred, making it all the more surprising that scholars still did not see gender as the central issue. Erik Midelfort's research on southwestern Germany is a case in point. While analyzing massive witch panics, such as Wiesensteig, where 63 women were burned to death, and Quedlinburg, where 133 witches, mostly female, were executed in one day, Midelfort suggested that "women seemed . . . to provoke somehow an intense misogyny at times" and asked that we study "why that group *attracted to itself* the scapegoating mechanism."[7] In addition to blaming the victims, Midelfort also denied that there had been a particular tradition of misogyny in the sixteenth century. Complaining that this alleged tradition had been documented "only in literary sources," he overlooked the fact that his own material was primary proof for it.[8]

By this time in the development of witchcraft studies, a pattern of denial is clear. Historians were denying that misogyny and patriarchy are valid historical categories and were refusing to treat women as a recognizable historical group. Reading these works is like reading accounts of the Nazi holocaust in which everyone would agree that the majority of victims were Jewish, but no one would mention anti-Semitism or the history of violent persecution against Jews, thereby implying that it was "natural" for Jews to be victims. Without mention of a tradition of oppression of women, the implication for the sixteenth century is that of course women would be attacked—and that it must somehow have been their fault. This is what historians conclude when they have no awareness of traditional misogyny or traditional oppression of women.

Earlier, in 1948, in the work of Émile Brouette, researcher of northern French witchcraft, misogyny had been related to the persecutions. Even if you believe that one can be antifeminist without burning witches, Brouette maintained, still it is theologically only one step from scorning a woman to believing that she is a servant of the devil.[9] Unfortunately for the future of witchcraft studies, this perception was rejected by Brouette's successor in northern French witchcraft studies, Fr. Pierre Villette, who insisted that it was "*psychologie féminine*" alone that explained the large numbers of female victims; in other words, that women indeed threaten men and drive them to attack. Villette even excused the virulent misogyny of the authors of the *Malleus Maleficarum* in light of this frightening "female psychology."[10]

Working twenty years later in the same northern French area that Villette had covered in the 1950s, Robert Muchembled drew quite different conclusions. Ascribing the preponderance of female victims (82 percent) partly to traditional misogyny, literary as well as theological, lay as well as clerical, Muchembled moved the argument along by tying female oppression to the general sexual repression of the Catholic and Protestant Reformations. His proofs were the increased punishment for prenuptial pregnancy, bastardy, and adultery, with heavier penalties against women than men. He also documented the intrusion of the state into village life, which brought in elite fantasies about witches and an impersonal bureaucratic form of justice, both of which seriously disturbed traditional village relationships. As society became more repressive, the charges against alleged witches became wilder: though some of the accused had had a reputation for lasciviousness, even women with a good name were now accused of having sex with the devil or keeping a demon lover. Muchembled was right to broaden the scope and to see that the witch hunt involved persecuting women for their sexuality.[11]

The years after 1972, when Midelfort's work was published, show a change in scholars' interpretations of this evidence, a change that must be credited to the nascent movement for women's history. Midelfort himself took a different position nine years later, claiming that "one cannot begin to understand the European witch-hunt without recognizing that it displayed a burst of misogyny without parallel in Western history," and suggested that future research should investigate the fantasies of the bishops and university professors who presided over the German trials.[12] This indicates an approach more sympathetic to the victims, one perhaps influenced by the work in women's history accomplished in the intervening decade.

In a general interpretation of early witchcraft up to 1500, Jeffrey Burton Russell made a major attempt to place women at the center of the problem.[13] Russell understood that medieval women were leaders in some heretical groups; he appreciated the extent to which medieval heretical groups appealed to women by offering women roles from which they were excluded by the church. But he failed to see that the practices of *folk religion* (folk magic and witchcraft) were another valid alternative for women. Throughout, he accepted the demonologists' definitions of witchcraft, calling it a "violent form" of "feminine discontent" involving "criminal" activity. Because he insisted on associating witchcraft primarily with heresy, rather than folk religion, and saw it as ultimately subversive, he was forced to conclude that alleged witches engaged in violent, even criminal activity, leaving the issue not far from a "woman as hag" position. In a more recent work, Russell makes an even stronger association between suspected women and hags: "in Christian Europe, the hag image was projected upon human beings. The European witch, then, must be understood not just as a sorceress, but as the incarnation of the hag."[14] This point of view will be challenged in chapter 6.

One publication that deserves mention in every discussion of European witchcraft, Carlo Ginzburg's *The Night Battles: Witchcraft and Agrarian Cults in the Sixteenth and Seventeenth Centuries,*[15] served as a corrective to Russell's point of view. Discovering the records of a fertility cult in the Italian Friuli region, Ginzburg showed how the cult had functioned to *protect* its members from witches but was then itself demonized by the Inquisition. But though he made folk religion an unquestionable factor in understanding sixteenth-century religious practice, and though his material shows that women played a large role in these grass-roots practices, Ginzburg did not comment on the issue of gender.

Two new comprehensive studies that cover the entire witch-hunting period go further in searching for gender factors. In Joseph Klaits's 1985 book, misogyny is identified as part of early modern theology, medical attitudes, law, art, ageism, and poverty. Woman-hatred is evident in familial attitudes and in sexual exploitation. That Klaits devotes half a chapter to "sexual politics," a discussion placed early in the book, shows that he understood the institutional nature of the problem—that the social order felt threatened by nonconformist women, that church and family, and even the state, were threatened. He is one of the few (Muchembled is another) who has analyzed the sadistic impulse in the witchcraze.[16]

However, Klaits sees not women but the Reformations (both Protestant and Catholic) as the main factor in the persecutions, blaming both the religious upheaval and, chiefly, the antisexual reforms of the Reformation period for the extremes of the witchcraze. In doing so, he shifts the focus away from women. Women, after all, were not the main actors in the Reformation drama, so Klaits brings us back to looking at what men did. I will argue that it matters little to witchcraft studies whether one explains it by what lawyers, judges, doctors, theologians, bishops, or Reformers did—all these explanations miss the central point, because all pull the focus away from the victims, from the women themselves. And Klaits states categorically that gender is not the central issue.[17] Even his emphasis on women as sexual *objects*, true though it is to the trial material, has the effect of showing us the victims from the outside.

Brian Levack's balanced, thorough study, intended like Klaits's to be used as a textbook, affirms at one point that accusations of witchcraft were sex-related and discusses the many ways in which women were more vulnerable than men to charges of evildoing.[18] But Levack seldom mentions gender in the rest of his book, stressing instead the importance of legal changes and a general air of anxiety throughout Europe.

A model of gender analysis had appeared in 1976, E. William Monter's study of the witchcraze in the Swiss-French borderlands.[19] Affirming the widespread use of black magic and white magic in preindustrial Europe, he was sympathetic to women's use of magic as a compensation for their legal and economic disadvantages. He attributed their persecution to their gender and maintained unequivocally that gender was the crucial factor, more important than poverty, age, or any other. Defining misogyny in family and in theology as more than just woman-hatred, Monter connected it also with legal attempts to control women's bodies. He observed that witch prosecutions rose and fell with legal action against two other sex-linked crimes: infanticide and sodomy. Infanticide was resorted to almost entirely by single women, and both infanticide and sodomy were seen by sixteenth-century society as "unnatural." Because witchcraft was seen as "unnatural," sinful, and a single woman's crime, it is not surprising that the sixteenth century became "interested in executing women as witches." Concluding that "women were the specially designated victims," that "witchcraft, as the demonologists had repeatedly insisted, was sex-linked," Monter set the stage for the type of gender analysis that must be done on the witchcraft materials, but he did not follow up on these insights.[20]

The late Scottish sociologist Christina Larner produced a thorough gender investigation of Scottish witchcraft materials.[21] Using her triple skills in sociology, history, and religion, Larner accepted the positive use of witchcraft by poor village females ("women embracing witchcraft"), saw the persecutions as motivated by a desire to control independent-minded women, and made male hatred of the female body into a real, believable factor in the witch hunts. Larner made a major contribution in pointing out that women as a group were criminalized for the first time by the witchcraze. One expects her to conclude that gender is the central issue, and she did affirm that "all women were potential witches," "the witch hunt was part of the sex war," and "witch-hunting *is* woman-hunting." Yet she was not satisfied with these formulations and repeatedly modified them: "the reasons why witches were hunted are not directly related to their being women, but to their being thought evil"; "the crime of witchcraft, while sex-related, was not sex specific"; the hunt was "no more a persecution of women than the prosecution of killers was a persecution of men." Finally concluding that "witch hunting is *not* woman-hunting," Larner maintained that, at any rate, the questions raised by the issue of woman-hunting were too narrow. Recommending instead that we ask broader, presumably more important questions of the craze, questions about Christianity as a political ideology, about crises in law and order—that is, the more traditionally political questions—she turned away from the theory of persecution by gender, which she, more than anyone, had validated.[22]

Once again women as a gender group seem not to matter, and the questions of women's history are considered too narrow. Larner's conclusions are the most disappointing of all, for she had a keen awareness of how the oppression of women works in history (see the epigraph for chapter 1). She does not make clear why one must forgo the questions about woman-hunting in order to work on the political issues, nor does she see that the woman-hunting questions *are* political. I will argue that material that shows women as "threatening to patriarchal order" or religion as "relentlessly patriarchal" is neither narrow nor apolitical. Meanwhile, feminist writers Andrea Dworkin and Mary Daly discussed the witch hunts in their studies of the oppression of women. By advancing the subject of violence against women as a serious issue in feminist discourse, they prepared the way for future work on topics such as rape and witch hunting.[23]

Two important studies of New England witch trials shed light on gender-related questions. By subjecting his material to psychological reflection, John Demos enables us to see the importance of the age and gender of the accusers as well as of the witches: the typical scenario pitted young girls against middle-aged women. Because this generational conflict appears in many trial records across Europe, it needs to be investigated further by psychologists. Beyond that, Demos focused on the conflicted social relations of the accused, asking if witch accusations were actual, as well as symbolic, ways of holding women down, and concluded not. Although he described colonial witches as typically assertive and aggressive "beyond what the culture deemed proper," and although he documented many stormy Puritan marriages, he is convinced that there was no general conflict between the sexes. I suggest that he did not take into account the limits on how a woman may rebel in a patriarchal society and did not see that his own material disproves his rejection of patriarchal tensions.[24]

Carol Karlsen's research on the New England witch trials placed gender at the center, a decision that paid off with some new insights into women's economic roles.[25] Discovering that women without husbands, brothers, or sons were especial targets of witchcraft accusations (as a means of getting hold of their property), Karlsen opened up the particular connection between witches and economic tension upon which I will expand in chapter 5.

Yet though Karlsen, Larner, Monter, and Muchembled provided us with careful analyses of the role of women in the witch hunts of their respective areas,[26] none factored in adequately either the savagery of persecution enacted or its sexual nature. One study that does so is Marianne Hester's reevaluation of trials in Essex, England. [27] Arguing with Macfarlane's conclusion that very few women were accused of both sexual offenses and witchcraft, Hester points out that about one-third of the Essex witchcraft cases also included charges of unacceptable sexual behavior. Hester makes a strong case for the amount of sexual violence in the prosecution of witches. Pointing out "the general male-dominated context of the witch-hunts" (males as judges, torturers, theoreticians), Hester concluded that "the witch-persecutions constituted sexual violence against women within a context of male supremacist social relations," and "that women's lives were profoundly controlled through the threat of witchcraft accusations."[28] Though Hester's material is confined to the county of Essex, I will offer documentation on sexual violence and the control of women from across Europe (see chapters 7 and 8).

The problems one faces in studying witchcraft as a persecution by gender are many. First, as Muchembled and Ginzburg have shown, one must acknowledge that "wise women" such as folk healers and diviners were useful, sought-after members of society, pre-1550. Although they were reperceived after that as suspect, even as evil, by elite groups, and eventually by villagers as well, the historian has no grounds to caricature them as hags or superstitious old fools. The distinction must be observed, therefore, between folk religious practices and the accusations of causing harm that they sometimes engendered, on one hand, and witchcraft accusations of serving the devil. The latter were grotesque distortions made by the European elite of the actual, useful functions of folk healers and counselors, distortions made in order to discredit them.

A lack of understanding of patriarchy as a historical category and of how it functions in a society is another weak point in most of the works cited here. Without this understanding one does not fully recognize that women were accused primarily by men, tried by male juries, examined by male searchers, sentenced by male judges, tortured by male jailers, burned to death by male executioners—while being prayed over by male confessors. The patriarchal system also explains why many women accused other females: if a woman displeased or threatened the men of her community, she would also be seen as dangerous by the women who depended on or identified with those men. The internalization of "who is not acceptable" goes even deeper than that. Women—and other oppressed groups—sometimes try to outdo their oppressors in scorning persons perceived as outsiders, in hope of being accepted, or tolerated, themselves. In the witchcraft trials, the poor attacked those even poorer; marginalized women attacked those women even further out of power than they. Women accusers often acted at the behest of their menfolk, as part of a family strategy of accusation.

There is another point that has been neglected: no historian of the period has considered the *effects* on European society of one hundred thousand or so public executions for witchcraft or of the targeting of its own women as victims (see chapter 8). The nature of beliefs about the crime itself, considered so horrifying that it justified any means of punishment, indicates a high level of fear; the form of execution, most often by burning, confirms a high level of violence. That torture and execution took place before large crowds shows not only the blood-thirst of the age but even more the desire of church and state, local and national, to control their citizens through intimidation. In the witch hunts, violence bred violence. The effects of the "solution," which I will argue were unsettling rather than healing, became in turn the cause of further persecution.

Finally—and this is very difficult with witchcraft materials—one must distinguish between women as victims and as agents of their own fates. Alleged witches were often both. Despite the emphasis on female sexuality in the trial records and procedures, the historian is ill advised to interpret the victims, no matter how sympathetically, only as sex objects. Women were more than sex objects in sixteenth-century society: they served as midwives, healers, counselors, farmers, alewives, spinners, domestic servants, assistants to their husbands in craft work, and so on, and their productive as well as reproductive roles made them potentially threatening to men.[29] Yet these women lived in a society fully capable of victimizing them. The historian must distinguish between both roles and work to understand how women could be both strong and persecuted.

THROUGHOUT, I will analyze the material in the context of woman-hunting. What difference does it make to apply categories of gender analysis to the events of the witch hunts?[30] The basic answer in applying these categories to any historical material is that we will uncover the element of power in relations between the sexes. In fact, Joan Scott argues that, in a broader sense, "gender is a *primary* way of signifying relationships of power."[31] Because this study covers many areas of Europe, it will throw light on questions of power in a comparative way. It is thus suggestive about whether the possibility of male fear and hatred of women is universal in Western civilization. For the same reason, it elucidates *how* misogyny functioned in different societies (see chapters 3 and 4).

To look at the witchcraft materials as a persecution by gender informs us beyond the fact that European men exerted the power of life and death over their women. It puts the women, not the powerful men, at the center of the story. By giving detailed analyses of how women were treated during the hunts, we uncover much about how women were valued or devalued and what they stood for as symbols. Among the possible meanings of a woman's life in early modern Europe, the most shocking was that she could stand for all that was utterly evil. By nature, because she was female, she was eligible for this role, and the meaning of this identification, strange to say, was that certain women served an important function as symbols of all that the society claimed that it was not. The utility of this role was such that the image of the "victim" changes constantly before our eyes, at one moment reviled, at another emerging as almost essential to her community.

In order to examine closely the processes by which these women became important symbols for their world, we must concentrate on the very parts of the story that have been most neglected: the ways they were tortured, the methods by which they were put to death, and the words used to describe their crimes. These crimes were seen as so heinous that they justified the most horrifying punishments that could be devised. My response to studying this material has often been the same as reading the daily newspaper, namely, that I learn more about human cruelty than I want to. For that reason, I admit having considered excising these unpleasant facts from this book, just as they are missing from most witchcraft studies. But I take seriously Scott's admonition that in order to do gender analysis "it is the processes we must continually keep in mind. We must ask more often how things happened in order to find out why they happened."[32] A convicted witch *could* be let off by being admonished, fined, or banished; that many were instead tortured to the point of death tells us something not only about the hatred of witchcraft among those in power but also about their loathing of women.

It is the high level of sadistic sexual torture that tells us most about how power functioned in early modern European society and about how men and women related to each other. How did beliefs about witchcraft, which began as often-harmless folk magic, become a belief that some women had sex with the devil, were won over to Satan's service because they were oversexed? Carroll Smith-Rosenberg has observed that sexual beliefs will tell us as much about the social construction of power as they do about actual sexual behavior.[33] For influential European men, the opportunity to punish in a sexually sadistic way became both a teaching tool and a prime exhibition of control. For this reason we will have to consider the men in power as well as the women victims, an investigation that links up with themes of European imperialism and racism (chapter 8). The witch hunts took place at the same time as colonial expansion and the Atlantic slave trade, and they were made possible by some of the same ecclesiastical policies and legal changes. The European ruling elite valorized certain European women much as it did African slaves and conquered natives, as objects to exploit and as useful symbols of all that European men claimed they were not.

It is appropriate to consider women as a group and to compare them to these other oppressed groups, for this places women's history in its proper context, interconnected with the major political events of the time. In direct contradiction of Larner's conclusion that the witch hunts were not sufficiently political, I find them to be at the heart of what men were doing and highly illuminating of the "men's world." When Smith-Rosenberg reminded us to invert the question that historians usually pose, by asking not what society can tell us about gender but what gender tells us about that society, she gave us a key to understanding the witch hunts.[34] I will discuss how our insights into the witch hunts challenge some traditional paradigms of sixteenth- and seventeenth-century history.

Finally, by using gender as an independent category of historical analysis and tracing the status of women through this period, I found that the witch hunts affected the traditional image of women in European society. The dramatic events of the witch persecutions reinforced the received traditions of misogyny and patriarchal control, narrowing women's status and demonizing the image of women in a damaging way. That women were criminalized for the first time as witches left its mark. Not until the mid-nineteenth century did the status of Western women begin to recover from the witch hunts. It can be argued that we have never entirely recovered since.

A scholar of Hebrew scriptures, Phyllis Trible, explained why she retold biblical "texts of terror" using a new feminist perspective: "It interprets stories of outrage on behalf of their female victims in order to recover a neglected history, to remember a past that the present embodies, and to pray that these terrors shall not come to pass again. In telling sad stories, a feminist hermeneutic seeks to redeem the time."[35]

So the reader is forewarned: these are not pretty stories. But they must be told, for they are happening, in new forms, in our own day.

The devil making love to a witch. Women, widely believed to be sexually insatiable and weak in character, were considered vulnerable to the devil's seductions. From Ulrifig Molitor's *Von den Unholden und Hexen,* Constance, 1489. Courtesy of Dover Pictorial Archive Series.

CHAPTER ONE

Why Women?

Gender, Numbers, Class

On average, witchcraft, the ultimate in human evil, was sex-related to women in much the same proportion as sanctity, the ultimate good, was sex-related to men.

—*Christina Larner,* Witchcraft and Religion

JOAN PETERSEN, a healer, "was searched again in a most unnatural and barbarous manner by four women" supplied by her accusers, who found "a teat of flesh in her secret parts more than other women usually had." After bribed witnesses testified against her, she was executed.[1]

Searching an accused woman's body for the devil's teat was one of the chief proofs of witchcraft. Though the investigation was normally done by women (and not done gently, as Joan Peterson's case demonstrates), the sessions were often witnessed by male court officials. When the constable of Salisbury, New Hampshire, undressed Eunice Cole to be whipped for witchcraft, he saw "under one of her brests. . . . A blew thing like unto a teate hanging downeward about three quarters of an inche longe not very thick." Men standing by saw him "rip her shift down"; moving in closer, they affirmed that Eunice "violently scratched it away," implying that she tried to remove the evidence from her body. When women were appointed to examine her further, they found instead "a place in her leg which was proveable wher she Had bin sucktt by Imps."[2]

This lewd scene can set the tone for much of what will be investigated in this book. An analysis of violence such as this exposes the sexual terror and brutality at the heart of the witch hunts, a topic too little discussed. The American historian Lois Banner has observed that two of the cultural norms specific to patriarchal society—war and rape—have been little studied by feminist scholars, and a third, pornography, studied only by feminists and not enough by them. In matters pertaining to the abuse of bodies, especially women's bodies, we have been strangely silent.[3] To her comment I would add that writers on witchcraft also, feminist or otherwise, have tended to avoid the specifics of what happened to the bodies of the victims and have not asked aloud what difference it made that most of them were female. That historians to date, following traditional interests in legal and intellectual history, have concentrated more on the judges and theoreticians of the witchcraft trials than on the witches may explain this omission. But one must ask if revulsion at the public exploration as well as the torture of female bodies may also have caused them to make that choice.

Having a female body was the factor most likely to render one vulnerable to being called a witch. The sexual connotations and the explicit sexual violence utilized in many of the trials make this fact clear. Just which women were targeted and under what circumstances reveals much about the status of women in early modern Europe.

A Typical Witch

Reginald Scot, the English skeptic about witchcraft, began his definition of witches this way: "women which be commonly old, lame, bleare-eied, pale, fowle, and full of wrinkles."[4] If Scot, who was sympathetic to the victims, perpetrated this negative stereotype, it is not surprising that witch hunters like Boguet and Remy used such phrases as "this miserable and damnable vermin" and "[like] a bitch far more hideous to look at than all the others."[5]

Despite these venomous stereotypes, the records reveal that there can be no one definition of persons accused as witches: some, for example, were as young as eight or nine; others were in their prime; a few were male. Yet Scot's and the Frenchmen's caricatures capture the truth about the majority of persons accused of this crime: old, unattractive, disliked, and female.

From a trial in south Germany we find a portrait of a woman who typified the witch image, Walpurga Hausmänin of Dillingen.[6] Walpurga, an elderly widow, supported herself by midwifery. Long suspect as a sorcerer ("twelve years ago she had killed at birth . . . a girl child"; "ten years ago she had poisoned with her salve the second child of Anna Kromt"), Walpurga was finally brought to trial in 1587, charged with the deaths of over forty babies, two women in childbirth, eight cows, a horse, and numerous geese and pigs. Her neighbors claimed also that she had caused three adults to languish to the point of death and had brought on a damaging hailstorm.

Finding the real Walpurga in this record is not easy, for it is a mix of her words (given under duress), the judge's promptings, and the court recorder's opinions. But despite the absurd elements in the story, we can learn a certain amount about this woman. The account states that "upon kindly questioning and also torture," she confessed to all these acts and explained that the powers by which she carried out these impressive maleficia (evil acts) were taught her by the devil, or to be exact, her devil-Lover "Federlin," who gave her the ointment that killed babies and caused women to deliver prematurely. Yet despite these fantastical elements and a description of flying to the devil's sabbat on a pitchfork, the account begins in a natural way, in the real world. Thirty-one years before, widowed but still in her prime, Walpurga, living in poverty and need, earned some money cutting corn for Hans Schlumperger. Attracted to his servant Bis in Pfarrhof, she enticed Bis "with lewd speeches and gestures," and he agreed to come to her house one night. She awaited him with "evil and fleshly thoughts," but it was not Bis who came "but the Evil One in the latter's guise and raiment and indulged in fornication with her."

From that point on, the story followed a well-known pattern, familiar surely to Walpurga from other witch trials. Walpurga testified that when she saw and felt the devil's cloven foot and wooden hand, she panicked, calling on Jesus—and her lover vanished. But the Evil Spirit returned, made love to her again, and bound her to him by promising to help her overcome her poverty. At this, "she surrendered herself to him body and soul." Receiving the devil's mark below her left shoulder, she signed a pact with him in her blood as he guided her hand across the paper. Although she was illiterate, she was controlled by him simply by being reminded of this contract; it prevented her from thinking of God or attending church, actions that might have freed her from his grasp.

The question immediately arises as to why Walpurga confessed to this bizarre behavior. She had been, in reality, not a murderess but a respected and useful member of that society, "for nineteen years a licensed and pledged midwife of the city of Dillingen." That she confessed while chained and being tortured explains much. In hope of ending the anguish, she may have told the judge what she knew he wanted to hear, the already widely accepted belief that the devil was sexually irresistible to women. But we know of women who made similar confessions *without torture.* So we must look for further explanations, in two directions: to female sexual fantasy and feelings of sexual guilt and to the role of healer that many women filled, a high-risk job.

Walpurga, like most of her contemporaries, may well have believed these ideas about demon-lovers herself, internalizing them and fitting them to the circumstances of her own life.[7] When her jailers demanded a confession, Walpurga may have gone back to an old guilt, her uneasiness over fornication committed thirty-one years before, and dressed it up with the devil lore that the judges expected. A connection between old sexual transgressions and women's confessions of witchcraft turns up in records all across Europe. This story is unusual only in providing a natural beginning, one no doubt taken from Walpurga's own past; it is this portion that is most useful for women's history.

It is possible that Walpurga had connected her sexual desire with the devil long before the court pressured her for a confession, believing that sexual desire in itself is evil, as the account states. In short, she may not have committed fornication but felt guilty over wanting to.[8] Furthermore, sexual guilt can attract to itself other guilts, as, for instance, a sense of failure over the death of babies whom Walpurga as a midwife could not save. Walpurga may have blamed herself over a long period of years for her infatuation with Bis.

These questions, involving as they do an element of psychohistory, are extremely difficult to evaluate. Yet, given the importance of the victims' confessions to a study of witchcraft, they are essential to our task. Based on fantasy, they are important but limited clues, pointing to the importance of the material in chapters 5 and 6, where we ask what women were actually doing in their work lives and sexual roles.

We have glimpses of what else Walpurga was doing, besides her job as a midwife (which clearly kept her busy—she explained that she could fly only a little way to the sabbat "on account of her duties"). She shared a meal with the chamber scribe's wife, who then blamed her for her premature labor. She gave young Jacob, the late chancellor's son, a hobbyhorse to ride, but when he later died, people said she had given it to him "to ride on it till he lost his senses." Eight years before this, she had helped Michel Klingler to push a cart, but now that he is dying, she is blamed. She once gave a young girl a drink, but now, years later, she is ill, and Walpurga is suspected. In short, any act of hers, any gesture of friendliness, is twisted into an evil threat. Every unexplained misfortune in Dillingen is blamed on her.

Although people depended on Walpurga for healing, they were also willing to make her the scapegoat for much of their bad luck. How did this useful woman become a symbol for evil, attracting so much hatred? She qualified for this role because she had long been a single woman, hence suspect in her sexual behavior, was poor and a widow, hence had no man to defend (or control) her, and possessed the power of healing, a power that everyone believed was also the power to kill.

Under the jurisdiction of the bishop of Augsburg, Walpurga was condemned on these charges by a local judge and jury. Her public execution, which took place in her hometown, was carried out in the style of south German witch burnings: her breasts and arms were torn five times with red-hot irons, her right hand cut off, her body burned at the stake, and her ashes thrown into the nearest flowing river. All her goods and estate went to the bishop's treasury.

Walpurga's story contains many of the standard features from witchcraft accounts. The victim was female; she was old, poor, illiterate, widowed, and a midwife-healer. Although her "crimes" were everyday occurrences, her power was seen as supernatural, coming from the devil. She fell prey to him because of sexual desire and economic need; he laid claim to her through a pact and a bodily mark. She flew through the air to a sabbat where she worshiped him, denouncing and denigrating her Christian faith. Long suspect, she ultimately was made scapegoat for an absurd assortment of alleged crimes, accused by the very persons she had tried to help. Originally seen as a useful member of the community ("a licensed and pledged midwife"), she became a pariah ("a malefic and miserable woman"). Under torture she confessed to all the accusations, no matter how lurid; she was put to death in a savage public ritual.[9]

Most notably, Walpurga was a woman alone, facing "a venerable jury," a lower-class female judged by the male oligarchy of her town. We will find this combination of accused and jurors in tens of thousands of cases. Examining why European society singled out its Walpurgas to be its scapegoats will tell us much about class and economics in the early modern world; it will also throw light on how men perceived and treated women.

Numbers

This discussion does well to begin with a word about my working definition of the term *witch:* I use it, and without quotation marks, wherever the sources use it *(sorcière, Hexe, Zauberer, bruja, hechicera, strega, troll, taltos).* Although witchcraft is a crime that cannot be proven by modern standards of evidence—an "invisible" crime that provides no witnesses, hence is not dealt with in modern courts of law—still it was widely recognized as a major crime in the sixteenth and seventeenth centuries. Sir Matthew Hale, for example, judge of the witch trial at Bury St. Edmunds, believed that witches were real, as did most learned persons; he claimed this because the Bible, the laws of all nations, and England's Parliament had decreed it so.[10]

This study of European society's persecutions of the people perceived to be witches will use the term in the sense that it was used at the time. Since long before the sixteenth century, people had believed that some persons had supernatural power, the ability to perform good or harmful magic (or both). A good witch, or cunning woman, as these magic workers were often called, might, for example, heal persons or animals by incantations or potions; she might just as readily kill with a curse or the evil eye. In either case, she possessed a power to be reckoned with. By the sixteenth century, many—especially among the elite—began to hold a new belief, namely, that such supernatural power came from the devil, who bestowed it chiefly on women in return for their absolute obedience to him.

Numbers are essential to this investigation. It is through an analysis of the percentage of women and men accused and of the percentage condemned that the gender bias of this persecution emerges. But first we must look at the overall size of the witchcraze. Contemporary accounts are of limited use. Just as the account of Walpurga's trial shows us how contemporaries twisted the facts of a suspect's life, so they showed no more accuracy in estimating the number of witches: Henri Boguet, the French witch hunter active around 1600, claimed there were 1,800,000 witches in Europe. Because by "witch" Boguet meant persons dedicated to serving Satan, he therefore believed there was a terrifying and widespread conspiracy of witches against Christian society. Joseph Glanvill, holding out against the rising tide of skepticism in the 1670s, maintained that England was still home to thousands of witches, but the doubter Bishop Hutchinson concluded in 1718 that there had been only "above 140 [witches]" put to death in England since the Reformation.[11]

Somewhere between these wildly differing claims we must find a sound compromise, but many modern commentators have not used caution either. Unless speculations are based on court records and other contemporary accounts and adjusted only by educated estimates, they are useless. This limitation, however, has not stopped some modern writers from claiming numbers ranging from two hundred thousand[12] into the millions, and this not referring to witches in general but specifically to persons executed, thus implying a far larger pool of suspects among the population.

Working on the statistics of witchcraft is like working with quicksand. Because many of the records have been lost or are defective, in most areas we cannot even speculate about what the totals may have been. Of the surviving records, many have not yet been carefully analyzed, a problem especially for Polish accounts. Even the records that have been analyzed raise more questions than they answer, for many are lacking names (hence, gender), ages, and sentences; almost all are silent about class, occupation, and marital status. Worse still is the scattered evidence that many witch accusations and executions never made it into the records. How many persons were driven out of their villages or lynched by mobs, we have no idea. One may well then ask why the historian would attempt an essay on the statistics of witchcraft, and in fact many have eschewed it. Yet despite the hazards, it is well worthwhile to speculate.

One reason for the necessity to grapple with numbers is the unrealistic totals that have been circulated. The current trend among some feminist groups to claim three million, six million, or even ten million female victims is mistaken. A statistically based figure, though lower, still makes the same point: that this was an organized mass murder of women that cannot be dismissed by historians.

Among the feminist writers claiming millions of deaths is Andrea Dworkin. Working from the only estimates available in the early 1970s, Dworkin made the claim, "In Europe, women were persecuted as witches for nearly four hundred years, burned at the stake, perhaps as many as nine million of them. . . ."[13] The "nearly four hundred years" almost doubles the years of actual major persecution (1560–1760), and the "nine million of them" is off by about 8,900,000. Even further off the mark is the claim by certain German feminists that ten million women were killed.[14] Faced with such exaggerations, the historian is forced to make an estimate based on the records, no matter how incomplete they may be.

An immediate corrective to these modern inaccuracies can be found in surveying the estimates made by contemporaries, which, although lacking a statistical base, are in the realm of the possible. Looking back over the recently ended holocaust, Voltaire claimed that one hundred thousand witches had been put to death. Bodin believed that "many thousands" had died in France. Boguet wrote that there were "thousands and thousands of stakes" in

Lorraine and that "there are witches by the thousand everywhere, multiplied upon the earth even as worms in a garden." Whatever one makes of these figures, one must note that they deal not in millions but in thousands.[15]

An even more pressing reason for working on numbers, however, is the simple need to know how many persons shared this fate. Given the chaotic state of the records, the temptation to round off the numbers is strong. Yet I found myself carefully retaining each awkward figure, even though this added hours of work for each region I studied. As Joan Ringelheim, researcher of women in the Nazi holocaust, stated of her work, to drop numbers now is to kill these persons twice.[16] Wanting to record every known victim, to ensure that the historical record finally acknowledges her death, I offer the most complete record available at this time. (See appendix B.)

Though one cannot add up estimates like these and expect any meaningful results, still, in order to settle on a reasonable total of victims, in contrast to figures such as ten million, it is imperative to reach a sum. The most careful totals made so far are those of Brian Levack, who estimates 110,000 accusations and 60,000 deaths.[17] I believe that though his are reasonable figures, they are almost certainly too low.

There are two pressing arguments for raising Levack's estimate of 110,000 accusations. In addition to the fact that many cases were never recorded, and of those that were, many records have been lost or destroyed, many trial entries are for unknown numbers of victims. Furthermore, additional cases are steadily turning up. Especially in view of the rate at which we are learning of new victims, I believe that Levack's estimate should be doubled, bringing us to a figure of about two hundred thousand accused.

Death estimates are even harder to deal with. Many records do not list the verdict of the trial, a strange omission given the severity of the penalties for a verdict of guilty (death or banishment in most cases). Most records do not include those who died in prison, like Issobel Pain of Scotland, who "dyed the last winter through cold hunger and other inconveniences of the prison."[18] The three women who survived Issobel complained in 1672 that they were kept "in a dark dungeon in a most miserable conditione being always at the point of starving . . . and are in such . . . miserie that it ware better for them to be dead than alyve."

Others, driven to despair by torture, or, like Didier Finance of Lorraine, by fear of being burned alive, killed themselves in prison. As an alleged witch and parricide, Didier faced being burned by red-hot tongs and incinerated alive at the stake.[19] Many accused witches were murdered in prison: for example, when the wife of a cobbler in Constance was found strangled to death in her cell, her murder was blamed on a demon.[20] Others died in prison from the torture inflicted on them, like two female witches accused of spreading the plague in the French Jura. A widow in Alsace, after being tortured, managed to struggle home, where she was found dead lying on her bed, her neck twisted, bruised, and disjointed.[21]

To these deaths must be added lynchings and posse-style murders of alleged witches (three hundred killed in the Ardennes, for example) that because of their extralegal nature can only be estimated.[22] Given all these factors, one must enlarge Levack's estimate of deaths. Claiming two hundred thousand accusations (a conservative estimate, I believe) and using a death rate of 50 percent of those arraigned, one reaches a figure of one hundred thousand dead—exactly what Voltaire estimated.[23]

But the convicted were not the only ones harmed. Once accused of being witches, few women ever returned to a normal life. So great was the fear of witchcraft that suspicion and ill will followed them to their graves, even when they moved to other areas.[24] Those who were let go often struggled with themselves over having been associated with the hated proceedings. An old Basque woman, Mariquita de Atauri, had, under pressure, named names. She confessed to her own witchcraft and was reconciled at Logroño, but she believed she was damned anyway because she had accused others who were innocent. When she tried to cross their names off the list of the accused and spoke to the inquisitor about her guilt, he called her a liar and a hussy and drove her away. In a desperate struggle with her conscience, Mariquita drowned herself.[25]

Those whose lives were thus ruined must in some way be taken into account in the total number of victims; the number of accused, therefore, is as important to our story as the number executed. Yet estimates are the best that one can offer.

Gender

Almost everywhere more women than men were accused and killed. The figures show that in fact women were overwhelmingly victimized: on average, 80 percent of those accused and 85 percent of those killed were female. Some areas, however, hunted down women more ferociously than others.

Among the accused in Essex, 92 percent were female, true also for the English Home Counties. The same percentage applied to the witch hunt in Namur County (in today's Belgium), and an even higher figure (95 percent) to the bishopric of Basel.[26] I suggest that a restudy of the Essex materials, stressing women's declining economic roles and the increasingly patriarchal nature of England's society, will explain why 92 percent of those accused were women.[27] As for Basel, the prominence there of hail-making accusations, a crime traditionally ascribed more often to women than men, may have contributed to the high number of female victims there but does not fully explain it.[28]

What these numbers meant for women can be seen in the following facts. Not only were over 80 percent of the accused in some areas women, but even more frightening statistics emerge from local hunts: for example, all but two of the female inhabitants of Langendorf in the Rhineland were arrested. In twelfth-century Kiev, when periodic fears of witchcraft arose, all the old women of the area were seized and subjected to the ordeal by cold water (thrown, bound hand and foot, into the Dnieper). Christina Larner, the chronicler of Scottish witchcraft, observed that there were periods "when no mature woman in Fife or East Lothian can have felt free from the fear of accusation."[29] Given these cases, we see that some notorious examples are not unbelievable: the two German villages left with only one female inhabitant apiece, and the Rhenish village where one person, most often female, out of every two families was put to death.[30]

Though almost every area of Europe hunted women more than men, three countries reversed this ratio: in Finland, Estonia, and apparently Russia, the majority of accused witches were men (see chapter 4). Some other regions had relatively lower percentages of women. In the Swiss Pays de Vaud, for instance, the accused were "only" 58 percent female. The rate for men was high there because the Vaudois thought of witchcraft as heresy, and heretics were chiefly male. The Aragonese Inquisition (1600–1650) prosecuted the lowest percentage of women in any witch trials, 28 percent, but secular courts in Aragon restored the usual balance by accusing sixty-six women to only two men, raising the rate for women in Aragon to 58 percent.[31]

The fact that overall about 20 percent of the accused were male is less an indication that men were associated with witchcraft than it appears. Most of these men were related to women already convicted of sorcery—as husbands, sons, or grandsons—and thus were not perceived as *originators* of witchcraft. Of the few who were not related, most had criminal records for other felonies, such as theft, highway robbery, murder, the theological crime of heresy, or sexual crimes such as rape, incest, fornication, adultery, or sodomy. For them, witchcraft was not the original charge but was added on to make the initial accusation more heinous.[32] Witchcraft thus was perceived primarily as a female offense.

When brought into court on a sorcery charge, men were often let off with lighter sentences than women (hence the even smaller number executed, 15 percent, out of all persons put to death, whereas 20 percent of all accused were male). Laws favored men: for example, when the rulers of Flanders decreed no more death penalty for prepubescent witches, boys benefited more because they were seen as minors until twenty-one, whereas girls became adults at eighteen.[33] Also, women, unable by law to give legal testimony, did not traditionally know how to use the courts, either for initial defense or for appeal. Therefore, appeals to the Parlement at Paris, which greatly moderated the force of the witchcraze in France, helped fewer women.[34]

Legal bias led to a notorious French case in which a priest and his mistress were both accused: through money and the influence of friends, he was let go without punishment, whereas she was burned at the stake. In Lorraine, when Claudine Simonette and her son Antoine were imprisoned, she was convicted, but his fate was not mentioned in the record. When a gentlemen hired Jeanette Neuve to poison his wife, she was burned at the stake, but there is no record that he received any punishment.[35] Of the fifteeen married couples convicted in England's Home Counties, more wives were executed than husbands.[36] A combination of factors, including the greater value placed on men as workers in the increasingly wage-oriented economy and a greater fear of women as inherently evil, loaded the scales against women, even when the charges against them were identical to those against men.

The effect on the image of sixteenth-century women was dramatic: although women committed far fewer crimes than men, the chief criminal stereotype of the period, that of the witch, was female.[37]

For all these reasons, the basic fact remains that throughout Europe during the period of major witch hunts (1560–1760), on average 80 percent of the accused and 85 percent of those executed were women. These lopsided figures are sufficiently telling when one thinks of them as individual burnings or hangings, especially considering that many of the victims were not guilty of this or any other crime. There is no need to inflate the numbers into millions; these statistics are sufficient to document an intentional mass murder of women. By documenting a persecution by gender, these numbers form the basis for this book. To ignore them or acknowledge them and then put them aside is to deny the most persistent fact about the persecutions.

Class

Scot continued in his discussion of witches to describe them as "poore, sullen. . . . These go from house to house, and from doore to doore for a pot full of milk, yeast, drinke, pottage, or some such releefe; without the which they could hardlie live." In most areas of Europe the accused were very poor, and their accusers were better off than they. Even though most accusers were neighbors who also lived in poverty, still they possessed more goods than their victims. The witch in many cases was the poorest of the poor, dependent on her neighbors to stave off starvation.[38] In the sixteenth century, as we will see, the poor were becoming poorer; more peasants were forced to beg or steal in order to survive. Old, single women, especially vulnerable in this economic crunch, came to be seen as nuisances. When they turned them down, people felt guilty, an uncomfortable state often exacerbated when the beggar cursed them for their refusal. Then when misfortune occurred, people turned on the beggars, a classic example of "blaming the victim."[39]

Those who had a little—and the rising expectations that go with "a little"—took out their frustrations over crop failure and the high death rate of infants on those who were least able to fight back. They also used witch accusations to establish their social position. In northern France, for instance, accusers were often those villagers who could read and write, who may have identified with the new reforms of the Catholic Reformation and the central government and may have seen cooperation with the authorities as the way up in the world. They strengthened their power in the village by attacking the most vulnerable group. As John Webster remarked (in 1677) of women having a bodily mark that could be taken for the devil's mark, "few would go free, especially those that are of the poorer sort."[40]

In some instances, wealthy women were attacked. Late in a witch hunt, after the pool of typical women victims had been depleted, bourgeois and even upper-class women and men might be accused.[41] In some cases poor women sought revenge by naming well-to-do women.[42] Powerful men sometimes attempted to destroy other successful men through their wives—some even used their own wives and daughters in order to effect this.[43]

Temperament and Age

Scot's description furnishes some further clues as to just which women would be singled out for accusation: "They are doting, scolds, mad, divelish; . . . so firme and steadfast in their opinions, as whosoever shall onelie have respect to the constancie of their words uttered, would easilie beleeve they were true indeed."[44] In other words, uppity women—women given to speaking out, to a bold tongue and independent spirit, women who had what Scottish people called "smeddum": spirit, quarrelsomeness, a refusal to be put down. They talked back to their neighbors, their ministers, even to their judges and executioners.[45]

Consider, for example, the case of a woman in the Spanish Netherlands known as the village curser. A poor but proud and outspoken woman, Marguerite Carlier, married with three children, voluntarily presented herself to be cleared of charges of killing animals. When she appealed to the privy council of the Hapsburg archduke, a number of well-off men from her village testified against her, revealing the real reason for their hatred of her—their fear that she had harmed them personally, that she was obsessed with causing them misery. But they had no proof, and under torture she confessed nothing; when released, she defended herself to one and all. Her defiance and open hostility made them fear her all the more, however, and she was banished, sent away from her family. After seven years in exile, she appealed again and was pardoned. Marguerite's case illustrates the price that an independent, outspoken woman might have to pay when she was up against the big men of the village, even when there was no proof against her.[46] That women talked back in a time when they were increasingly expected to be submissive is a point to which we will return.

Still another way in which women were vulnerable to charges of sorcery was because of their age. Though the majority of alleged witches in New England were middle-aged,[47] most European victims were older, over fifty.[48] Older women were frequently notorious as scolds; those no longer beholden to father, husband, or children felt freer to express themselves and often said just what they thought. John Metcalf of Leeds, England, complained in court that Anne Dixon had cursed him, calling him, "Whoremaster, whoremonger and harlott and did sit her downe upon her knees and cursed and banned him, and his wife, and badd a vengeance light upon the wife of the said John Metcalf and upon that whoremaster and whoremonger harlott her husband . . . and prayed God that they might never thryve."[49] The ability of early modern women to attack with words was fearsome. Curses like Anne Dixon's were the basis for many witchcraft accusations.

The typical scold and the typical witch were older females, and both were criminalized during the same period. Each had their own kind of power. By laying curses and giving "lip," old women used what power they had to make others fear them, give them "space," and maybe respect them. The fact that people feared their curse was proof that their words carried numinous power. This trait can be interpreted in two ways, as sheer bad nature or as a defensive strategy. John Demos believes that the "uppity" quality of middle-aged and older women in New England was the chief reason they "attracted" witch accusations. Seeing them as quarrelsome and intractable, especially in their relations with their husbands, and as offering unwanted advice to their neighbors, he explains their persecution by their behavior.[50] He omits from discussion the way women were subordinated to men, especially to husbands, in Puritan New England, and thus does not include the observation that they might well turn to nagging to protect their space in their homes.

Another way of looking at this trait is as a sign of being independent-minded. Traditionally, peasant women in bad marriages had complained of how they were treated, but increasingly now when they did so they were branded as "traitors" to their husbands. The family, not only in New England but across Europe, was becoming more patriarchal in the sixteenth century, causing women's roles within the family to shrink.[51] Outspoken wives were called shrews and suspected of witchcraft; when they spoke out against neighbors who had been unfair or ungenerous to them, they were hauled into court for being a nuisance and a witch.

Scolding done by a female was considered a crime and was punished in Britain by the scold's bridle, which locked the victim's head inside an iron cage that drove spikes through her tongue, and by the ducking stool, used for witches as well, by which they were ducked under water in stagnant ponds or cesspools.[52] Sixteenth-century females, especially the older ones, *were* often scolds—and the punishment they received for scolding and witchcraft was so harsh that women kept a lower profile for several centuries afterward.

Another complaint against women, especially old women, was what was seen as their overassertive sexuality. Men fancied that old women still desired them and found the idea grotesque, hence Reginald Scot's saying that "to enforce a man, how proper so ever he be, to love an old hag, she giveth unto him to eate (among other meates) his owne doong." Likewise the Kent assize reported that Goodwife Swane "vehemently suspected by church authorities [as a witch]," boasted "that she can make a drink, which she saith if she give it to any young man that she liketh well of, he shall be in love with her."[53]

One aspect of the witchcraze, undeniably, was an uneasiness with and hostility toward dependent older women. Witch charges may have been used to get rid of indigent elderly women, past childbearing and too enfeebled to do productive work. As Barbara Walker has put it, these women "could be called witches and destroyed, like domestic animals past their usefulness. . . . The old woman was an ideal scapegoat: too expendable to be missed, too weak to fight back, too poor to matter."[54]

A final important lead from Scot, one seldom followed up on by historians of witchcraft, somewhat balanced out these female handicaps: these women were "so firme and steadfast in their opinions" that people listened to them. The alleged witch may have been sliding down into economic dependency, but she still had a certain authority, some standing in her community. As a healer, midwife, advice-giver, fortune-teller, spell-lifter, she was sought after; she could therefore boast "that she (as a goddes) hath brought such things to pass." People turned *to* witches as well as turned *on* them. Like female shamans in Korea today, they were both scorned *and* considered essential to the community, were both outcasts and authority figures.[55] That their day as folk healers and cunning women was passing was part of the tragedy in which they were caught.

A
B
C
D
Many poor women imprisoned, and hanged for Witches.
A. Hangman. B. Belman. C. Two Sergeants. D. Witch-
finder taking the money for his work.

At this public execution of witches, four women hang while others (left and center) mourn. Men officiate: note the witch-finder receiving his payoff at right. From Ralph Gardiner, *England's Grievance Discovered,* 1655. Courtesy of the Rare Book & Manuscripts Library, Columbia University.

CHAPTER TWO

The Structure of a Witch Hunt

WHAT DID PEOPLE expect to accomplish by calling for and cooperating in a witch hunt? A complex social matrix was created once an accusation was made: the accusers would hope minimally to prove the source of what had been troubling them, and ideally to gain control over that source by forcing her to back away and remove the curse. As a witch hunt progressed and local authorities intervened more decisively, accusers might hope to destroy a woman's reputation, banish her, or kill her. The accuser might hope in addition to gain part or all of her property. More than one victim might be targeted, with a group of friends or an entire family wiped out.

But before neighbors would turn against neighbors in this way, they must believe in the reality of harmful magic. Almost everyone in sixteenth-century Europe did believe. The importance of the connection between a belief in harmful magic and witch hunts is shown by southern Spain—such belief was not important there, and no witch hunts occurred.[1]

Simple belief in the hurtful power of magic, however, would not alone cause a witch hunt. Throughout the Middle Ages, a period when such beliefs were widespread, there were few prosecutions. The something further required was that someone in the regional power structure believe that the devil and his servants, the witches, were attacking the Christian world. Why this belief developed and spread during the sixteenth century will require our attention in the final chapter. The connection with the devil made the crucial difference between, on the one hand, local people working out tensions through charges of harmful magic and countermagic and, on the other, the regional elite laying down the death sentence in ever-widening circles.

The nature of the law further determined whether and how harshly an area would prosecute—whether the law allowed torture, as it did in the German lands, for example, but not in England. Where torture and other inquisitional procedures were allowed, major witch trials could occur; without them, no mass prosecutions could be achieved. But again, these factors do not fully explain the mass persecutions that broke out in the sixteenth century. Inquisitional courts had been developed during the thirteenth century by the papacy in order to eradicate heretical groups, so these measures had been available for several centuries before the major witch hunts began. True, the secular courts of Europe did not begin to adopt inquisitional processes until the fifteenth century and did not take up witch accusations in a major way (take them away from church courts, that is) until the sixteenth. This timing, however suggestive it is for our chronology, still does not fully explain why European society was willing for the first time to prosecute and execute women on a large scale.

A look at long-term changes in European legal customs is pertinent here. Medieval Europe had originally practiced restitutive justice, a form of community customary law that functioned through arbitration with a goal of reconciliation.[2] Because the objective was the restoration of communal peace, it was not advantageous to wipe out one's enemies or to inflict long-term punishment on them. In the effort to keep the community functioning as peacefully as possible, accusers were made responsible for their charges—a false accusation carried a heavy penalty. Early medieval justice, like justice in most primitive societies, was thus personal, requiring face-to-face accusation and judgment by a panel of one's neighbors.

In the twelfth century, however, a very different system of law developed on the continent. Based on Roman law, it stressed punitive justice, emphasizing fines, punishments, and the death penalty. Its goal was to protect and purify the state. Because this law was administered by the state rather than the community, it was impersonal law, with magistrates reporting to superiors in far-off towns and cities. Although this distancing allowed for a certain objectivity of judgment and in some cases provided for appeals, it interjected alien values into communal settlement customs. The judge became the initiator of charges, compiling evidence against suspects, interrogating the accused in secret, using torture when necessary to ascertain the truth, acting always in the name of the state. These changes have been described as "constituting a revolutionary change in legal methods and techniques of societal control."[3]

In addition to the use of torture and impersonal, punitive law, I suggest a third factor of equal importance: whether or not an area still maintained the medieval *lex talionis*, the mandate that an accuser must prove his or her accusation or suffer the punishment that the defendant would have received. Because the legal penalty for witchcraft was death, this law acted as a powerful restraint on potential accusers. But in many parts of Europe by the sixteenth century, the personal justice of the *lex talionis*, carried out by the injured parties in a way that restored community relations, was being replaced by a more abstract justice administered by state officials;[4] now one could accuse with impunity. This shift rendered European justice more rational but less humane, and it opened the door wide to witchcraft accusations.

Given the necessary beliefs and legal conditions, what might prompt a witch hunt to begin? Though personal calamity was the most frequent trigger, natural disasters like hailstorms, a desire for revenge, or possession by demons (bewitchment) also turned up frequently as the cause. Hard times, caused by political, religious, or economic upheaval, were often in the background. The ensuing accusations might lead to a restrained witch hunt causing no deaths but only the whipping, fining, banishment, or ruined reputation of one or a few persons. They might produce a witchcraze, however, a mass hunt involving the deaths of hundreds of victims. Whether or not these actions restored the longed-for reconciliation and health to the community is another question; I find increasing evidence that they usually did not achieve this goal. That they harmed the status of women and women's self-image is, I believe, not to be questioned.

In chapters 5, 6, and 7 we will consider evidence for the social and economic harm that it did women to become associated with demonic witchcraft. But first we must look at the process of the witch hunts themselves. What do they tell us about the way sixteenth-century Europeans settled their problems, or about the level of violence in that world? And what do they tell us about how men and women related to one another?

THE TRIAL of a young Dutch woman is instructive of how witchcraft accusations often served as a cover for other problems, and how the women of a family could be made scapegoats for men's quarrels.

When Neele Ellers was about ten years old, her mother and paternal grandmother were accused of witchcraft: some soldiers stationed near Neele's village of Nijkerk in the Netherlands warned a village neighbor not to let these women into her house, because they could travel one hundred miles in a night.[5] This obvious reference to a witch's ability to fly through the air was made, not by neighbors who might have the usual grievances against the two women, but by outsiders, leaving us unsure as to what they based their charge on. Perhaps it was retaliation for a slight; perhaps the two women had overcharged the soldiers for food or laundry. Or they may have already had a reputation for working magic that the soldiers picked up on—we do not know.

In any case, this slander seems not to have affected Neele's early life. She faced at least one other problem, family violence, for when she was thirteen or fourteen her brother Jan hit her in the face with a flail, scarring her forehead. When she grew up she married a local man, Hendrick Bessens, no stranger to violence himself—he and his father had killed a man of the Van Brenen family four years before. Still, Neele's husband stood by her later, in her time of trouble. She also became close friends with a new woman in town, Luyt Hermans, but Luyt, as we shall see, turned against her. We can surmise that Neele and her husband lived with her family, not his, because she often quarreled with the poor widow who was allowed to live on the strip of common land immediately in front of Neele's parents' farm. Neele (and her mother) took Communion every Easter and at midwinter.

Neele's story would not be known to history had not a local man accused her of bewitching a young girl; this occurred in January 1550, when Neele was twenty-three. Her accuser, Jochum Bos, was just her age and had known her since they were both small. When he was a penniless child, Neele and her mother Diel had, out of compassion, given him a piece of bread.

When Jochum made his highly damaging charge, he was the first person ever to associate Neele with witchcraft. True, there may have been something suspect about her, for when Luyt Hermans and Neele were enjoying their friendship, Luyt's husband and Neele's father-in-law forced the women to break it off, saying that there was too much gossip about it. The nature of people's suspicions was not spelled out: Were the women neglecting their work? Was Luyt neglecting her two children and her two young brothers who lived with her? Or was the husband's nose out of joint over the pleasure that Luyt took in someone other than himself? His dissatisfaction may indeed have had something to do with the children, for we know that Luyt's younger brother, Rutger Hermans, lived with Neele's family in the summer of 1549. But her husband's criticism of her friendship with Neele breathed no hint of witchcraft.[6]

The young man who first libeled Neele as a witch had returned to live in Nijkerk the previous spring after six years away. But Jochum Bos did not settle down, instead taking to the road again, this time accompanied by the nine-year-old son of Goosen Heynricxz, the immediate neighbor of Neele's family. Goosen had tried several years before to get them to give up their lease so that he could add their property to his. When they refused, he made them into his bitter enemies.

Jochum Bos's summer travels were profitable. An old friend taught him how to conjure the face of a witch in a bucket of water, and somewhere he picked up a book of magic. He was lucky to be out of Nijkerk during those months, for the village was struck with an epidemic of illness caused by bewitchment. Returning just before Christmas, he looked in on the local convent, stirring up the nuns in the bakery and brewery so much that they began to sing lewd songs and to run away; he even became engaged to one of them. Forbidden to enter the convent again, he replied that no lock could keep him out (meaning that he had the power to break locks). He got drunk at the local tavern, so drunk that on his way home he fell repeatedly into the ditch and a companion had to fish him out.

Basing himself now at Goosen's house, Jochum put his new magic skills to work, reading from his sorcerer's book to the bewitched victims, including Goosen's fifteen-year-old daughter, Geertgen. He enlisted the hired hand, Peter van Brenen, to find more patients, such as Luyt Hermans's young brothers Rutger and Derrick.

Jochum's reputation as a cunning man depended on his ability to name the person responsible for the bewitchings. Finally he named Neele Ellers—he added four older women to his list, including Diel, but he mainly accused Neele. All four of the others already had reputations for witchcraft, but not Neele.[7] One can only speculate what led him to name her: Did thirteen-year-old Rutger Hermans nurse a grudge from the previous summer when he had lived at Neele's house, a grudge that he passed along to Jochum? Or did fifteen-year-old Geertgen have reason to fear her? Every time she saw Neele (who lived next door) she fainted, and on recovery had seizures and vomited up horsehair, iron nails, and other strange objects.[8] Or was there bad blood between Jochum and Neele, so that hers might be the face he would conjure up in the bucket of water? Although he was vague about his charges against the older women, he singled out the young one, blaming her for all the bewitchments in Nijkerk.

We cannot know at this point in the story what led the cunning man to Neele, but we do know the reaction of her family. Her husband, father, and father-in-law chased Jochum, intending to thrash him, once even driving him with a drawn bow to the home of Goosen's brother, one of the bewitched. At this point the sheriff stepped in, arrested Jochum, and accepted Neele and Diel's charge of slander against him. But the women were not let off; presumably there was too much fear surrounding the epidemic of bewitchments to let them go. Finally everyone involved, the five accused witches and the cunning man, were taken by cart to the regional capital, Arnhem. One of the women escaped, but Neele and Diel gave testimony before the court of their own free will.

Neele's husband procured a letter of good character for them from the chaplain of Nijkerk, confirmed by the opinion of several leading citizens. They needed all the help they could get, for Jochum, through his helper Peter van Brenen, arranged for nine Nijkerkers, all suffering from bewitchment, to come to Arnhem and give evidence against the accused women.[9] Goosen's sister-in-law claimed that Diel had bewitched her cattle and made them ill; Geertgen complained that she often saw Neele's face in the fire and then fainted and had seizures. Rutger and Derrick Hermans averred that Neele had given them apples and pears that made them ill, and that while bewitched by her, a black cat, which no one else could see, jumped over them and could only be chased away with holy water. Luyt, Neele's former friend, did not accuse her but struck instead at Neele's sister, who she implied had bewitched Luyt's young daughter, causing her twice to see the devil. Another neighbor claimed that after giving Diel's granddaughter a piece of bread, her butter would not churn; Jochum had the nerve to accuse Neele of knocking him into a ditch when he was walking with a friend. The court inquired about the scar on Neele's forehead, implying that it was the devil's mark.

All these claims were the stuff of local magical beliefs, typically found in cases throughout Europe. They concern misfortune to one's person or animals. There was a whiff of demonological belief in references to seeing the devil and the devil's mark, but none of the more frightening myths appeared, such as having sex with the devil or worshiping him at a sabbat. The most dangerous moment for Neele came when Geertgen insisted that Neele bless her. If Neele did so, and the girl was healed, then that was strong proof that Neele had indeed caused the curse, that is, that she was a witch. When the court ordered Neele to give the blessing, she did so, and Geertgen was healed. When the other victims asked to be blessed also, the case looked dangerous for Neele.[10]

But Jochum, a known alcoholic and womanizer, was not a credible accuser. When the court applied torture to him, he broke and retracted his accusations. Still not satisfied about Neele's innocence, they cross-examined her again but finally let her, as well as the other women, go free, with the admonition that no one was to hurt them in word or deed. The fact that none of Neele's accusers had been willing to call her a witch before the unsavory Jochum did so stood in her favor. The magician got off light, sentenced only to banishment from the duchy of Gelderland for life.

Though the court's restraint in not using torture against the women and in not pressing charges of devil worship contributed to making this a mild witch hunt, it was probably mostly limited by the threat of the *lex talionis,* still in effect in Gelderland. Although this law did not prevent the rash Jochum from making accusations dangerous to himself, it did seem to restrain the witnesses, who held back from direct accusations of witchcraft out of fear of receiving the punishment themselves.

It was typical of many hunts in that it was based on a bitter quarrel over property in which men used a woman as target. Note that Jochum, acting for his protectors, the Heynricxz family, did not accuse the men of Neele's family, their obvious enemies in the property dispute, nor did he help his assistant, Peter van Brenen, get revenge for his relative's murder by smearing the Bessens men. Instead he got at them all through the one young woman who connected the two families by marriage, Neele Ellers. As the researcher of this trial, Hans De Waardt, concludes, "Whoever got her, got both families."[11] Although women were seldom acknowledged as heads of families, they could serve as scapegoats in family feuds, thus gaining a perverse kind of power. An accusation of witchcraft therefore could be based on troubles quite unrelated to harmful magic itself.

A witchcraft accusation casts a long shadow. Over forty years later Neele was accused again as a witch, along with her daughters, son-in-law, and grandchildren. By this time they were living just across the border in the province of Utrecht, where they may have fled to escape from continuing persecution in Nijkerk. By the 1590s, Utrecht was undergoing a fresh wave of witch hunting, and Neele and many of her family were burned at the stake.[12]

Once accused, few persons lived down the label of witch. Thus the cunning man Jochum Bos had the last word—his naming of Neele in 1550 destroyed her and her family in the end. People believed that witchcraft ran in families, was handed down from mother to daughter, and passed along to in-laws. Neele, granddaughter and daughter of witches, and mother, mother-in-law, and grandmother of others, could not escape the onus of being seen as an enemy of her society.

Though this trial did not identify the source of the illnesses (bewitchments) in Nijkerk, it did take care of the witch scare. True, by ruling that it was the cunning man rather than the alleged witches who had disturbed the peace, it offered a twist to the usual scenario. The court was wise enough to see that if Jochum had not returned to Nijkerk to practice magic, there would have been no witch hunt, and it dealt with that problem by banishing him. But it cannot be said that it restored the village to peace or harmony; that Neele and her family moved to another province probably means that they continued to be harassed, and their later executions show that the charge of evildoing followed them.

That the trial itself was moderate is all the more remarkable, given the level of violence in Nijkerk, where among our small cast of characters we know of two murders in the previous four years. As for how men and women related to one another, we find cases of marital loyalty, even in the face of witchcraft charges, though families often deserted an accused relative, so greatly were the charges feared. We also find restraint on the part of local and provincial authorities, who did not stereotype the women as criminals. These positive signs were contradicted, however, by several indications of the powerlessness of women and a general suspicion of them. Neele's close friendship with Luyt was broken up by her father-in-law and Luyt's husband, indicating that patriarchal family power was stronger than the ability of women to bond. Community suspicion of witchcraft in five generations of women exposes the depth of belief in women's weakness for witchcraft, and in its inheritability. But it is primarily the rash attacks of the cunning man against five women that confirms how vulnerable women were in Gelderland. In order to set himself up as a village healer, Jochum would have sent the women to their deaths.

The events in Gelderland might have had worse results for the accused if the Netherlands had had its own centralized government instead of being one small part of Charles V's great empire. We may draw this conclusion by contrasting the events in Nijkerk with those in another rural area, the Lancashire of James I's England. A famous trial there in 1612 reveals the powerful effect of royal edicts on local witchcraft customs—and on the lives of village women.

ANY DISCUSSION of sixteenth-century witch persecutions must mention the growing power of the state. In England in 1604, for example, in the second week of King James I's first Parliament, the House of Lords passed a much stricter witchcraft law. Whereas before the death penalty was invoked only when a witch's powers caused death, now merely causing hurt through evil spirits or a second offense of using magic for finding stolen property, causing unlawful love, or *intending* to hurt or destroy a person would also bring the death sentence. The king's intense interest in witch hunting bore early fruit.[13]

The ducal and royal governments of Europe were becoming more efficient, centralized, and powerful, in other words, more capable of controlling many aspects of more people's lives. Taxation, which fell primarily on the peasantry, increased greatly.[14] Royal agents asserted their influence in parts of Europe never before interfered with. They demanded not only taxes and military levies but also a new ideological conformity: nationalism as we know it first reached rural western Europe in the seventeenth century. Secular courts took over prosecution of sexual crimes, matters formerly reserved for judgment in the more private sphere of church or neighborhood. The state was willing to take on the responsibility and expense of this jurisdiction because these moral judgments helped to define what it stood for and allowed for the control of the most intimate aspects of the lives of its citizens.

These governments were as intolerant as they were interfering. In an important study, R. I. Moore demonstrated how the European state became an organ of persecution, how, in the eleventh and twelfth centuries, European governments began, for the first time, to identify groups as enemies of the state—heretics, Jews, lepers, homosexuals—and to *create the myths* that would enable rulers to destroy those groups. Observing that there have been two major periods of persecutions in Europe since, the sixteenth and seventeenth centuries (the witchcraze) and the twentieth (the Holocaust), Moore states that intolerance "became part of the character of European society," and that in each case it was the rulers, not the people, who originated and carried out the pogroms. In short, the chief motive behind European racism and bigotry was the drive for political power. Even though none of the victims were powerful enemies, they served as an excuse for governments to use powerful weapons against their own people.[15]

This new system of social control in which centralized governments were willing to prosecute on sexual and religious matters fell heaviest on the lower class, those unable to use the law to protect themselves—too uneducated to learn to use its ways or too poor to afford it. The women who suffered from these handicaps were particularly vulnerable when the state turned its attention to witchcraft.

As for the status of women in European legal history, one notable fact about them is their absence. Until the sixteenth century, women made up a very small number of the defendants, accusers, or witnesses in legal cases,[16] and the personnel who ran the courts, whether secular or ecclesiastical, were, of course, male. When women were arrested it was primarily on sexual charges. Married women, in fact, as dependents of their husbands, were not held accountable for many types of crimes.[17] Few females appeared as witnesses, because a woman's testimony was not legally acceptable. Furthermore, women rarely took the initiative in bringing charges, because whatever problems their lives contained were settled mostly outside the courts, by extralegal methods.

Women seldom engaged in violent crime, but when they did, they typically attacked other women. In England, for example, Joan Marvel hit Agnes Fordan during church service, and Joan Sleap attacked the woman who blocked her way into a field by hitting her in the teeth.[18] Women were known to steal—behind many witchcraft charges lie small thefts of domestic items. The courts took little interest in domestic theft, however, seeing robbery of business property as much more threatening to the right ordering of society.

Because women were frequently suspect as infanticides, we know that they were capable of murder. European courts, however, did not begin seriously to prosecute infanticide until after the middle of the sixteenth century. Medieval women therefore appear to have committed less crime than men, and to have done so in less observable ways, settling their minor thefts among themselves, covering up the murder of a baby whenever possible. The courts, meanwhile, busied themselves with the affairs of men, matters such as quarrels between heads of families over property and issues touching male honor.[19]

Even when women did take part in what were seen as major crimes—receiving stolen goods, poisonings, and so on—they were often acting as their husband's agents, carrying out a supporting role in the schemes and vendettas of the family. The courts regarded women as minors; married women, it was assumed, would be kept in line by their husbands, and single women, a more problematic group, were left to the community to control. I conclude that until the late sixteenth century the European legal system lumped women, children, serfs, and slaves into the category of dependent property and therefore largely ignored them, except when they got too far out of line.

Then around 1560 European secular courts began to hear accusations of witchcraft and sexual crimes, and women began to appear in court in large numbers, an entirely new phenomenon. Larner was correct to point out that women were criminalized, as witches and infanticides, for the first time in this period.[20] These were heinous crimes, newly perceived as so threatening to society that they could no longer be left to the control of the women's world. But in the process of bringing these offenses under their jurisdiction, sixteenth-century courts were forced to admit their perpetrators to a new legal standing.[21] No longer seen as too dependent to be prosecuted, women were now held accountable in court for their actions. Because witches were believed to freely choose their craft, they were held responsible for the harm they reputedly caused. Even though they acted through the power of the devil, they alone (and certainly not their husbands) must be punished. The surprising number of husbands who joined others in accusing their wives of witchcraft makes it clear that on a charge so dangerous many men would not be responsible for their wives nor dare to be identified with them.[22] That European women first emerged into full legal adulthood *as witches*, that they were first accorded independent legal status in order to be prosecuted for witchcraft, indicates both their vulnerability and the level of antifeminism in modern European society.

The trials that followed these two major legal changes were in many ways a clash of cultures, with the elite theories of diabolical conspiracy set against the traditional sorcery, magic, and clan loyalties of the folk culture. Nowhere was this better illustrated than in the mass trial of the Lancashire witches in 1612, when two rival families of self-identified witches were dragged into the juridical net of England's royal circuit judges.

Living in a remote area called Pendle Forest, the families of Old Demdyke and Old Chattox were the poorest of the poor, living mainly off begging and the proceeds of their charms and curses.[23] Old Demdyke, the matriarch of all the witches in Pendle Forest, was an eighty-year-old widow who ruled over her daughter, son-in-law, and three grandchildren at Malking Tower. Too poor to own a cow, she sent her grandchildren out to beg for milk and forage for old clothing. Although now blind, she was still in demand as a healer: when John Nutter's cow became ill, she was called to "mend" it.

But Demdyke's reputation was mixed. Her daughter Elizabeth Device asked her to go to the miller Baldwin to collect pay for Elizabeth. When Demdyke, led by her teen-aged granddaughter Alison, approached, the miller shouted, "Get out of my ground, whores and witches. I will burn the one of you and hang the other." To which Demdyke replied, "I care not for thee. Hang thyself." When Baldwin's young daughter took ill soon after and eventually died, there was murmuring against Demdyke.

She had become a witch forty years before, when she gave her soul to "a spirit or devil in the shape of a boy," in return for a promise of having whatever she wanted. The spirit appeared to her as a dog named Tibb, who sucked blood from under her left arm. The first time he came, she went mad for eight weeks.

Five years later she initiated her neighbor, later known as Old Chattox, a wool carder, "a very old, withered, spent, and decreped creature," "her lippes ever chattering," who supplemented her income with a protection scheme, promising not to harm those who gave her an annual bribe of meal. With Demdyke she found three skulls in the graveyard and extracted eight teeth, sharing them equally between them. Chattox knew how to place curses through clay images, and several local children died after she made images of them.

Both women taught their daughters witchcraft, and Old Demdyke initiated her granddaughter Alison Device as well. The two families competed for business as conjurors and cursers, and because they were forced to share the trade with a number of other women and several men, competition was fierce. Bad feelings between the two families were not eased when Old Demdyke's daughter Elizabeth Device was robbed of clothing and food and later found some of these items in the possession of Old Chattox's daughter Anne Redfearne.

Thus the clans feuded for years, far from the reach of royal justice. Had a wealthy local family not intruded into their lives, they might have continued their practices of magic and sorcery for generations more. But when Robert Nutter, a son of local gentry who were the Redfearne's landlord, tried to seduce Anne Redfearne and she refused him, their troubles began. Nutter threatened that he would evict Anne from her home when he inherited the land. In retaliation Old Chattox attempted to kill Nutter by witchcraft, egged on by three women, Nutter's cousins, who coveted the land. When three months later he died, Old Chattox and Anne were in deep trouble. At this point cooperation arrived from an unexpected source, the rival clan, when Elizabeth Device made a clay image of one of the Nutter women.

Shortly after, the granddaughter Alison had an altercation with an itinerant peddler whom she met on the road. A few minutes later he suffered a stroke, for which he blamed Alison. The teenager accepted the charge and asked his pardon. In doing so, she followed custom: a bewitcher was expected, when faced with the damage she had done, to ask pardon *and receive it.* But no doubt Alison did not know about the strict witchcraft law of 1604, which greatly increased the penalty for white or black magic. The peddler's family may have known about it, however, for the peddler's son complained to the local justice of the peace. Alison not only confessed again that she had lamed the peddler, but described how her grandmother had many times urged her to accept a familiar;[24] finally Alison had allowed a black dog to suck at her breast. Then, no doubt pressed by the J.P., she described several examples of Demdyke's harmful magic. Not content with implicating her grandmother, she added that Chattox had bewitched her (Alison's) father to death when he fell behind in paying her a bribe. On Alison's evidence, Old Demdyke was brought before the local J.P. on a general charge of witchcraft. She soon implicated her granddaughter Alison and Old Chattox, and the three females were imprisoned in Lancaster Castle, some thirty miles away, to await the next royal assizes.

Families involved in the Lancashire Trial of 1612

OLD DEMDYKE — OLD CHATTOX

ELIZABETH DEVICE — ANNE REDFEARNE

ALISON, JAMES, JENNET

CHRISTOPHER NUTTER (d. 1594)

ROBERT, JOHN, MARGARET

ALICE NUTTER (*relation to above unknown*)

Witch hunting was in the air in that region—eventually nineteen persons were arrested, fifteen women and four men. But before the roundup occurred, the clans tried to strike back. United by this outside threat, about twenty persons met under Elizabeth Device's leadership at Old Demdyke's home at Malking Tower and planned to rescue the prisoners. While plotting a jail escape, they feasted on a mutton that Elizabeth's son James Device had stolen.

Events up to this point are believable enough, a narrative straight out of the culture of folk magic. But from the meeting at Malking Tower on, that is, from the moment a conspiracy of witches was spotted, details begin to get out of hand. A constable was ordered to question Elizabeth Device and her two younger children, James and nine-year-old Jennet. The two young people blabbed on and on, naming about sixteen persons who had been present at the cabal; most likely they had no idea that they were implicating them in a crime that since 1604 had carried the death penalty. They even included Jennet Preston from nearby Gisburn, recently released from her trial for witchcraft in York. Astonishingly, instead of lying low, she had come to this gathering, even though she was not implicated in the Pendle Forest troubles. Either she wanted revenge on her accusers and came seeking allies (as Elizabeth Device claimed) or she was a confederate of the Pendle witches and feared they would name her if she refused to help them in their time of trouble. In either case, she made a fatal mistake, for she ended up being retried, and this time she was found guilty and hanged. Her presence adds greatly to the sense of a coven or "working group" of cunning women and cursers in the Pendle area.

Equally damaging was Jennet and James's declaration that their mother had been a witch for a number of years, that she carried out curses by making clay images of her victims, and that she had caused the deaths of several men. Elizabeth at first denied all charges, but when faced with the accusations of her children, she admitted all, adding the information that she had brought about the death of John Robinson because he had accused her of bearing an illegitimate child.[25] After these revelations and James's showing the constable where to dig up the teeth his grandmother had buried, the J.P. ordered Elizabeth, her two younger children, and seven more whom they had named to be jailed in Lancaster with the others.

The court's account of the Good Friday cabal claims that they plotted to kill the jailer of Lancaster Castle and then blow up the place, an obvious steal from the Guy Fawkes plot to blow up Parliament seven years before.

Elizabeth Device denied this, but not the description of the gathering's end, when they all "went out of the said house in their owne shapes and likenesses. And they all, by that they were forth of the dores, gotten on Horsebacke, like unto Foales, some of one colour, some of another; and Preston's wife was the last; and, when shee got on Horsebacke, they all presently vanished out of sight." This first English description of a sabbat implies that they had changed shape at the sabbat, and then changed back again, and perhaps that they flew away at the end. Yet despite these far-fetched notions, all the court witnesses who mentioned the Good Friday meeting agreed on these details.

Before the royal justices arrived at Lancaster, the prisoners had incriminated one another, and the case was built. Old Demdyke had died in prison, raising the question of brutal treatment. Her death left ten from Pendle Hill to be tried on charges of signing a pact with the devil in blood; turning into dogs, cats, or rabbits; and making clay images in order to cause others to languish or to die. Perhaps because of the numbers involved and the consequent notion of demonic conspiracy, or perhaps because of the outlandish image of "wild" rural folk, the case drew unprecedented attention around the country. It stirred up so much furor in Lancashire that it even drew a member of the gentry onto the accused list, Alice Nutter, identified by Jennet as present at the Malking Tower cabal and as the murderer, together with Elizabeth and Demdyke, of a local Pendle Hill man, Henry Mitton. Although she was wealthy, respected, and apparently well liked, she could not extricate herself from charges that she had attended the Good Friday gathering and had previously assisted Old Demdyke in bewitching a man to death. It seems that the court did not find it strange that a woman of the gentry would take part in peasant black magic. Once the Devices, mother, son, and younger daughter accused her, nothing her family did could save her. As for the Devices, perhaps they figured that if they were going down, they would take a member of the hated gentry with them. What had the local upper class ever done but pour scorn on them?

In prison family loyalties further broke down. Elizabeth, who had already accused her mother, was accused in turn by Jennet and James; they claimed that she used a spirit in the form of a brown dog called Ball to bewitch and kill people. Jennet in turn accused James of using his demon spirit, a dog named Dandy, to bewitch to death, a charge he then confessed to. Killing was the main charge against Old Chattox, Elizabeth and James Device, Anne Redfearne, Alice Nutter, and Katharine Hewitt. Causing illness or "wasting away" was charged against Alison Device, Isabel Robey, and a husband and wife named Bulcock.

The case of Anne Redfearne stands out: accused of Robert Nutter's murder by his brother and sister and further tainted by Old Demdyke's claim that she had seen Anne make an image of Robert, she nonetheless maintained her innocence and was acquitted. But the crowd cried out against her, and she was charged again, this time for the bewitchment and murder of Robert's father, Christopher, eighteen years before; this time the charge stuck.

In the end, five members of the Pendle families confessed (all except Anne), but none of the others did, raising again the question of where reality ended in this testimony. Perhaps the five who had indeed practiced black magic confessed to it, and those whose names were added as accomplices, but who were in fact not sorcerers, refused to confess what they were not guilty of. If so, Anne Redfearne was not guilty of sorcery; thus her story needs more analysis. Known as a witch and daughter of a witch, she might have been as much a sorcerer as any of them; a number of witnesses accused her of "many strange practices," whatever that meant. But she had clear reason for hating the man she was accused of killing; Robert Nutter had tried to seduce her and had then threatened to throw her off her land. That, having been cleared in his death, she was then charged with the murder of his father many years before, implies that the Nutter family was out to get her, come what may. This tells us less about Anne than about Robert and his family: it was *he* who was guilty (of sexual harassment) and *they* who were left to deal with that guilt. In blaming Anne it seems that they were engaging in the classic projection of guilt outward onto the victim, a transferal documented in hundreds of witchcraft accusations. Yet it was Old Chattox who had actually hexed him—why were they not content to see her condemned? The Nutter family and the crowd appeared determined to destroy Anne. The case is an example of the price a woman paid for refusing a man's sexual advances and of how vulnerable a poor woman was to attack by a family of the gentry.

And neither was Alice Nutter guilty, if refusal to confess is the criterion. Historians and novelists have pondered why this respectable woman of the gentry joined the cabal that Good Friday.[26] It is possible that out of hatred for her neighbor Henry Mitton she had earlier asked Demdyke to hex him, that she now feared that she would be named by Demdyke or the Devices, and had therefore gone to Malking Tower to try to buy them off or otherwise silence them.

Whatever the cause, enmity between the two peasant clans and this gentry family ran deep, eventually ending in the execution of seven of their numbers. The court sentenced in all ten persons to be hanged, acquitted five, and sentenced one to a year's imprisonment. It was the largest trial and second largest hanging thus far in the English witch hunts.[27] This case stands in sharp contrast to the continental trials we will consider next: no mention was made of searching for the devil's mark (thus no body searches were carried out), and no apparent force was used to generate testimony or confessions. The judge was credulous enough about nine-year-old Jennet's testimony about demonic animal spirits.[28] Nonetheless he acquitted five of the prisoners and three more women brought in on witchcraft charges in the midst of this trial.[29] It was not a hanging jury. Still, the prosecution destroyed two peasant families in the name of explaining and punishing some recent deaths.

These families were matriarchal clans, where knowledge of witchery was handed down from mother to daughter, from mother to son. They survived on their wits and their ability to conjure and heal— survived, that is, until the alien language of J.P., jailer, and judge was put to them. Then this female-dominant society unraveled fast, mothers, daughters, and son accusing one another. What deep hatreds were triggered in the presence of officials of the law? Why did Old Demdyke name her own granddaughter to the officials—and almost immediately at that? Even more unnatural was Jennet and James's turning on their mother. James, a prisoner, may have tried to save his own skin, but Jennet, being underage, was not even under indictment. Too much poverty or too much magic or (most likely) too much community rejection had left this family vulnerable to attack from outside. But how many peasant families could have stood up to close examination by the J.P. and a notorious trial before the king's judges?[30]

We cannot know the answers, but perhaps the surest clues lie not in family relationships but in how village people experienced the new impact of the law. Neither paralyzed nor divided by the first arrests (Elizabeth, remember, had organized the defense of her mother, her older daughter, and Old Chattox soon after they were arrested), once in prison they fell on one another like wolves. Did the jailers promise them release if they incriminated one another? Or, more likely, were they panicked by the apparatus of the law? Having lived their lives like outlaws in Pendle Forest, settling their squabbles among themselves, they may have become desperate when caged in prison, pursued by judges sent from London. To face even a minor charge as defendant before a court is an overwhelming experience; to be brought up on a charge carrying the death penalty was apparently sufficient to tear this family to shreds. The long arm of royal justice reached into a remote corner of English society, destroying two matriarchies of sorcerers and dragging down one gentlewoman with them all. The centuries-old female bonding that went on around magical practices of healing and harming was no match for the threat of being hanged by a royal court. The force of a witchcraft accusation was powerful indeed.

The amount of sexual content was low, compared with that in many continental trials, but it is present. Elizabeth was known as the mother of an illegitimate child; Demdyke and Alison were called whores. Anne Redfearne's tragedy stemmed from her rejection of an upper-class man's sexual demands. It was as dangerous then as now for a woman to tell certain men no.

As we saw in the Dutch trial of Neele Ellers, the tragedy does not end with the trial. The residents of this small rural area had to go on living together, across barriers of suspicion and hatred. Class tensions must have been raw, and women were suspect by their very nature. Young Jennet was left an orphan. We don't know who took her in, but we do know that the shadow of her family's history stayed with her. Rumors of witchcraft continued to be whispered around Pendle Hill until they built up twenty-one years later into a second witch hunt, again one that rested on the accusations of a child, an eleven-year-old boy. One of the women charged was Jennet Device, now about thirty.[31] After the 1633 trial found seventeen guilty and acquitted several, four of the women were sent to London for examination by royal physicians, including William Harvey, and midwives. This time the search for the devil's mark was a prominent part of the procedures, so body searches were carried out. Harvey's report was in favor of the women, who were returned to Lancaster but, strangely, not released. In 1636 a sheriff's report listed nine still in jail, including Jennet.[32] Because four had died from the harsh conditions of prison life, the outlook for her cannot have been good.

THESE CASES produced only mild witch persecution. Utilizing almost no torture other than psychological and not concerned with the classical accusations of devil worship, they did not spread beyond the immediate circumstances that produced them. Witch hunts in south Germany, drawing heavily on both torture and demonology, had a very different structure and result.

These hunts, deserving of the name *witchcraze,* could not have happened unless a major legal change had taken place: the adoption by secular courts of inquisitional procedures. Secret sessions, withholding of the source of charges, denial of counsel, acceptance of evidence from prejudiced sources, lack of cross-examination, passing of indeterminate sentences, assumption of guilt—all these were justified to protect the church from heretics and society from witches. The judge was both prosecutor and confessor, trying to condemn the defendant as a follower of Satan but to do so in such a way as to save her soul.[33] Undeniably the most influential change brought in by inquisitional procedure, however, was the use of torture to force confessions and the naming of accomplices.[34]

By the sixteenth century both municipal and royal courts freely used these procedures, especially in cases of witchcraft, sexual crimes (including infanticide), and treason. This was an ominous trend, for the secular courts turned out to be more murderous than the church courts had been. Although the church must be charged with developing the demonic theories, the misogyny, and the extreme legal processes that made massive witch hunts possible, and with offering continuing encouragement to secular authorities to prosecute, still one must remember that the major witch hunts were carried out not by churches but by temporal authorities. In that process, witchcraft became a secular crime, one seen, rather like treason, as an assault on the very existence of the community or commonwealth. To understand the full damage that these persecutions could cause to women and to communities, one must look at several typical sets of German trials. Keeping in mind the case of Walpurga Hausmänin of Dillingen, consider events in Eichstätt and Offenburg.

A Catholic town in Bavaria, Eichstätt was ruled by its prince-bishop. It suffered three waves of witch persecutions, in 1590, 1603–30, and 1637.[35] The exact number put to death is not known, but about 1629 a judge claimed he had examined 274 witches "who had to all appearances died." For the period when the gender of the victims is known, the ratio of women to men was about fourteen to one. Every village in the region had its victims; for almost fifty years the area can have known no rest from the terror, because between the waves of arrests, accusations were constantly being made. *Terror* is the accurate word, for the accused were tortured not once but repeatedly, convicted witches suffered the hot pincers, and one had her right hand cut off. Add to this the psychological terror of neighbor accusing neighbor, and one begins to see the disruption that a witchcraze caused.

The trial of a poor woman at the end of the Eichstätt witchcraze (1637) epitomizes the mind-set of the times.[36] Known to us only as "N. N.," she did not know the names of her parents or where or when they were born or died. Apparently she kept a little store. Forty years old, she had been married twenty-three years and had borne eight children, two of whom had died of smallpox and a six-year-old of unspecified causes, all some years ago. Because of "these suspicious circumstances of death" she has now been summoned to the Town Hall. But there is more to the case: she is accused by fifteen persons of passing through locked doors, riding through the sky, attending the sabbat, having a demon lover, raising storms, exhuming corpses—but, surprisingly, not of harming humans or animals. South German definitions of witchcraft had by this time been so demonized that they no longer depended on maleficium at all.

Imprisoned, subjected to an "indecent" examination, and identified as having a devil's mark, she begins bravely enough, laughing heartily and denying all charges, until she is stretched on the ladder. Then she confesses she is a witch, only to retract the statement as soon as the ropes are loosened. This process of denial, torture, confession goes on until she admits to practicing evil magic. One night after she had just given birth to another child, her husband had come home drunk and cursed her, wishing the devil would take her and all the children. And she thought, "Oh, when would he come! Oh, soon!" She then had a love affair with the hangman, who turned out to be the devil himself. The devil-hangman forced her to deny God and do evil everywhere.

As the torture continues, day after day, she confesses to many crimes, even some she was not accused of: poisoning her six-year-old and causing her former mistress's four-year-old to die of plague. When she is not repentant enough to satisfy the court, she is flogged, and then admits that some years ago she had killed her own horse and cow and had had intercourse with the devil in her prison cell. She also tries to commit suicide there, by scratching open an old wound in her arm so she would bleed and by suffocating herself. But each time they lessen the torture, she denies all that she has said.

Throughout her trial the judges have assumed her guilt and worked only to get her to confess and to name others. Although this was a secular court, it opened each day's session with prayer (was a priest present also?). Finally her mind grows confused; she now confesses without the prompting of the ladder. Describing in detail her visits to the sabbat, she names (and thereby implicates) a number of other persons whom she saw there. The twelfth day into the trial, the court presses charges relating to harm to the community, namely, storm raising. In order to elicit her confession to this monstrous crime, she is placed in the Spanish boots (which crush the leg bones) and is lashed "while the bells tolled the Ave Maria." Discord is suspected between her and her husband.

Her most shocking confession is of exhuming the corpse of her own child, buried six years and all rotted away, in order to cook the remains to make a magic powder that she gave to her devil. But what haunts her most are her sexual failings: because of her seduction by the devil she cannot pray anymore and fears she will not go to Heaven. Yet she got no pleasure from her affair, for the devil beat her and caused her pain when they were in bed together so that she screamed out, waking her husband, who then began to sleep in a separate bed.

Confessing finally the one action she may in fact have taken out of all this fantasy, she says that she often seduced her servant, "indeed, he had let her show it to him often." She dies penitent, having assured the judges that they have helped her to salvation.

I will argue that this fully developed form of witch trial was designed to drive the accused insane. First, the stark imbalance of power, between the top officials of the district and a poor woman who does not know her parents' names, would be enough to paralyze her with fear. Condescendingly, they repeatedly assure her that they can protect her from the devil, all the while torturing her to force her to confess her "guilt," playing with her as cat with mouse. They have every advantage over her—of education, community prestige, and, of course, of access to the implements of torture.

Second, the gender imbalance, one woman against at least six men (for we must count in the torturers too), would further intimidate her. Not even a female jailer is mentioned; N. N. says that "being alone, she feels afraid and does not know why." When she confesses to having a devil-lover, she describes him as "the hangman," possibly a clever jibe at a hated local figure, possibly a sign of the disintegration of her mind. Or it may be that she was indeed having a forced relationship with him; it was the hangman who searched the bodies of accused women for the devil's mark, giving him every opportunity to rape his prisoners.

Her relationship with her husband had been fractured long before; she implies that it was his rejection of her that made her long for the devil in the first place, and we know of many women who claimed that the devil seduced them when they were down. It is not surprising that the husband does not support her at the trial.

In fact, no one supports her. Fifteen of her acquaintances *accuse* her, and she takes revenge by naming forty-five individuals as co-witches. But she was alone indeed—although she was a religious person who went to confession and took communion, no priest is mentioned as advising or consoling her. She had to go through this physical and mental ordeal unaided.

The charges cleverly tear down all that she might have been proud of. Attacking her as a mother, the court blames her for the deaths of her three children, even though two died of smallpox, a common contagious disease. The worst of it for her, however, seems to have been the issue of the truth about who and what she is. Again and again she risks being sent back to torture in order to protest that *she is not a witch.* To clear her name, to make the world acknowledge the truth about her, seems to have been what drove her. When the torture breaks her down and she describes every possible lurid detail of the sabbat, confessing finally even to infanticide, the shock of telling these lies deranges her mind. When she pleads, "O Jesus Christ, be with me, and because I have grievously sinned against thee, please, dear God, open your ears again to me," she is not begging to be released from torture but to be forgiven for having *said* that she had sex with the devil. The extent of her derangement is shown in the alarming number of persons she was willing to implicate, her attempts at suicide, and the way she finally groveled in front of the authorities.

The case of another woman of Eichstätt, Anna Kaserin, wife of an innkeeper, shows again the lengths the authorities went to in order to crush suspects. Brought to trial in 1629 and accused of crimes almost identical to those of N. N., Anna was even more severely tortured (thumbscrew and strappado) and chained to her cell wall, in this case with a female jailer as guard.[37] First denying everything, she finally admitted that twice when she was drunk and had lain down, "someone" had come in and had sex with her. Trying to satisfy the court, she names him "Beelzebub" and says that he placed his devil's mark on her right foot. She also confessed to having killed her own child. What ties her story most closely to that of N. N., however, was her attempt at suicide; emptying her bowels and bladder into a bowl, she broke bread into it and tried to eat it, hoping this would kill her. But she vomited it up and survived to be beheaded and burned. The way in which these trials were carried out was designed to reduce people to animal-like behavior, to break their spirits and minds.

N. N.'s family was apparently not implicated with her; in fact, the witchcraze ended in Eichstätt shortly after her execution. But as we have seen in both the Dutch and Lancashire cases, blood relationship, and even relationship by marriage, counted heavily in identifying witches. The way in which family relationship triggered witchcraft charges is amply illustrated in Offenburg, a strongly Catholic free city near Strasbourg.[38] Five mother-daughter groups, three mother-son, one father-son, one husband-wife-son, and two groups of three generations of women suffered from trials. In Offenburg and the immediate vicinity, 102 persons were killed and one banished between 1557 and 1630. Reaction to witches was vicious from the start: in 1557 two women were burned alive, and confession was often extracted by placing the accused in the witch chair, a metal seat heated from beneath. One woman died from torture; another had her right breast torn by hot pincers; still another committed suicide in prison; a fourth went mad.

Several women claimed that the devil appeared when they suffered from their husbands' cruelty. This echoes N. N.'s *hope* that the devil would come to her after her husband cursed her. Others testified that their demon gave them a switch that would kill man or beast with a single blow, a useful weapon to raise against an abusive husband. This motif of the demon as protector of battered women is strengthened by frequent references to marriage to the demon: a woman's relation with her demon often began with a wedding celebration and was called a "marriage." Lea comments that this motif became an indispensable part of witch lore in the Offenburg area.

Families were bound to an accused witch, come what may. Required to pay not only prison costs but execution expenses as well, some families were ruined financially as well as by reputation when members were convicted.

What stands out in the Offenburg record is the way accusations tore through important families. The first executions that took place in the city proper included the wife of Georg Laubbach, a member of the Rat, the ruling council.[39] Soon his three daughters were accused, two by another councillor, Silberrad, the leader of the witch-hunting faction. Counteraccusations ended in the arrest of Silberrad; totally polarized, the town must have been paralyzed by this time. What underlay this crisis is not clear; it may have been debates over whether or not the town should turn Protestant. Although in the end it remained firmly Catholic, the town fathers had to bar the gates on Sundays and feast days to prevent people from attending Protestant services elsewhere, and only sworn Catholics could be citizens. These precautions indicate a volatile ecclesiastical situation.

Two of the Laubbach daughters were let off, but the third was not so fortunate: after heroically enduring torture, Else finally broke when her young daughter, after being beaten, confessed to practicing witchcraft. This, of course, implicated the mother, who was soon put to death. The young girl was spared death but was banished. In the prominent Laubbach family a grandmother, mother, and daughter were accused, and two lost their lives.

Trials continued apace, the victims drawn heavily from the women of the ruling class, until 1629, when finally a member of the council itself was executed. The death of Ratsherr Hans Georg Bauer so shook the town that Offenburg killed no more citizens on the charge of witchcraft.[40] The use of elite women as surrogates for their powerful husbands, men far harder to get at than the wives, exposes the strange value of women in an early bourgeois urban setting: powerless to defend themselves against witch charges, still they *counted* in the political struggles of the Rat. Killing them smeared the reputation of their families. The inability or unwillingness of their husbands and fathers to protect them must be noted: one official, his wife incarcerated, tried to write to her to convince her to confess to unfaithfulness and said she should be tortured about her relationship with a certain young man. She was executed. Add this hostility to the fact that many women spoke of their longing for marriage to the devil and their need for protection from men, and we are left with a disturbing picture of marriage in Offenburg.

The process in this secular court followed inquisitional method throughout. No defense was allowed, nor communication with the accused; torture was used repeatedly, and a promise of lighter torture was traded for the naming of accomplices, virtually assuring that more trials would be needed; priests worked with the court to obtain confession, worked so hard that they asked for (but did not receive) pay.[41] But the town fathers went beyond even what inquisitional procedures called for: gratuitous torture was applied even after conviction; women's bodies were repeatedly examined by the executioner; two male guards were ordinarily stationed in the cell with the woman, exposing her to the possibility of constant sexual harassment.

During the years of these trials, an orgy of hatred against the convicted was built up, as evidenced by the fact that as the condemned were carried in a cart to the place of execution, they were "accompanied by a mocking and abusive crowd yelling with hatred and derision." Even more disturbing are the bizarre entertainments and banquets for the judges and priests that often preceded the executions—all of which had to be paid for by the family of the victim. Because the victims were overwhelmingly female, these events must be considered an orgy of hatred against women. The image of woman in

Offenburg cannot have been positive during these years, and the self-image of women must have suffered as well.

We have seen remarkable differences in patterns of witch hunting in three countries, from the restraint shown in the Netherlands to the frenzy of the south German towns. In every case, however, it was women primarily who suffered. An overview of the patterns of witch hunting across Europe will shed light on attitudes toward women in different areas.

In the sixteenth century, a rise in sexual violence in European society was exacerbated by pressure from church and state to change basic sexual customs. In the next two chapters we will consider each of these causes as they affected different countries. As the centuries since have shown escalating levels of both violence, general and sexual, and of state control, the witchcraze can be considered a portent, even a model, of some aspects of what modern Europe would be like.

In *Linda Maestra* ("Pretty Teacher"), Francisco de Goya parodies the relationship between an older and a younger woman, and emphasizes the obscene nakedness and evil intent of women. This is a late example of the popular imagery that effectively fueled negative public opinion toward women throughout the witchcraze. Spanish, 18th–19th century. Etching and aquatint, 208 x 149mm. Courtesy of The Harvard University Art Museums.

CHAPTER THREE

Witchcraze in the Central Regions

The persecution of social fringe groups is relatively easy to explain; but the persecution of a whole sex . . . calls for a more thorough attempt at explanation.

—*Sylvia Bovenschen,* "The Contemporary Witch, the Historical Witch, and the Witch Myth."

PURSUING THE QUESTION of why the persecution broke out when it did, not sooner, not later, we can find clues in economic history, particularly as it affected women. For a start, Richard Dunn's account is useful. Given that in about 1560 Europe began to experience population saturation, food scarcity, and runaway inflation, its ruling class "had a desperate need for scapegoats to meliorate the impact of social disasters for which they had no remedy: poverty, disease, crime, famine, plague, wartime carnage, and revolutionary upheaval, all characteristic of [this] troubled society." Taking a primarily economic approach, Dunn concludes that "it was no accident that the great witchcraft hysteria, one of the most distinctive phenomena in the age of religious wars, began in the 1560s."[1] Other historians stress as triggers for the witch hunts the pressure put on commoners by absolutist central governments and reform-minded churches.[2]

Some parts of Europe hunted witches longer and more vigorously than others. That persecutions developed different regional patterns reflects not only contrasting legal, political, and religious structures but also differing attitudes toward women. That most regions persecuted women more than men, however, reveals the prevalence of misogynistic attitudes, laws, and theology throughout Europe. Another variable must also be kept in mind: the willingness in the region to stage a persecution against *any* group or gender.

The European witch hunt was not uniform. The death rate was highest by far in the German-speaking lands and their immediate neighbors, especially Poland; all experienced a pattern of mass panics. Witchcraft in Francophone lands was less intense but marked by belief in demonic possession, providing some of the most dramatic trial accounts. The British Isles must be considered separately from each other, witch hunts having occurred frequently in Scotland, seldom in England, almost never in Ireland; the brief but intense persecutions in New England were related to but not identical with the English outbreaks. Dutch witch hunts were similar to the English, moderate in number but with a few mass killings. Prosecutions in Estonia became heavy twice, in the mid- and late seventeenth century; in Scandinavia they began late, not peaking until the 1670s, but were fairly intense; in Hungary they reached their height even later, in the 1720s, involving similar numbers. In Russia, however, they apparently never became widespread. In Italy and Spain there were numerous investigations but few executions. Iceland and Portugal were scarcely touched.

Though regional variations in witch hunting reveal much about the ecclesiastical and political structures of these lands, the social implications are much more difficult to dig out, especially on the question of how each region treated women. The state of witch trial records is an obstacle; they often lack information on the class, marital status, and even gender of the accused. Still, historians could have done more gender analysis, recognizing this material as part of women's history. As it is, they have shown less interest in social than in legal or theological aspects; which is to say, less has been written about the victims (mostly female) than about their victimizers (mostly male). As I give an overview of the witch hunts, I will draw out the implications for women in each region.

Lands Influenced by German Customs

> *Wenn du eine Frau siehst, denke, es sei der Teufel, diese ist eine Art Hölle.* (Whenever you see a woman, think, it is the Devil, this is a hellish breed.)
>
> —*Eneas Silvius*

> [Demons] take no account of males . . . and among a hundred witches there's scarcely a man to be seen.
>
> —*Augustin Baumann, Munich, 1600*

Over half, perhaps three-fourths, of all executions for witchcraft were carried out in what Erik Midelfort called the heartland of the witchcraze: the Holy Roman Empire, centered in Germany.[3] Because the death rate was also high in the surrounding lands, especially the western provinces of Poland where large numbers of Germans had settled and German merchants traded, those areas must be discussed with the German lands. Neighboring areas such as Lorraine, Luxembourg, and Franche-Comté, although culturally and linguistically different from the empire, shared certain of its legal customs and religious beliefs, a heritage that turned them toward intensive witch hunting.

The most horrifying attacks in the German lands were made in the Catholic territories. Though the new Protestant magistrates also prosecuted for witchcraft, they did not keep up with the prince-bishops and archbishop-electors of the Catholic ecclesiastical lands, executing one witch to the Catholics' three.[4] At Trier between 1587 and 1593, for example, under the direction of the Jesuit demonologist Peter Binsfeld, 368 witches were burned from twenty-two villages, a hunt so devastating that two villages were left with only one woman apiece. The abbot of Fulda was responsible for the deaths of over 700 witches at the beginning of the seventeenth century. A particularly vicious outbreak occurred at Ellwangen, where 390 persons were burned between 1611 and 1618. The Teutonic Knights ordered the deaths of 124 in just two years, 1628 to 1630. In the conventual land of Quedlinburg, 133 witches were executed on one day in 1589. At Eichstätt, 274 persons were burned at the stake apparently in one year, 1629.[5]

The first wave of German trials victimized mainly women of the poor or middling sort, midwives like Walpurga Hausmänin, but as the supply of poor women ran low, accusers turned to women and men of the establishment. The nine hundred persons put to death by the prince-bishop of Würzburg, for example, included nineteen of his priests and his own nephew. The archbishop-elector of Cologne ordered the deaths of the wives of his chancellor and his secretary. And at Bamberg the bishop executed six hundred witches, including his own chancellor and the burgermeister. Most grotesque was the execution of forty-one young children at Würzburg, a custom that grew in Germany until most major trials included children as both victims and accusers. These later witch hunters turned to younger victims, to men, and to persons of their own class. This last apparently led to a slackening of the craze (as in Offenburg), as the elite, fearful for their own lives, used their clout to stop the madness.[6]

The fierce religious differences revealed by the Reformation added another point of instability in this tumultuous century. Lutheran theologians and pastors stressed a demonology different from that of the Catholics. Regarding the devil's power, they taught that misfortune was caused not by the devil but by God's providence, and that the devil, and certainly his servants, did not have the enormous power with which popular belief, and especially Catholic belief, credited them. Although traditional demonology also existed in Protestant minds, enabling Protestant magistrates to send many victims to their deaths, still, the new teaching had the effect of moderating the witch hunt in most Protestant lands.[7]

The question has been raised whether, by suppressing folk magic, Protestantism forced its followers to turn to witchcraft or devil worship. Günther Lottes finds no evidence for this, indicating instead that Protestants went right on practicing the old magic but did so surreptitiously.[8] They also produced a different, if ambivalent, doctrine of woman.[9] Rejecting the Catholic association of witchcraft with female sexuality, Luther identified sorcery with the disobedient wife, thus freeing women to affirm their sexuality but putting them into the bind of an increasingly male-dominant family. What Protestantism gave to women by encouraging them to become literate and to share religious life at home it took away with its ideal of the submissive wife. Catholicism, by maintaining its insistence on the dangerous nature of female sexuality, kept the identification of all sexually active women with witches.[10] All German women were endangered by the prevailing ideologies, but Catholic women had the most to fear.

Useful as these distinctions between the two major Christian groups may be, they do not take us far. The fact remains that, in a period when the two communions tried in every way to prove how different they were, they both believed in witches and prosecuted them. On this important point they were in basic agreement. Surprisingly, they seldom used witch accusations against each other,[11] turning them against their own women instead.

But even if we cannot use the Reformation as the key to why central Europe perpetrated massive witch hunts, we cannot ignore religious upheaval as one factor. The violent breakup of the unity of Christendom led not only to a creative religious ferment within both Protestantism and Catholicism but to massive religious confusion, anxiety, and suspicion as well; not all of this was focused against the other faith, part being defused through witch hunting.[12]

The mass panics for which the Catholic German lands were famous were made possible by two beliefs. The first, that Satan intended to destroy Christian civilization and required hordes of witches to do so, led to the "conspiracy theory" of witchcraft, in which sorcery was seen as treason, as an attempt to overthrow state and church; fear was concomitantly intense. The second followed from this, that therefore witchcraft was so heinous a crime that the use of torture was justified. This policy, which, we have seen, originated in the church's inquisitional courts, was greatly reinforced by the Holy Roman Emperor. He decreed in 1532 in the "Carolina" code that malevolent witchcraft could be determined by judicial torture and was punishable by death, specifically death by fire.[13] This belief produced huge trials, for the more torture was applied, the more the victims named names. The practice of consulting university professors and prominent inquisitors also intensified the witch hunt, by adding prestige to local trials and by spreading the empire's law that witchcraft was punishable by death. All these factors produced the mass trials that made the German death rate the highest in Europe.

These beliefs came from the elite, not from popular lore (see chapter 6). A further ideological injection from "above" was purely theological. We saw in the charges against Walpurga Hausmänin how Catholic churchmen had shaped devil worship to be the inversion of Christianity: for example, the sabbat feast on the flesh of an innocent child as the substitute for communion.[14] Above all, they asserted that the power to perform evil is as strong as the power to create good—or perhaps even stronger. A frantic fear runs through these accounts, fear that the devil's power may be greater than God's. This fear accounts for the charges that Walpurga desecrated the Blessed Sacrament, giving the wafer to her demon, stamping it underfoot until she actually saw drops of blood on the wafer, that she denied God, Christ, the saints, "and the whole of Christendom." That behind Walpurga's power to kill her neighbors' children and animals lay the power to destroy Christianity—this was the paranoia that fueled the major German trials, that created the largest persecutions that Europe experienced.

That Germans put to death far more witches than anyone else must be connected also to the general history of persecution in German lands. Prior to the witchcraze, the two major types of European repression had been against heretics and Jews. As the penalty for heresy was death by burning (sometimes reduced to banishment), these persecutions accustomed the populace to the sight of women and men being killed at the stake. During the fourteenth century in the German and Flemish lands and northern France, beghards and beguines, groups of lay men and women who followed a life of sacrificial poverty, were hunted down by papal inquisitors. But as these groups were tamed, the inquisitors, especially in Germany, turned on fringe groups such as witches. Free of control by local authorities, the inquisitors began to get out of hand.[15]

The transfer of these attitudes and practices from heretics to witches is seen clearly in the work of Kramer and Sprenger, authors of the *Malleus Maleficarum*, Dominican inquisitors armed with papal authorization to purge Germany of witches. Defining witchcraft as treason against God, the authors described it primarily as female rebellion. Using stereotypes of women already familiar from the centuries of heresy hunting, they set out to demonize certain types of women: witches make a pact with the devil and have ritual sex with him; they sacrifice unbaptized infants, change shapes, fly through the air, cook and eat children, render men impotent, even cause a priest's penis to disappear. The document reeks with fear and hatred of women, concluding with thanks to God "who has so far preserved the male sex from so great a crime."[16] When the senile Kramer launched a witch hunt at Innsbruck in 1485 (accusing fifty-five women and two men), he acted so arbitrarily that he offended the populace and the bishop, pressing intimate sexual questions on the accused women and even holding some of them captive illegally.[17]

The attitudes expressed in the *Malleus* explain how Germans justified wiping out a sizable portion of their female population. Germans accused and executed women at the average European rate (82 percent and 82 percent). But because they put to death about 30,000 persons, that means that they destroyed around 24,600 women—a believable figure, given the devastations described above. In one town, Rottenburg, for example, by 1590 at least 150 women had been executed, and worse was to come.[18]

The German lands held an additional tradition that ultimately trapped women. Though the Germans came late to heresy hunting, they had been almost the first to carry out violent persecution of Jews, another group that, as we shall see, became identified with women.[19] From the initial outbreaks in 1095, Germans maintained vicious anti-Semitic practices throughout the Middle Ages, repressing Jews more harshly than in any other European area.

The numerous German pogroms accustomed people to blaming a defenseless minority group for misfortune, to scapegoating an outsider group. The most harmful aspect of this practice was the dehumanizing of the Jews: thought of as less than human, they could be dealt any mistreatment, and it would be justified.

The Germans thus had a dangerous heritage of violent persecution to use against any group perceived as deviant. Women as a gender group suffered a special liability in that they had begun to be identified with Jews.[20] Both groups suffered from being associated with magical practices: making potions and poisons, wearing amulets, possessing the evil eye, sticking pins in dolls, having abnormal knowledge about dreams, fortune-telling, or the magical properties of gems.[21] Rumors circulated about their bodies, that Jewish men menstruated (because they were circumcised), that witches bore the devil's mark, that both could turn themselves into animals, that Jewish women practiced bestiality and produced animal babies and that witches had sex with the devil and gave birth to demons. Both were believed to cause storms and plagues. An especially damaging belief held against Jews was that they celebrated a travesty of the Christian mass in which they worshiped the devil, requiring for Communion either the bodies of Christians or their own sperm.[22] These allegations against Jews became the sabbat of the witches, often referred to as the witches' "synagogue," but made even more lurid by the claim that witches had sex with Satan. And the Jewish synagogue in turn was referred to as a brothel.[23]

Jewish men were portrayed as Satan, with goat's beard, horns, swarthy complexion, and hooked nose. Witches were pictured as crones, wrinkled, with warts and hooked nose. Both groups were rumored to be lascivious and sexually insatiable. All these stereotypes rendered both Jews and women as less than human, thereby justifying the inhuman treatment unleashed on them. But the witches, unlike Jews, saw themselves as Christians, as insiders in the Christian realm. In order to prosecute for witchcraft, European society had to turn against its own.

Most threatening to both groups was the belief that they were servants of Satan, who committed ritual murder against Christians, mutilated crucifixes (causing Christ to suffer yet again), concocted poisons from the bodies of Christian babies, and desecrated the Communion wafer. It was a witch's power to mock Christianity that was especially feared and hated.

In order to gauge the extent of German misogyny, it is instructive to see what additional charges were laid on women that Jews were spared. Jews were never, to my knowledge, accused of inflicting miscarriage, causing a man's sex organ to disappear, or having sexual orgies with demons. These important points of demonology, applied only to women accused of witchcraft, point to a particular fear of female sexuality and a belief that women are evil by nature. For the most part, however, witches and Jews were persecuted interchangeably. In Hungary, for example, witches were sentenced for a first offense to stand all day in public, wearing a Jew's hat.[24] Both witches and Jews were perceived as traitors to Christian society who must be eradicated. The majority of Jews had been driven out of western Europe by the early sixteenth century.[25] That it was only a few years later that the witchcraze began there indicates Europe's continuing need for a scapegoat.[26]

In addition, women became more vulnerable to persecution in Germany in the sixteenth century because of changing economic and political conditions. At the same time as a sharp population rise forced peasant incomes down, a new political order emerged: the states began to intervene in village life, devising new ways to draw off every bit of surplus income from farmers and craftsmen.[27] In order to pay for their new bureaucracies and wars, the princes imposed steep taxes, redistributing wealth from the private to the public sector. At the same time, inspired by the moral reforms of both Catholics and Protestants, they began to interfere in daily customs, imposing uniform village bylaws, supervising village assemblies, regulating dress codes, ruling how many guests a smallholder might invite to his wedding, how much one might drink at a festival. Reforming puritanism combined with princely greed to make the average person's life more onerous.

As incomes dropped and taxes rose, women, who worked mainly in marginal jobs, were the first to feel the economic pinch. They also found that they had less say in their communities: local power now flowed through the village assembly, where each household had a voice, but that voice was spoken by the male head. As families and community structure became more patriarchal, women found it harder to express their grievances or to protect themselves.

A final factor in German persecutions was the lack of central authority in the Holy Roman Empire. Attacking outsider groups was easier to do in Germany than elsewhere because of its fragmented political condition; there was no strong central power to restrain local zealots, as there was, for example, in France and England. This heritage of unrestrained persecution traveled wherever the empire's jurisdiction had been planted, carrying the plague of mass panics to neighboring lands.

In the duchy of Lorraine, for example, these German customs combined with local economic changes to trigger a witchcraze. In Lorraine, the gap between rich and poor was widening, especially during 1580 to 1630, the exact period of concentrated prosecutions. Peasant landholdings were being absorbed by wealthy landowners, and communal rights disappeared, forcing many peasants into debt.[28] This background sharpens our understanding of the many witch charges relating to loss of wealth and property; hapless peasants, discovering that no matter how hard they worked they ended up with less, blamed their poverty on the witchery of neighbors.

A particular concern about the sabbat and sexual crimes fueled the Lorraine trials, most of which took place in local secular courts under semiliterate judges who showed no mercy; the conviction rate was nearly 90 percent. The chief judge, Nicolas Remy, who boasted that he sent eight or nine hundred to their deaths and tortured as many more, sentenced the children of convicted witches to be beaten with rods as they watched their parents being burned alive (and then wondered if he had been too lenient) and stressed women's sexual crimes such as abortion, infanticide, castration, and attempts to murder their husbands. About women, Remy believed that mothers passed the power of sorcery to their children, that women changed themselves into rabid dogs or wolves and killed babies before or after birth to make magic powders. He was especially suspicious of old women and female healers. Remy concluded that witches were usually female "because the rabble of witches is chiefly composed of that sex which, owing to its feebleness of understanding, is least able to resist and withstand the wiles of the Devil."[29] Believing in witchcraft and practicing countermagic himself, Remy recorded some of the most realistic accounts of the sabbat, complete with orgiastic circle dances and cannibal feasts (see chapter 5).[30]

In Franche-Comté, mass panics took place on only a slightly smaller scale than in the German-speaking lands. During years of crop failure and famine, especially 1628 to 1630, the province condemned forty witches at Lugeuil. In the wake of a case of demonic possession, the judge Boguet condemned twenty-eight (St. Cloud, 1598–1609). An inquisitor who ordered every parish to hunt out its witches sent "more than a hundred" to their deaths in 1657 to 1659 before his excesses were stopped by papal authorities.[31]

Boguet's treatise remains our chief document for witch hunting in Franche-Comté. Stressing the sexual element, including male homosexuality, he quoted the maxim that the devil is interested only in those past puberty. Still, he condemned young children, believing that, once possessed, no one could struggle free of the devil's hold.[32] Boguet is best known for his extreme cruelty, insisting on burning some victims alive (that is, rather than strangling them first) and lashing and burning children. One frantic woman, Claude Janguillaume, tore herself free from the stake three times, only to be dragged back each time by the executioner.[33]

Though Boguet included men as well as women among the twenty-eight persons he condemned (four more died in prison), he thought of witches as female, believing that mothers passed the craft down to their daughters. Connecting witchcraft with female sexuality, he maintained that the devil seduced women more easily because of their inordinate love of carnal pleasures, that Satan spoke through a female's "shameful parts," and that all witches were abortionists.[34] He even identified werewolves as female. Because of the detailed instructions he gave for witch hunting, Boguet's treatise was one of the most influential in France. Had it not been that Franche-Comté's parliament began accepting appeals in witchcraft cases the year after Boguet began witch hunting (1599), thereby reducing the number of deaths by over half,[35] Boguet might well have launched a craze the equal of those in the German lands.

The history of witch hunting in Luxembourg is especially instructive, a beginning having been made there on gender analysis. Bilingual, as was Lorraine, Luxembourg illustrates further the power of German influence: its witch hunt began in the German-speaking part (c. 1580), peaked there upon receipt of the Jesuit Binsfeld's treatise, produced more arrests than its French persecution (316 to 231), and executed a far higher percentage (76 percent of the men and 84 percent of the women to 38 percent and 42 percent).[36] Nevertheless, the French persecution too was sizable (1615–30), also benefiting from the arrival of a Jesuit treatise, that of the Spaniard Martin Del Rio.[37] The energy of Jesuit inquisitors was everywhere evident as they began enforcing the reforms of the Council of Trent. Aided by Franciscan friars and Capuchin monks, backed by the archduke, and in close cooperation with municipal authorities, the Jesuits preached against the "superstitions" of the folk religion and utilized lay courts to enforce their reforms.[38]

Thanks to the work of Dupont-Bouchat, we can see the effects of these reforms on Luxembourg women. The newly enforced strictures against adultery, abortion, and infanticide were especially dangerous for women, who were punished for sexual transgressions more severely than men. Women condemned for doing away with their newborn children, for example, were buried alive, whereas the fathers, if known, were either fined or let go free. Charges for sexual crimes and for sorcery often went together; for example, the daughter of a poor manual worker at Sanweiler was executed for sorcery and for killing her child. The word *witch* in Luxembourg was associated with *putain* and *ribaude*, meaning "whore." It is not surprising that prosecutions for witchcraft peaked during the same period as those for abortion and infanticide.[39]

Poland offers further proof of German influence,[40] its persecutions beginning in western Poland, long heavily settled by Germans, and spreading eastward into lands where Germans had immigrated, such as the Ukraine and Transylvania. Especially heavy in strongly Catholic provinces, they seldom took place in lands controlled by the Orthodox church. Although the Polish craze began late (1676–1725), peaking only after the witch hunt was ending in western Europe, it was especially severe, accounting for as many as ten thousand deaths.[41]

Polish witch accusations often had a political twist, burgers aiming charges at political rivals or, more often, at their wives and daughters. The main force in the Polish persecutions, however, appears to have been a militant Catholicism that finally, after a remarkable period of tolerance, asserted itself, a militancy instigated by priests but in fact carried out by laymen.[42] But as for gender, not even the barest statistical breakdown has been made. Until the records are studied more closely and more is known about early modern Polish attitudes to women, the issue of gender in the Polish trials cannot be evaluated.

Switzerland, trilingual and in process of becoming politically independent of the Holy Roman Empire, shared a number of witchcraft characteristics with both the empire and France and was full of internal contradictions. The Calvinist Republic of Geneva, for example, executed only 21 percent of its accused witches (excepting those accused of spreading plague, who were killed at a rate of over 40 percent), whereas the neighboring area, the Pays de Vaud, also Protestant, put to death 90 percent of those indicted. Basel and

Lucerne, both Catholic and German-speaking, each executed just over 50 percent.[43]

The Genevan leniency is misleading, as authorities there permanently banished many accused witches. Nonetheless, the lack of bloodshed in Genevan witch hunts is remarkable; Monter attributed it to the Calvinist view that witchcraft was a theological fault rather than criminal activity, was heresy more than sorcery. The *maleficium* of the standard accusation could thus be separated out and punished simply as a misdemeanor, not as an offense against the Almighty. But elsewhere in Protestant Switzerland such sanity did not prevail. In Vaud, guilt was assumed in advance and torture applied.[44] In the Catholic bishopric of Basel, the greatest number of trials and executions occurred in its small Protestant areas. Thus in Switzerland Protestants pursued witches as zealously as Catholics, in contrast to the record in most of the German lands.[45]

Finally, the question of why the Swiss persecuted women in such large numbers, 80 percent of those executed overall, 95 percent of those executed in the bishopric of Basel, points again to increasing hostility toward female sexuality. Prosecution for sexual crimes rose here in the sixteenth and seventeenth centuries, just as it did in Luxembourg and elsewhere in Europe, and had the same deleterious effect on the female population. For example, in the century from 1595 to 1695, of the thirty-one women tried in Genevan courts for infanticide, twenty-two were condemned to death, a very high execution rate. Prosecution for sodomy, previously largely ignored, also increased, augmenting witchcraft charges because both were seen as unnatural.[46]

As Monter observed, like abortion and infanticide, witchcraft was a woman's crime. He notes further that, in addition to these sex-related crimes, sixteenth-century Swiss women suffered from being socially and legally powerless, having only the magic of folk religion to protect themselves. He stresses that during these centuries they became the victims of an unusually hostile patriarchy, a male-dominant society that, previously having shown little interest in executing women, now turned on them. More broadly, one can apply Monter's statement about Jura witchcraft to the entire Swiss context: "misogyny was a basic force underlying these trials."[47]

The question of why the German-speaking lands and their neighbors under the imperial Carolina code carried out a veritable witchcraze is thus a complex mystery, one that I believe belies a "single-factor" solution. Religious upheaval, the precedent of persecutions of heretics and Jews, centralizing of power within many duchies without the restraint of an effective overlord, the weakening of women's economic and social position—each of these explains part of the puzzle but not the whole. To better understand this sixteenth- and seventeenth-century gender-based holocaust is especially important, however, for it may shed light on the dynamics of the twentieth-century holocaust based on anti-Semitism.

The French Lands

Mais quoi, on dit que toutte femme sont sorcière! (What now, they say that every woman is a sorcerer!)

—*Aldegonde de Rue,*[48] *Cambrai, 1601*

The second heaviest concentration of European witch trials was in the French-speaking lands, especially on their margins. Where royal control was firm, the panics were kept in hand, but the outlying provinces, resistant in every way to central control, at first hunted down witches with little restraint.[49]

The northern province of Flanders (Département du Nord), under Spanish control during much of the witch hunt era, persecuted four women for every man, plus numbers of young children. Robert Muchembled concludes that women were targeted because of both theological and societal biases against them. The Catholic Reformation's drive to control the sexuality of its members fell heaviest, of course, on the female sex. Heavy penalties for illegitimate births and irregular marriages, and the death penalty for abortion and infanticide, placed new limits on women's control over their bodies and their lives. It required a century or more after the Council of Trent for French society to fall into line, but by the end of the seventeenth century French women were producing only one-third as many illegitimate births as their English (Protestant) sisters.[50]

The church also cut deeply into women's traditional roles at this time. By ruling (in France) that baptisms must take place within twenty-four hours of birth, it prevented women from gathering their extended families to celebrate the arrival of the new child; by forbidding wakes to be held in churches, it cut women out from their chief quasi-liturgical role, that of public mourner. Along with this went a major attack on midwives and female healers. The church thus undermined women's mastery of folk healing, adding to the parish priest's control over the laity's lives at every point possible. Add to this ecclesiastical attack the traditional societal disgust for old women and envy of the power of folk healers, and one finds a potent wave of antifeminism growing in rural sixteenth- and seventeenth-century France. Muchembled believes that basic to these customs was "*une méfiance fondamentale*" (a fundamental distrust) of women.[51] To this summary must be added the deterioration in women's economic possibilities.

As for what triggered witch hunting in this area, belief in demonism seems not to have been the cause, such matters appearing in trial records only on the prompting of the judges. Here it was a case of prolonged disruption of daily life, the almost continuous wars and frequent plagues[52] and increasing poverty. Because of this long period of turmoil, the economic conditions of the peasants steadily worsened throughout the late sixteenth and seventeenth centuries. The number of paupers increased as rural taxes became heavier; wealth became concentrated in the hands of a few rich peasant families, those eligible to attend the communal assembly, those few who had recently learned to read and write and could thus cooperate with the new religious reformers. As the gap between rich and poor increased, social tensions rose and were dealt with by the powerful families via witchcraft charges against the indigent. Always the accusers were better off, even if only slightly, than the persons whom they accused.[53]

A further cause of change in rural France was the vigor of the Counter-Reformation in punishing the old, accepted moral laxities, as noted also in Luxembourg. Yet again the blame cannot be placed entirely on the zeal of reforming priests, for it was not until the French secular courts began to prosecute for sorcery that a true epidemic began.[54]

The southwestern French area of Labourd had its first witch hunt in 1576, but it was in 1609, when the king and the Parlement of Bordeaux commissioned judge Pierre de Lancre to investigate sorcery there that the Basque lands made their main contribution to demonological history. Relying mainly on the testimony of young girls and confessions obtained under torture, de Lancre described elaborate sabbats where witches danced naked in circles back to back and a cock's crow announcing the dawn ended the orgy.[55] So convinced was de Lancre of the reality of these reports that he believed a sabbat had been celebrated in his hotel room.[56] De Lancre was especially suspicious of assertive women, criticizing the Basque women who assisted priests during church services.

The other major French witchcrazes were very different from either the northern or the Basque, being urban and centered in convents, where nuns were afflicted with demonic possession. Occurring in many cultures in every part of the world, possession is experienced chiefly by women, especially those who are oppressed and lack legal means to redress wrongs.[57] During possession, the individual goes into trance, that is, loses normal consciousness. She loses memory and may hallucinate, experiencing an alternative form of consciousness; she may speak in tongues. Easily observed physical changes occur: the eyes become glazed and possibly bulge, limbs may stiffen, the body may lose sensitivity to heat or cold. Some persons are able to endure fire—for example, handle, walk on, or roll in hot coals without being blistered, indicating that an actual chemical change in their bodies has occurred. Some even experience levitation.

Trance can happen without being accompanied by possession. In the cases we are concerned with, however, possession did occur, causing a further transformation: the person's body and mind were entered and possessed by a foreign spirit, perceived as evil by Christians, although experienced as good in many cultures. The bewitched person then speaks in a different voice, moving and acting in a way characteristic of that spirit. I have witnessed striking examples of benevolent (that is, desired) spirit possession, for example, in contemporary American spiritualism, Haitian vodoun, Hindu popular culture, and Korean shamanism; the phenomenon is also well documented in African religions, Cuban Santeria, and Native American religion.[58] These good spirits bring powers of wisdom, prophecy, and healing, and honor the devotee by their presence. But a spirit perceived as evil indicates the presence of the demonic, or as specified in European culture, of the demons of Satan himself. These spirits torment their victims and force them to speak and act in shameful ways, blasphemous or obscene. The tension that runs through all possession-practicing cultures concerns *who* speaks: the gods or the demons?[59]

When possessed, the French nuns accused priests, or in one case, a mother superior, of bewitching and seducing them. The outbreaks at Aix-en-Provence, Loudun, Louviers, and Lille are well known and much written about.[60]

These earlier convent cases, which had scandalized France and drawn international crowds to witness the nun's exorcisms and the priests' public burnings, had shown striking similarities to one another; both the possessed and the exorcist must have heard accounts of the previous outbreaks. The Ursuline sisters at Auxonne, however, produced a different version of the story; they accused their mother superior, Barbara Buvée, of bewitching them (1660).[61] Blame for these possessions had been passed around in a confusing way. First, eight nuns accused their father confessor of stimulating them sexually, but he claimed that he was not responsible, because he had been bewitched by two peasants. The peasants were ordered banished but were lynched by a mob. The confessor then tried to exorcise the disturbed women, both publicly and by lying in bed with them. Because Barbara Buvée had opposed the exorcisms, she was seen as guilty of the nuns' continuing possession. Charged with witchcraft, she was tried by the Parlement of Dijon.

Before the judges, the sisters accused Buvée of kissing them, of lying down on them wearing a false phallus, of putting her fingers in their vaginas. Because charges of lesbianism almost never reached seventeenth-century courts, the Parlement did not know how to deal with the case and finally dropped it. Buvée moved to another convent, and the trances ceased.[62]

At any rate, by 1662, many French judges and doctors had become skeptical of demonic possession. Several declared that the women were frauds. The case of Elisabeth de Ranfaing occurred earlier, however, in 1620, at the height of public fascination with spirit possession, and Elisabeth earned years of attention from leading priests because of her affliction.[63]

Leading to the execution of an innocent man and woman, the case of Elisabeth de Ranfaing illustrates amply the extent of French popular hysteria about witchcraft in the 1620s, among judges and clerics as well as the populace. Yet even given this store of common belief and fear, backed by a wealth of demonological treatises, the French witch hunts did not come near the level of the German, perhaps ten thousand trials compared with the empire's one hundred thousand, and around five thousand executions to about thirty thousand.

Alfred Soman has argued that the French had an early skepticism about witchcraft to thank for this, particularly a skepticism about proving witchcraft charges in court. Added to this was the reluctance of the high court, the Parlement of Paris, to approve convictions on appeal. Soman shows that from the beginning of major witch hunting in France in the 1560s, the Parlement had rejected a high percentage of convictions. Furthermore, a royal edict of 1624, decreeing that all witchcraft sentences prescribing capital or corporal punishment be automatically appealed to Paris, was in fact a reflection of restraints already being applied locally.[64] The extremism of French demonologists such as Jean Bodin, far from indicating a *national* mania over witches, was in fact the product of their frustration with the Parlement's leniency![65]

That French culture evidenced no lack of misogyny, no less than in the German lands, explains the basis for the French persecution of women. That repression in France did not equal German repression must be understood by France's more centralized government and different legal system.

A witch and her demon riding the phallic broomstick to a Sabbath. This image underlines the blatantly sexual aspect of most witchcraft accusations. From Ulrich Molitor's *Hexen Meysterey*, 1545. Courtesy of Dover Pictorial Archive Series.

CHAPTER FOUR

Witch Hunts on the Periphery

The British Isles and New England

EVERYWHERE ON the periphery of Europe the witch hunts were milder—in the British Isles, the Netherlands, Scandinavia, Russia, Hungary, the Mediterranean lands. The Balkans, under Muslim (Ottoman Turk) control, scarcely experienced the persecutions at all.

In general, where demonological beliefs were weaker, creating less talk of the sabbat, sex with the devil, and so on, and where torture was forbidden, there the persecutions were smaller. England is a case in point; although the devil's pact was sometimes mentioned in English records, the sabbat played little part, and a conspiracy theory even less. There are few references to women having sex with the devil, to eating babies, or to the rest of the usual diabolical lore. Without these beliefs about the devil, witchcraft was seen, not as heresy, but as straightforward criminality, and was therefore punished not by burning but by the less cruel method of hanging.

As for the legal background, England was governed by common law, not Roman law, and had no experience of inquisitional courts. Because torture was forbidden by law, only a few witch hunters, like Matthew Hopkins, managed to get away with it. Without torture and belief in the sabbat, there was little likelihood of mass panics, and in fact English trials concentrated typically on one, or perhaps a handful, of witches.

The English prosecuted on the basis of causing harm to one's neighbors; therefore, English trials tell us more about social conditions, especially among villagers, and a great deal less about the demonic fantasies of priests and judges. Keith Thomas and Alan Macfarlane have argued that witch accusations served a social purpose, to end an intolerable relationship among neighbors or to put an inferior in her place. In a typical instance, John Woddle and his wife accused "Goody Hall of Crawly that cometh and beggeth and hath it." Irked at the woman's nerve, Woddle forbade his wife to give the beggar any more alms. Falling ill and seeking for an explanation of his misfortune, he feared that Goody Hall was taking revenge on him. In his guilt over having refused her, *he* accused *her* of sorcery.[1] Accusations were functional in other ways as well, providing the aggrieved party with redress and, by identifying the evildoer, providing the possibility of defense by countermagic.[2]

Everyday incidents such as this began to be prosecuted as witchcraft in England during the 1580s, and before it was over, a thousand or more persons had been put to death.[3] The one uniquely English contribution to witch lore was belief in the imp or familiar, a demon who took the shape of a cat, dog, or toad, assisting the witch with her *maleficium,* and being allowed to suck from her special teat in return. In England there were also a large number of accusations by children, mostly by young girls against older women.[4]

All in all, however, English witch persecutions were restrained and remained localized. Some have argued that they were mild because the position of English women was improving.[5] As I will discuss in chapters 4 and 5, the condition of women Europe-wide was in fact worsening, reaching its nadir in the early nineteenth century. Nor was English society lacking in misogyny, a quality that was growing in the early modern period,[6] so that the percentage of women prosecuted was high, and their treatment in court was harsher than that received by men.[7] Explanations for the relative restraint of England's witch hunt must therefore rest in its lack of Roman law and an inquisition, thereby permitting a prohibition on torture, and the absence of belief in the sabbat and the conspiracy theory of witchcraft, not in an alleged privileged position of women.

The witch hunt in Scotland was far different, however, approaching the ferocity of the Continental trials: 1,337 executions, plus or minus perhaps 300, and additional deaths from suicides and from torture and neglect, all from a small population less than half that of England. The analyst of Scottish witchcraft, Christina Larner, concluded, "The Scottish witch-hunt was arguably one of the major witch-hunts of Europe," and named its use of inquisitorial procedures and its belief in sabbats and a diabolical conspiracy as the causes. Church and state appear to have competed to see who could be the most Godly, that is, the most anti-Satan. Each time the royal courts would act to restrain the hunt, the General Assembly of the Presbyterian church (the state church) would order its ministers to seek out witches in every parish; when the church relaxed, the Privy Council would issue decrees for a new hunt. Between them they kept southern and eastern Scotland in an uproar over much of the period 1590 to 1700.[8]

As for the victimizing of females, Larner maintained that Calvinism set a trap for women, making them adults newly responsible for their souls while at the same time blaming them for using their free will to choose to practice witchcraft: "As witches [women] became adult criminals acting in a manner for which their husbands could not be deemed responsible. The pursuit of witches could therefore be seen as a rearguard action against the emergence of women as independent adults."[9] Noting signs of intensified misogyny at this time, Larner blamed it on the increasingly patriarchal nature of Scottish society. Observing that "women are feared as a source of disorder in patriarchal society," and that "the women who were accused were those who challenged the patriarchal view of the ideal woman," she believed that Scottish men, as husbands, judges, and ministers, were placing a tighter reign on the women whom they feared. She concluded that in early modern Scotland, "all women were potential witches."[10]

Although Ireland was the scene of one of the earliest and most influential witch trials, it has received little attention from witchcraft scholars. The trial of Dame Alice Kyteler in 1324–25 was typical of fourteenth-century trials in that the accused was wealthy, in this case from a prominent merchant and banking family, and that the charge was in part politically motivated.[11] Dame Alice was accused of causing her husband's death. Once the case heated up, the women involved were accused of having sex with demons and were vilified as evil by nature. In the end Dame Alice escaped, but her maid was burned at the stake.

Several important European precedents were established by this trial: that women were associated with demonic sex, man-hating and man-harming, and harming of dead infants, and that wives hostile to husbands were witches; that sorcery was heresy and that sorcerers would receive the same punishments as heretics, especially torture and death by fire; that the poor would be made scapegoats for the rich. It would be useful to know the future of these beliefs in further Irish witch accusations, but court records reveal only sporadic, isolated cases.[12]

The New England witch hunt, where "only" thirty-five persons were put to death, came like a coda to the European craze, reaching its peak in the 1690s as the persecutions were being repudiated in Britain and western Europe. (Americans today, unaware of the European persecutions, tend to think of the New England outbreak as *the* witch hunt, but it was, of course, only an echo of the parent phenomenon.) Still, 334 persons were accused in the new, sparsely settled colonies, so the hunt was fairly intense. A study of its beliefs and practices, however, makes it clear the New England hunt was part of the main persecutions that we are discussing.[13]

We find that the witches were predominantly women (78 percent of the accused, 80 percent of those executed), mostly poor, mostly married or widowed, between the ages of forty and sixty. At Salem, where 20 were condemned and 165 were accused, most of the accusers (defined as those who experienced fits at the trials) were young girls between the age of eleven and twenty; three-fourths of the witnesses were men. Like many British witches, several of the accused had reputations for eccentricity, outspokenness, petty crime, or dubious religious practices.[14] Most of the accusers were neighbors of the accused, so it is not surprising that the trial reveals many village tensions, economic,[15] sexual,[16] ecclesiastical.[17]

Women's economic status explains much about the New England persecution. Carol Karlsen's research shows that women who were inheritors were at high risk for accusation.[18] Anxieties about inheritance, in fact, lay at the heart of most accusations. This was a society designed to keep property in the hands of men; when a woman had no husband, brother, or son and therefore inherited in their stead, she was liable to harassments of various kinds, including arraignment for witchcraft.[19] And once arrested, she was more likely than other suspects to be condemned and executed. Women who were successful at business were also at high risk, as were those who acted on behalf of sick or absent husbands. Single women and postmenopausal women without sons were especially vulnerable. That in Salem widows were allowed to own property outright may have been the reason that the witch hunt there was especially intense.

That a woman might gain financial independence was one kind of threat, but aggressive action of any kind was dangerous. Any woman whose actions were seen as sexually unrestrained, or any wife who refused obedience to her husband, was likely to be punished.[20] Puritans, in emphasizing the sacred nature of the family even more than other Protestants, defined women's roles narrowly: they were to be faithful wives, and they were punished more severely than men for infidelity. This combination of religious and economic control created an exceptionally patriarchal society. As Karlsen concludes, in Puritan New England, gender issues *were* religious issues.

Though the roots clearly lie in the English trials, such as at Warboys, complete with demonic possession and the generation gap between young accuser and mature victim, and though much of the Puritan theology invoked against the devil was English too, there was a greater harshness in the New England hunt. The Massachusetts Bay Colony legal code of 1648, mandating the death penalty not only for homicide but also for witchcraft, blasphemy, bestiality, sodomy, adultery, rape, and stubbornness or rebelliousness of son against parents, went beyond English law, which exempted blasphemers and insubordinate children; the New England code, furthermore, claimed the Bible as its authority for these stern measures.[21] It was this religious zeal, so prominent in theocratic Massachusetts, that accounts for much of the intensity of the Salem panic. Knowledge of Continental diabolism beliefs also influenced the prosecutors; I have found that Increase Mather's library included a translation of a portion of the *Malleus* and other Continental demonologists as well.[22] This material may account for the ferocity with which some Puritan preachers and magistrates hunted down the suspects.

Russia and Scandinavia

There were witch hunts on the eastern edge of Europe, but far less has been published on them, only one article in a western European language, Russell Zguta's work on trials appealed to Moscow from 1622 to 1700.[23] Although this report, based on the ninety-nine persons tried on appeal to Moscow courts, can represent only the tip of the iceberg, it offers useful parallels with the West. Here too more powerful people punished those who were more vulnerable: over half of the victims were peasants, a significant number of whom were transients or foreigners, and their accusers were nobility or military men. The Russian witch hunt began after the mid-1550s. Until 1552 witchcraft was in the hands of the Russian Orthodox church, which seldom prosecuted for it,[24] but when the czar transferred jurisdiction over witch cases to the civil courts, both church and state began to show greater concern about witchcraft. Though they may have been responding to news of witch hunts from the West, it was only the unrestrained methods of their secular courts that permitted a hunt to begin.

The courts applied tortures known in the West, such as lashing, the rack, the strappado, and ducking, as well as methods unique to Russia: burning wedges placed between hands or feet, pincers tightened around the scrotum, cold water poured continuously on the head. Believing in a conspiracy theory, they tortured prisoners to force them to name others. Officials could initiate trials, and physical objects (supposedly used by witches) were considered damning evidence. Death was by burning.

Russians also experienced demonic possession. Zguta mentions the *klikushi*, women "who ranted and raved hysterically during church services, calling out the names of those who they said had bewitched them." On this basis so many innocent people were tortured that local authorities appealed to the czar for help; at Shuia, for example, seventy *klikushi* were reported in 1670. Were they like the possessed girls of Warboys and Salem, or like the French nuns? Were their victims old women, or handsome clergy? Unfortunately the record does not give their ages or describe whom they accused.

But other features were remarkably different from Western witch hunts. The secular court that tried these cases was a military court, which may account for the extraordinarily harsh use of torture. No children were involved, either as accusers or as victims. Aside from the conspiracy theory, Russian judges did not subscribe to satanist theories; there was little use of spectral evidence or charges of weird behavior such as baby-snatching. Witchcraft was viewed as straight malefice.

Zguta believes that most cases reached the Moscow appeals court. If so, ninety-nine cases in almost eighty years is a small yield indeed. He argues that the defendants' right to call witnesses, added to the absence of theories of diabolism, kept the hunt small. There were, for example, no multiple burnings.

One remaining factor in the Russian material claims our attention: the ratio between men and women is unlike that of most of the West, fifty-nine men tried on appeal to forty women, 60 percent male to 40 percent female. Did Russians persecute women less severely than western Europeans? One must be warned by considering the gender ratio of appeals to the Parlement of Paris: although French women were accused in local courts at a rate of four to one over men, they *appealed* far less often than men. Men, even poor peasants, moved more easily in the public world than women and were more aggressive about demanding their rights. This may well have been the case in Russia also; if so, the high percentage of men making appeals may not indicate a low percentage of women accused.

Zguta gives us glimpses of Russian witches: the Tatar (foreign, Mongol) woman of Lebedianskoe, whose reputation for fortune-telling and healing was so widespread that a crowd followed her wherever she went, who was tried as a witch in 1630; the grandmother of Ivan IV, accused by his advisers of setting fire to Moscow in 1547, attacked by a mob; Dar'ia, Jewish wife of a village cantor, arrested for causing a bridegroom's impotence by placing a blazing splinter under his staircase and urinating on it; the old women who in earlier times (twelfth century) were rounded up during famine on charges of sorcery, their hands and feet tied together, and thrown into the river at Kiev.[25] These cases are types familiar enough to Western persecutions: the successful healer, the woman from a different ethnic group or different religion, the noblewoman caught in a male political struggle, the old women ritually sacrificed to purge the land of evil or to break a plague or famine. Because these Russian stories connect with Western stereotypes, we can surmise that Russian women were subjected to a type of gender persecution similar to that practiced on western European women.

These women, both humble and royal, could be found in Western trial records. What is different about the Russian material is the high number of male witches and the number of trials involving the imperial court—the two warlocks, for example, accused of softening the heart of Czar Peter I to prevent his sending an elderly officer to a distant post; the warlocks were burned, the old man beheaded, and his wife incarcerated in a convent. As in the earliest days in the West, witch hunting in Russia involved high-level politics, and, therefore, men.

I have three reasons for suspecting that witch accusations were more numerous and more often directed at women than Zguta found. First, attitudes of the Orthodox church toward wise women and indeed toward any practice smacking in the least of "paganism" were even more hostile than in the Western churches. Second, sexual customs were strictly enforced by the church, in even greater detail than by the seventeenth-century Western churches, and sexuality was viewed in a strongly negative way. And finally, the low status of women throughout the Slavic world was similar to that in the West.[26] These are three of the main conditions for witch hunts, as we have seen. The only social factor lacking in Russia was strong interference by the government in sex life; apparently the czars' bureaucracies left those matters entirely to the church.

As Eve Levin has shown, the Russian family was patriarchal, husbands being responsible for wives, women being physically subject to husbands. In a culture lacking a concept of romantic love, marriages were arranged and were not expected to be passionate; the strongest emotional bond developed between mothers and sons. The church taught that women must be obedient to fathers and husbands, who were allowed, even expected, to beat their women for "great offenses" such as disobedience or inattention. Bridegrooms were presented with whips at their weddings!

Sex was considered of the devil, and women were thought to be more sexual by nature, thus more susceptible to the devil. If a man could not resist a woman, it was, by nature, her fault. Women were frequently condemned for being "evil-tongued" and openly sexual. Though these derogatory views sound identical to those of the misogyny of the West, they carried an extra force in Russia. There was a "blame the victim" twist to antiwoman sentiments there: if a woman had a spontaneous miscarriage, she must do penance because her sins had caused her to lose her pregnancy; if her infant died, it was because she had sinned.

The church ceaselessly opposed wise women and female healers. Curing infertility with herbs was condemned as witchcraft, as was dispensing aphrodisiacs or bringing on an abortion. Women were forbidden to seek the help of wise women to conceive or to patronize the *baby bogomerzskija* (God-insulting grannies) for any reason. Thus attacking the female-centered world of healing, the church cut at the root of female power.

All women, healers or not, suffered from being controlled by violence. Although laws, both ecclesiastical and secular, protected women from rape, little was in fact done to carry them out. If a woman got out of line (insulted a man, for example), she was considered deserving of being raped. Levin concludes that "medieval Slavic society had a high level of tolerance for violence against women"[27]—which makes fertile ground for a witch hunt.

As for why this beginning did not evolve into a witchcraze, Zguta notes that the scene was ripe, given the Russians' belief in a witch's ability to effect harm and the intense period of disasters that Russia underwent in the seventeenth century, including a major schism in the Orthodox church. He points to religious differences as the saving factor, the original Russian belief, not in a pantheon of gods as in the West, but in nature herself: "Among the Eastern Slavs, consequently, the intellectual rationale for witchcraft was predicated on a pantheistic concept of the universe rather than a demonological one, as was true in the West. Without Satan and without the Sabbat, Russian witches bore little—and sometimes no—resemblance to their Continental counterparts."[28]

I would add that in the West, where pagans had venerated the great gods and lost them to Christianity, *there was Satan.* So Satan is the Westerners' lost God(s). This speculation comes close to the oft-disputed theory of Margaret Murray that Western witchcraft was a continuation of the ancient European pagan religion.[29] It illuminates that part of her argument that I have never been able to dismiss, namely, the evidence for ancient "folk religious" practices throughout the Western witchcraft material. Murray erred by forcing her evidence too far, by re-creating late medieval witchcraft as an "alternative church" instead of a loose collection of magical practices, a decision that pushed her into many anachronisms. Still, her attention to *what people were doing,* to folk ritual and belief, was on the right track (see chapter 6), and Zguta's material from Russia reinforces her approach.

The moderation of the witch hunt in Russia, and in all the lands ruled by the Orthodox church, needs further study. In addition to the fortunate lack of demonological obsession among Orthodox priests, we need to know more about how they related to the Russian government's attacks on witchcraft, and, especially, we need to know more about the attitudes of priests and people to women.

THE SCANDINAVIAN witch hunts produced one notable anomaly, the fact that in Finland and Estonia the typical witch was male. To see what this can tell us about the issue of gender in these accounts, we first need to trace the history of the witch hunt in the other northern countries.

Though witch trials never reached panic level anywhere in Scandinavia, each country went through a period when the witch hunt might have turned into a craze. Norway's two peak periods, the 1620s and 1660s, seem to have been caused by economic pressure—or to be exact, by population pressure on land, causing the emergence of a new underclass. By around 1600 a poor class of crofters who lived on small plots of marginal land made up about 10 percent of the population; with the even poorer beggars, they became a criminal class. The historian of Norwegian witchcraft, H. E. Naess, found "a connection between the circumstances leading to indictments for witchcraft and the social standing of the suspects. In 160 of the 196 trials containing documentation on the economic situation of those accused, they were characterized as extremely poor. . . . Several witches owned nothing but their old, torn clothes, which barely hid their naked bodies."[30] Differing from people in most countries, where the middling poor accused those only slightly less well-off than they, Norwegians in most cases went after those who lived below the poverty line.

An exception was the famous trial of the widow of a distinguished humanist scholar and Lutheran pastor, Anna Pedersdotter Absalon.[31] Attacked by traditionalists who wanted to keep the old pre-Reformation statues in the churches, she was accused of familiar *maleficium*, of making ill a man who had refused her wine, beer, and vinegar, of killing a young boy with a bewitched biscuit. Adding a charge of diabolism, her servant claimed that Anna had transformed her into a horse and ridden her to a sabbat; there a group of witches plotted a storm that would wreck all ships arriving at Bergen and then burn the town and cause it to be flooded. This demonological testimony sealed Anna's fate, and she was burned as a witch. Her case, similar to many in Germany and Poland, showed that enemies would attack a man's wife when he was too powerful to be disposed of, or would take revenge on him posthumously through his more vulnerable spouse.

Naess, who records but does not comment on the fact that 80 percent of the accused were female, concludes that economics is the explanation for the hunts, that "it is difficult to see how the trials could have started off in communities where the economic as well as the social and cultural conditions were progressing." I would add that one must then ask, What was the economic condition of women? How was it changing in those decades when Norwegians carried out those "ruthless trials against burdensome members of society"?

Denmark had all the usual conditions for a witchcraze, including widespread belief in sorcery and an important set of ordinances in 1617 declaring that the power of witchcraft indicated a pact with the devil. These decrees also attempted to reform the sexual mores, ruling harshly against adultery and fornication and ordering what types of clothing different classes might wear. In short, as Jens Johansen comments, "The laws of 1617 were an attempt to tighten the [government's] hold on Danish society."[32] As had happened in northern France, the interference of central government in daily life had a deeply unsettling effect on the Danes. Immediately, in that same year, the number of witch trials began to rise, and in the next eight years, Denmark had 297 trials, the greatest concentration in European annals. Church and state apparently worked hand in hand, as the most powerful bishop at that time was a strictly orthodox Lutheran.

Evidence from elsewhere shows that moral crusades such as this, combined with demonological witchcraft beliefs, were devastating to women. But Johansen neither comments on the gender issue nor informs us how many victims of the witch trials were female. Establishing that poverty was probably not a factor (Denmark was prosperous at the time), he concludes that the key to the course of the Danish trials was judicial: the Danish statute of 1576 requiring appeal in witchcraft cases (the earliest such law in Europe) saved the country from a holocaust.

From Sweden comes an example of how secular courts interfered in women's sexual lives—and of how women might close ranks when that happened. In Ribe in 1548, a poor girl faced the death sentence for having killed her baby. Because she had been seduced and abandoned by the child's father, the wife of the Protestant superintendent of pastors took her side and led the leading women of the town into civic court to protest the sentence. The girl was convicted but let off with public penance and banishment.[33]

But, more often, moral crusades triggered witch trials. This time the impetus came from the church, in the form of ordinances in 1664 challenging sexual customs and community traditions. The church ruled that sexual offenses, formerly punished with a fine, would now receive corporal or even capital punishment. Premarital sex, communal feasts and processions, public singing and dancing, maypoles and wedding processions, all were proscribed. This attack on cherished customs produced an immediate effect—in 1668 witch accusations that approached panic level broke out among children and young women in the provinces. Twenty-three persons, mostly women, were sentenced to death. Although testimony of minors younger than fifteen was not acceptable, judges cheated by adding several minors together to make "one witness." Ankarloo has evidence that the children collaborated on accusations, concocting stories of being bewitched and taken to "Blakulla" to attend the devil's sabbat. Encouraged by men from the new middle class, priests, small bureaucrats, judges, and officers who approved of the conservative trends, thousands of children took part in the hysteria. Some were even paid by priests to continue with their testimony. Their targets were 86 percent female, mostly older women, married or widowed. Ankarloo surmises that they had it in for older women either as a group of "mother-figures, of sexual rivals, of old hags, or of demanding employers, whatever it may be. We shall probably never know."[34] I believe that we must know, that the deaths by beheading and burning of 640 or so women can tell us something about the Sweden of the 1660s and 1670s.

The trials in Finland and Estonia (along with Iceland, which did not have a true witch hunt)[35] offer a rare phenomenon, the typical witch as male. Finland's trials were concentrated heavily on its west coast, where most people were from Sweden, spoke Swedish, traded with Sweden, and therefore were acquainted with the Swedish outbreak of 1668 to 1675. Accusations flourished among moderately well-off peasants and burgers, successful from their export trade with Sweden. Inland, where people were mostly subsistence farmers, there were few outbreaks.

Finns had always associated sorcery with males, and as the trials began with sorcery accusations, they focused on men. But as the trials increased, the number and percentage of women accused also increased. The longer an outbreak of witch fever lasted, and the more that people resorted to charges of diabolism, the more women were targeted.

In Estonia 60 percent of victims were males, who were middle-aged or elderly, married, peasants, and known as healers or sorcerers.[36] They were accused mainly of poisoning, their main weapons being hexed beer, fish, strawberries, or bread. When women were accused, it was mainly for laying a curse on someone. An exception emerges in the first major trial, a case of class bias in which an estate owner accused his wife of poisoning his father and almost killing him. The wife escaped, but not before denouncing her maid and an old woman. These peasants and three accomplices were burned at the stake, whereas the lady was only ordered into exile. As in the Alice Kyteler case in Ireland, servants were made to serve as scapegoats for the upper class.

Torture was commonly used, and death was by burning. Diabolism was not taken up by the common people, even though judges did inject it into proceedings. Estonian witchcraft remained mainly a matter of the power of magic to inflict harm; its connections with the ancient European beliefs about magic were shown through widespread concern over werewolves, who figure more often in trials of women than of men. These creatures were believed to be humans who changed themselves into wolves (or bears) using animal skins. At Meremoisa, for instance, a peasant named Ann admitted that she had been a werewolf for four years and had killed a number of animals; she had hidden her wolf skin under a stone in a field. Another woman confessed that she had become a werewolf when an old woman had led her into the forest and fed her sweet roots. People believed that werewolves roamed in packs.

Another prominent Estonian belief, widely held across Europe, was that witches rode at night through the air. Some believed that they did so only in order to commit destruction; others held, as did the peasants of Friuli whom we will consider in a moment, that they were good witches who rode out in spirit to protect the crops.

This survey of Scandinavian and Baltic witchcraft shows that it was deeply rooted in European folk customs and that the common people never did adopt much of the demonological lore of the judges and theologians, thereby probably sparing themselves a major witchcraze. But whenever beliefs about the devil did spread at the grass roots, as in Sweden in the children's myths about "Blakulla," the numbers of accused women soared.

Hungary and the Balkan Lands

Hungary, including Transylvania, engaged in heavy prosecutions of almost panic intensity, over sixteen hundred trials and over eight hundred deaths, most of which occurred in a 140-year period. The peak came in 1710 to 1760, during and following a major, failed war for independence. Hungary found itself dominated from the north by Hapsburg Austria and from the south by the Ottoman Turks and badly divided internally. Its struggle for national autonomy, stretching throughout the eighteenth century, kept the country in turmoil.

Hungary qualifies without question as a laboratory for gender bias: 90 percent of accusations and 91.8 percent of death sentences were against women. Many accusers were female also, children and teenaged girls. Gabor Klaniczay, compiler of these statistics, offers one explanation for them: women gained so much power in the late Middle Ages as mystics and saints that men diabolized women in self-defense.[37] Considering that acceptance of a mystic's power, and the concomitant accolade of sainthood, were dependent on the approval of the male ecclesiastical hierarchy, Klaniczay's theory does seem sound. Yet when we consider how many women with spiritual gifts were not accepted but were condemned as heretics or witches (mystics like Joan of Arc and Marguerite Porete), we must consider the possibility that they were, as a sex, consciously demonized.[38] But there is surely more to the deaths of so many women than this one motivation. As Klaniczay and his colleagues continue to analyze twenty thousand Hungarian narratives pertaining to magic, one can hope that a broader gender analysis will be forthcoming.

Most interesting about the Hungarian material is the considerable amount of archaic folk magic it contains. In addition to the infiltration of demonic lore from German lands, there was already a broad base of folk religion to build on. Hungarian society included shamanic figures called *taltosok*, more often female than male, created wise in their mother's wombs, born with teeth, whose souls could travel out of their bodies (the shamanic "soul-journey") in order to fight with other *taltosok* or to visit God, where they would receive the gift of healing. They served Hungarian society by finding hidden treasure, warning of fires, preventing hailstorms, and healing. These magical activities brought them into the territory of witch lore, of course, and many traces of shamanism have been found in Hungarian witch trials. They could heal the bewitched and identify witches, and they sometimes met in spirit at gatherings. They became bulls that witches rode up the chimney and to their sabbats.

The Hungarian material also contains many references to the "healer who also kills." We will return to this theme in chapter 6. All these folk customs link Hungary with the Italian *benandanti* (see the section on Italy and Spain, p. 89) and the shamans of Slovenia, Croatia, and Estonia. We are here at the edge of a vast stratum of folk religion, ancient and possibly Europe-wide, that underlies the trials of the sixteenth and seventeenth centuries. They are only the signal to alert us to what had been going on for centuries.

The Netherlands

An anomaly among northern European lands in terms of witch hunting was the Netherlands. Although under control of the Hapsburg emperor of the Holy Roman Empire until 1579 and thus ruled by laws that encouraged the witchcraze, the northern Netherlandish provinces that became the Dutch Republic endured only a mild witchcraft persecution.[39] Fewer than 150 were executed, and there were virtually no mass panics, raising the question of how much influence one should give to legal and political factors. The Dutch Republic is known for its tolerance in many matters; its enlightened response to tensions over witchcraft may be part of a general pattern of restraint. In any case, the death penalty for witchcraft was not permitted after 1600, and the number of accusations dropped dramatically after that. Agitation about witchcraft returned to what it had traditionally been, namely, local charges of slander, cursing, and so on.

During the brief period of active persecution (c. 1540–1600) both folk magic and injurious sorcery were prosecuted as witchcraft.[40] Though the devil's pact was a factor, mention of the sabbat and sex with the devil, and of a conspiracy of witches, was rare. The new Reformed church was concerned about its parishioners consulting cunning people but did not panic over the devil's power; church councils in fact encouraged legal authorities to give mild sentences in dealing with witchcraft.[41] The church saw itself as responsible for reconciling quarrels among its members, not exacerbating them. Reformed theologians also worked to lessen the belief in magic; church councils therefore punished those who consulted witch doctors and practiced counter-magic but treated accused witches leniently, not panicking over their offense.

Evidence from the Netherlands questions other generalizations about European witchcraft. Consider the well-known connection between witch hunts and rising poverty: the Netherlands was prosperous during this period, but still produced a witch hunt. As for the observation that political turmoil increased witch hunting, although the chief decades of Dutch witch hunting coincided with the tumultuous years of the struggle for independence from Hapsburg Spain and the founding of the Republic, the attacks on witches were brought under control—just as the rest of Europe was entering its heaviest years of persecution.

That 90 percent of the accused in the Netherlands were women has not been sufficiently addressed.

Italy and Spain

Signora Oriente rules the society as Christ rules the world.

—*Pierina de Bugatis, Milan, 1390*

The society to which Pierina referred met every Thursday night in Milan to pay homage to the woman Oriente, who taught them magic and divination, let them feast on animals, and led them in stealing food and drink from rich folks' houses. This example of folk religion in the form of a fertility cult flourished for years until the *podesta* (the secular court) took notice.[42]

Because some early, fourteenth-century trials against "superstition" took place in Italy,[43] and the basis for demonological theory was laid by Italian and Spanish inquisitors, one would expect that these Mediterranean lands suffered a witchcraze, but in fact they did not. Though they prosecuted many, they executed few. The reformed, "modern" Inquisitions of Spain and Italy, strictly regulated, inquired into thousands of cases of harmful magic, but seldom turned over their prisoners to the secular arm. Secular courts, shocked at this leniency, contested the church's right to adjudicate in these matters, but never gained control of them. Especially in Italy, exhibiting an intense interest in the activities of female fortune-tellers and male magicians, inquisitors perceived these activities as wrong belief rather than diabolic magic and sought to convert the practitioners to a papally approved form of Catholicism. Punishments therefore consisted of penances and, in extreme cases, whippings and banishment, but not death.[44]

Research on witch persecutions in these lands, embedded as it is in the records of their Inquisitions, is in its beginning stage. With forty-four thousand cases in the Spanish archives alone (covering heresy as well as all kinds of magic) to be dealt with, it will be years before we have the kinds of social and gender analysis we need.[45] Some preliminary speculations can be made, however.

The only Mediterranean examples of typical witch hunts occurred in northern Spain and Italy, influenced by the more savage French and German hunts across their borders, but both were aborted. Around 1500 in the diocese of Como, a Dominican inquisitor claimed that he tried a thousand and burned a hundred witches a year, mostly poor peasants. When the peasants took up arms and appealed to the bishop, an episcopal commission condemned the hunt.[46]

Likewise in Spain, when the witch mania stirred up by Pierre de Lancre spilled across the Pyrenees into the Spanish Basque provinces, a thorough investigation by the inquisitor Salazar caused most of the cases to be dismissed. True, harm was done and reputations were ruined: one accused woman (Mariquita de Atauri) committed suicide, and five others died in prison. But Salazar's skepticism, especially of tales told by children, saved thousands of persons from the stake (over five thousand had been accused).[47] In the end, only six persons suffered death in the *auto-da-fé*.[48]

In the Italian lands, Carlo Ginzburg has discovered that in 1575 the Inquisition uncovered at Udine, northeast of Venice, one of the more remarkable examples of folk religion in its annals, a sect of Friulian men and women called *benandanti*, the "do-gooders."[49] Born with a caul, which they still wore around their necks, they went out at night (although still sleeping in their beds) to *do battle with witches.* These specially chosen persons fought in military order, brandishing sticks of sorghum and fennel stalks against sorcerers who would destroy the crops. Four times a year, at each seasonal equinox, they fought to protect the livelihood of their community, and on the way home, they broke into houses and drank wine in the cellars.

This cosmic struggle, reminiscent of fertility rites across the world, is a version of the salvation journey motif.[50] And that is exactly how the *benandanti* saw themselves when they first explained their activities to the inquisitors; they were proud to be protectors of their neighbors. The Inquisition, understandably, suspected them of devil worship, that is, of *being witches,* and began imprisoning them. Perhaps because the court did not use torture, it took a very long time to break down the group's self-image, several generations in fact, but by 1650 *benandanti* were confessing that they *were* witches, and the ritual came to an end.

Benandanti (mostly men) opposed witches (mostly female) not only in night battles but on the streets of villages in broad daylight. These "do-gooders" played the role of shaman for their communities, sometimes working as healers but mainly policing the boundaries between the ordinary world and the supernatural.

Ginzburg has been able to connect the Friulian magicians with the werewolves of Livland (Estonia), good men who took animal form and walked down into Hell on three special days each year to fight witches who had stolen seed needed for crops. The Estonian testimony avers that German and Russian werewolves performed the same beneficent deed and insists that werewolves are "the hounds of God," not servants of Satan. Ginzburg has also tied in his extraordinary material with the cult of the goddess Diana (also known as Abundia, Holda, Satia, Perchta), in which during Ember Days women travel at night with the goddess, surrounded by the souls of the dead, demanding food and drink at the houses they visit. This legend turns up all over Europe. Ginzburg also found a parallel between the *benandanti's* military formation and the claim of Hungarian witches that they went to their nocturnal meetings at the sound of trumpets, led by captains and corporals carrying black banners.[51]

After an initial preoccupation with Protestant heretics, the majority of Italian inquisitional cases were directed against folk healers and diviners,[52] the church insisting that its own methods of healing by blessing, applying holy water, and exorcising were to be used exclusively. Many of the healers were priests who mixed folk and Christian magical methods in their exorcisms, thus incurring the wrath of the church.[53]

A specialty of Italian folk culture was the love potion. As with the *benandanti,* the women who administered such potions thought of themselves as doing good, but the Inquisition offered its most severe penalties, whipping and banishment, for this type of magic, hoping to destroy people's belief in it and the business that prostitutes enjoyed from it.

These magicians and folk healers, were they predominantly men or women? One fragmentary piece of statistical evidence gives some idea. Between 1596 and 1785 in the Friuli, 777 accusations were made of performing magical arts: divination, necromancy, love magic, healing, making spells for acquiring wealth or avoiding bullets, causing storms, witchcraft *(maleficium),* and of course, being *benandanti.* Of these 777, exactly half were women, who prevailed in healing, witchcraft, and causing storms, but not in any other category. After 1670, in fact, the defendants were overwhelmingly male.[54] But these are bare statistics and give us no glimpse of why men were particularly suspect as magicians at this time in this part of Italy, or what the attitudes toward women were.

One speculation can be made: that the Roman Inquisition treated magic workers more leniently than many courts north of the Alps because it doubted the power of the devil. Believing that these practices stemmed from ignorance, that is, from a mistaken belief in satanic power, the church wanted to correct, not destroy, the practitioners. Its intellectual skepticism places it with Reginald Scot and some of the English magistrates who also denied the power of Satan. Thus, moderation was found in Protestant England and Catholic Italy, but seldom in between.

The same common sense ruled the Spanish Inquisition.[55] Reformed and controlled by the monarchy after its excesses against Jews, its leaders declared in 1526 that witchcraft was a delusion, a matter more of madness than of heresy, and thereafter, with the exception of the Basque outbreak, no one was killed for witchcraft in Spain except by secular courts.[56] The Inquisition turned its energies instead to spreading the moral reforms of the Counter-Reformation, insisting, for example, that one must have religious instruction before procuring a marriage license, teaching that, contrary to popular belief, fornication was a sin, and prosecuting for concubinage, bigamy, and having sex with prostitutes.[57] Sodomy was punished by castration and the stake, bestiality by being burned alive or sent to the galleys. For witchcraft, by contrast, the most severe sentence was two hundred lashes and exile.[58]

The Inquisition was in many ways a negative force in Spanish life. Utilizing thousands of agents known as *familiares*, it acted as a secret police force, accountable to no one. Spreading fear and suspicion, it increased Spanish anti-Semitism, institutionalized bigotry, and by strict censorship narrowed intellectual life. Furthermore, it attacked the scapegoats of Spanish society: Marranos, foreigners, deviants, heretics, Jews. Yet there was not a mass murder of women in Spain. Although it interrogated several thousand women for "superstition," it punished only a few and killed but a handful. The usual misogynistic attitudes were present in Spanish society: for example, Martin de Castanega, the priest who carried out a small, early witch hunt in Navarre in 1529, claimed that women were more likely to be witches. He gave a number of reasons, including that they are more talkative and could not keep secrets, want to know about secret matters, are more angry and vengeful, and being powerless, have no way other than witchcraft to get what they want.[59] Still, women as a gender group were not attacked.

I believe that Trevor-Roper was on the right track when he argued that the Spanish Inquisition did not instigate a witchcraze because it was already sated with victims, chiefly Jews and Muslims.[60] I would like to combine his idea with Kamen's observations about the power of the Spanish family, however, and suggest that it was not simply crude satiation but a more subtle combination of forces based on gender roles. Given the power of family, especially of clans, in Spanish social and political life, and the fervor of its Christianity, I can believe that the Spanish, whether lay or clerical, would not attack their own women. Spanish men guaranteed their honor and their identity as Spaniards through the purity of their race and religion, a purity they traced through family blood ties and religious orthodoxy. Heretics, Jews, and Moors were therefore suspect on grounds of religion, and the latter two on grounds of race as well. But Christian Spanish women were seen by Spanish men as part of their group, not as outsiders. As mothers they were in fact the guarantors of group purity. I conclude that before they can become the targets of a mass persecution, women *as a group* must be perceived as outsiders, as capable of turning against those who see themselves as insiders in a society. And this is precisely what did not occur in Spain.

FROM THIS COMPARATIVE survey emerge several important preconditions for intense witch persecutions. First, the secular courts must have gained jurisdiction over witchcraft cases from the church and must have adopted the procedures of inquisitional courts, especially the right to torture prisoners until they accuse others. That these legal conditions existed by the mid-sixteenth century explains why municipal judges were the chief persecutors of alleged witches. Second, where a weak or distant central government enabled these local officials to pursue witches without restraint, as in the Holy Roman Empire, it was more likely that mob rule might take over. Third, as for belief, there were major witch hunts almost everywhere that judges and theologians believed in diabolism, that is, in the devil's ability to work evil through human beings. When this belief developed into a conspiracy theory, as it did in Lorraine, Franche-Comté, the German lands, and elsewhere, it produced a holocaust for witches. One can trace a rise in persecutions as this belief spread. Where witchcraft was conceived of only as *maleficium,* as sorcery, a witchcraze did not develop.

Furthermore, this elite persecution of witches was part of a much larger elite attack on folk culture, a reform movement carried out by both state and church that *in itself* sometimes triggered witch hunts, importing a strong class bias into the proceedings. And because these prosecutions grew out of religious reforms, both Catholic and Protestant, we must consider the role of the two Reformations in the witch hunts, not only as direct attack on witchcraft but more broadly as an attack on basic customs and values of the people.

This survey raises several issues for a gender analysis of the persecutions. The first and most important is that where prosecution for sexual crimes rose, there charges of witchcraft were likely to rise also (Spain and Italy were exceptions). We must look also at differences in family patterns. Where women were protected by their families, especially by extended kinship networks, they were less likely to become targets for accusations or, if charged, to be brought to trial. Where the medieval clan system was breaking down, women were more vulnerable. These factors will be discussed in the next chapter.

Further, we have seen that worsening economic conditions produced tensions that led to witchcraft charges. As marginal workers, women figured prominently in the groups who were first to suffer from the late sixteenth-century inflation, unemployment, and higher taxation. Because very little has been written about women's economic roles in relation to the witch persecutions, a separate chapter will be devoted to it.

Finally, misogyny, a tradition of antifeminism, turns out to be pervasive and dynamic, appearing in both the folk customs and the learned literature of every area. Though it tells us much about men and how they asserted control, it also indicates an important point about women: that they were powerful enough to be feared. This factor does not surface in a survey such as I have just made, yet it explains better than any other why women were victimized. Chapters 5 and 6, which concentrate on what women were doing, is therefore fundamental to this study: the interplay between the very real power of women in the minds of men and their vulnerability when caught up in the institutional world is what the witch hunts were about. It is to the question of what women were actually doing, where their power lay, that we must now turn.

A witch brewing up a storm. Although women were marginalized as workers and as productive members of their communities, they were frequently accused of having caused death and economic destruction. From Olaus Magnus's *Historia de gentibus septentrionalibus*, Rome, 1555. Courtesy of Dover Pictorial Archive Series.

CHAPTER FIVE

Women and Work

Economic Marginalization

No labor scorning, be it ever so mean . . .
So many hardships daily we go through,
I boldly say, the like *you* never knew.

—*Mary Collier to Stephen Duck, London, 1739*

A WOMAN could be killed for going to work. A young woman, Margaret Flower, was employed by the earl of Rutland at Belvoir Castle near Lincoln, where she served as keeper "of the poultrey abroad and the washhouse within dores." Her sister and mother also worked there, and Mother Flower, a cunning woman, occasionally gave the earl advice.[1] Sometime around 1613 fault was found with Margaret's performance, and she was fired. When her mother protested, she in turn was sent away. As Mother Flower left "she cursed them all."

Soon after, the earl, head of one of the wealthiest families in England, lost his eldest son, Henry Rosse; when his second son, Francis, sickened in the spring of 1618, he suspected the women he had gotten rid of. After all, wasn't Mother Flower rumored to be a witch? And wasn't she known as "a monstrous malicious woman, full of oathes, curses, and imprecations irreligious"? Furthermore, everyone knew that "like mother, like daughter" applied where sorcery was suspected.[2]

The pamphlet describing this case, written entirely from the earl's point of view, accuses Margaret of stealing supplies from the castle and refers vaguely to "some indecencies in her life." The younger daughter, Philippa, was said to be "lewdly transported with the love of one Thomas

Simpson" whom she had bewitched; he had no power to leave her and was "marvelously altered both in minde and body" since she had taken up with him. As for Mother Flower, she had begun to look strange, "her eyes were fiery and hollow, her speech fell and envious, her demeanor strange and exoticke . . . so that the whole course of her life gave great suspicion that she was a notorious Witch"; besides, she was known as an atheist. To top it all, she "dealt with familiar spirits, and terrified them all with curses and threatening of revenge, if there was never so little cause of displeasure and unkindnesse."

In all this there is little substance, except perhaps the charge that Margaret stole from her employer. But it makes clear that someone (or a number of people) did not like the Flowers and were out to destroy them. Whether it was envy of their jobs at the castle, or fear of an aggressive old woman, or possibly that Mother Flower dabbled in magic, or a former lover's revenge, we cannot be sure. Given that the daughters were young, single women, there is the possibility that the earl's sons had seduced them, grown tired of them, and driven them away. What we do know is what happened when this gossip reached the earl. He had no need to add to the slander against the three women, having much more powerful weapons at his command.

What happened next illustrates the injustice possible when the aristocracy leveled an attack of witchcraft against commoners. The three women were arrested for witchcraft and sent to the assizes at Lincoln. Mother Flower died along the way, raising the possibility that the prisoners were maltreated. The two young women were tried before Sir Edward Bromley, who had recently judged the notorious Lancashire trials. The *inability* of these commoners to cope with the alien customs of the court is evidenced by the way they incriminated themselves: Philippa confessed that she had stolen the right-hand glove of Lord Henry Rosse and given it to her mother, who rubbed it on the back of her cat Rutterkin, her familiar. The old woman had then placed the glove in boiling water and buried it in the yard (presumably causing the young lord's death). A similar glove story was offered to explain the second son's illness. Rutterkin was alleged to "leap on [Mother Flower's] shoulder and suck her neck."

That both daughters confessed to such damning actions indicates the possibility that they were threatened with torture. That the earl of Rutland was a close adviser of King James I, author of a treatise on witchcraft that urged the use of torture, raises this speculation to the level of probability.[3] In any case, the outcome of the trial emphasized the way the elite could manipulate the courts to further oppress the poor: both daughters were hanged.[4]

A story that began by describing three working women, self-supporting (there were apparently no men in their lives) and united as a family, ultimately illustrates the destruction of that family. The Flower women were sacrificed to the grief and fear of a rich family of powerful men, well connected and thus able to provide themselves with scapegoats from the laboring class. That the earl chose women who had no male relatives to protect them was a further exploitation. We do not know who claimed their property, but it was probably the earl.

But perhaps the earl was on the right track after all. In firing the women and depriving them of their livelihood, he had reason to fear their hatred and revenge. This is a classic case of the original offender being unable to deal with his guilt, then projecting the guilt outward onto the original victims, making them into witches *so that they could be done away with*, thus ridding the original offender of the source of his guilt.

In analyzing village discontent in sixteenth-century Württemberg, David Sabean concludes that "in a village with rich and poor, the generalized envy of the poor could bring about a [rich] person's illness." When illness broke out (plague was frequent in Württemberg), everyone was to take communion with and pray with the sick, but the prosperous members of the village were told also to send food and drink to the poor.[5] In this way the rich could atone for their largesse and hope to placate the envy of the poor, and redistribute a bit of the wealth as well. The envy of the English villagers living around the castle of Belvoir could well have been great, an envy that would turn to hatred and revenge in women who lost their livelihood at the hands of one of the wealthiest men in England. In a society that believed in evil magic, hatred could kill, and the earl's sons could be believed to have died from it. Witchcraft beliefs thus had a double effect: to interpret misfortune (the deaths of the two young aristocrats) as intended evil, and to pollute or seduce or draw certain vulnerable persons (the Flower women) into an identification as witches.

TO EXPLAIN the increasing vulnerability of working women in the sixteenth century, one must not overlook the way that two events in that century converged: the rise of witchcraft accusations, beginning about 1550, and the steep rise of inflation, charted from about that same year. At midcentury, crisis gripped Europe, based on population growth that had reached the saturation point, exacerbated by a flood of wealth from the new colonies in the Americas. Overpopulation created a land shortage, followed by the inevitable food shortages, hunger, unemployment, and unrest.[6] Crime, both rural and urban, increased all across Europe.[7]

This brutal combination had occurred before, notably in the early fourteenth century, but had not then triggered a witch hunt. The earlier crisis had been diverted by the massive deaths caused by the bubonic plague (the Black Death) beginning in 1348, an almost providential killing off of Europe's excess population. No such Malthusian salvation rescued Europe two hundred years later when it faced the same squeeze. This time extraneous events conspired instead to make the population crisis even worse.

The influx of silver and gold from the Americas, flooding Europe's markets through Spain, drove prices up. Although much of the merchant class that controlled this expanding wealth enjoyed prosperity throughout the century, the poor suffered. Soon people living at the poverty level could not afford many basic necessities. Begging, vagabondage, homelessness, and theft increased; a vast underclass was created. As the rich grew richer and the poor grew poorer, tension between them rose. Into this economic gap came a method for resolving social tensions, at least on the surface, namely, witchcraft accusations.[8] For though rural Europe had long been familiar with the occasional charge of *maleficium,* the rulers of village and town had not taken such charges seriously, had not put people—especially women—to death for them on a regular basis, until after 1550. That the accused persons, mostly poor themselves, were not responsible for this economic suffering was beside the point; they were *perceived* as the cause, and that perception sufficed to justify scapegoating them.

The seventeenth century brought no relief: a crisis in industrial production ended the boom for the wealthy and only worsened the suffering of the poor.[9] A century-long depression affected all of Europe except the Netherlands, Denmark, and Sweden. Along with economic and demographic stagnation, there was rigidity in the old industries; the only institution to increase in power was the monarchy, as monarchs continued the process of centralization, tight taxation, and militarization they had begun so auspiciously the century before.

During this one hundred fifty years of hard times, the exact period of major witch hunting in Europe, women suffered economically and socially more than men. Before we analyze the connections between that fact and their victimization as witches, we must see what roles women played in the economy before 1560.

Though medieval women's work had always been defined by their role in the family, and though they had always worked for less pay and had less control over their earnings than men, still, their contribution to Europe's economic life was impressive and essential.[10] Almost all rural women kept gardens and cared for domestic animals, preserved food, chopped and carried wood, transported water, cared for and educated children, nursed sick family members, and prepared the dead for burial. Beyond satisfying these universal expectations, they might also augment family income by serving as brewers, fortune-tellers, healers, midwives, pharmacists, milliners, seamstresses, spinners, tavern keepers, thatchers, road workers, lace makers, receivers of stolen goods, victualers (caterers), wet nurses, weavers, and sellers of their surplus at market. During harvest season they hired out as extra labor, although they received far less in wages for this work than men.

In towns and cities, as in the villages, women's work was limited to and by their family situation. The wife of a man who owned his own business routinely worked alongside her husband. Urban women might therefore become skilled at silk manufacture, weaving, tailoring, skinning leather, candle making, or other crafts, or assist their husbands in tavern-keeping. City women, both married and widowed, also worked as pawnbrokers, moneylenders, launderers. Women provided almost all the available medical services, male doctors being scarce in European towns until the nineteenth century; they also dispensed welfare for town and city councils.[11] Occasionally they took up arms. Like their country sisters, city women found brewing and selling ale to be a mainstay. Wives of poor men might sell handiwork, peddle bread, hire themselves out for wet nursing.

If a woman had no family, only the lowest jobs were available to her: prostitution, wool-combing, petty crime. The more enterprising poor not only served as prostitutes but also ran brothels. That women *worked,* putting in longer hours than men and accounting for a great deal of the productive labor, is no longer challenged. The questions that must be asked are, Did their efforts earn them any control over their lives, and did their working lives change during the sixteenth century?

The one time in a woman's life that she might prosper and have some say over what she produced was after her husband's death. Provided she was not placed under control of a grown son, a widow might inherit property, be allowed to continue her husband's business, even defend her interests in court. Some women added to their wealth, especially as merchants and renters of real estate. The attractions of widowhood are proved by the low rate of remarriage: in an era when marriage rates were high and women in demand as wives, few chose to remarry.[12] But none became equal in power or prestige to the big men of village or town: forbidden to hold membership in town councils, they did not have a say in crucial communal decisions, nor did they have access to the best resources or loans, to the financial "inside track."

In studying late medieval Exeter, Maryanne Kowaleski points out five basic characteristics of female employment that apply equally to the sixteenth century.[13] Women almost never received formal training for jobs; forbidden to be apprentices, they could not qualify for highly skilled work. In any trade, they therefore held the low-status, poorly paid jobs. In the textile industry, for example, they were pattern cutters and stitchers, not finishers or retailers. Furthermore, women usually had no visibility in the business world, their work being subsumed under that of their husbands or fathers;[14] this confined them to part-time, low-investment, home-related trade, work that fit in with their responsibilities to their households, especially to their children. It follows from this that their work was intermittent and they were thus incapable of keeping up with male competitors. Finally, unlike men, most women engaged in more than one trade, apparently needing to do so in order to support themselves; thus it was harder for them to become expert at any one skill.

How society viewed women as workers is revealed in the fact that English men, by law, were forbidden to practice more than one trade. Women's work was so little respected, however, that female producers were not restricted—they were not seen as a threat to male control of the economy. Communities showed where women stood by how they addressed them: when women were named at all in municipal records, they were usually listed as "wife of so-and-so the goldsmith," or "so-and-so the tanner." And no women were allowed to hold public office, anywhere in Europe.

In the long run, what held women back most, however, was their self-image and expectations. Their work identity tended to be vague and their ambition low.[15] Denied the professionalizing training of apprentices, they seldom learned to think of themselves as "weavers" or "pewterers," that is, as artisans; rather, they were jacks-of-all-trades. Neither did they learn to work together, to close ranks around their own economic needs. Always underrepresented in guilds, they were virtually forced out of them after 1500; this expulsion rendered them strangers to the very institution where most of the job-hiring rules were made, wages and prices were negotiated, and deals about resources and loans were struck.[16]

In discussing Lyon, Natalie Davis gives a telling summary of what women could not do, of how invisible they were: "The females did not march in their craft's parades; the few sworn guilds had no women as officers or in any significant role; the city council never selected women to be *maîtres de metier*, that is, the two persons from each craft who ratified the new consuls and attended meetings as notables. Mistresses . . . played no part in confraternity drama, and may not always have been invited to the banquets."[17]

I conclude that women were the marginal workers of Europe, kept on the fringes of the economy and serving as the main source of cheap labor in a society with few serfs or slaves. When times grew hard, women workers were the first to be forced out. When trade fell off in Bristol, for example, causing unemployment in 1461, local men were urged to remove their wives and daughters from the work force.[18] Their work was always seen as secondary to that of men: women kept alehouses, men kept inns; men were bakers, women peddled bread; alewives could not be ale-tasters, only male brewers could be.[19] Neither the laws of municipalities nor the customs of patriarchal families permitted them to compete openly with men or to keep control of what they earned. Because many women headed single-parent households, most of what they earned went to the support of children and elderly dependents, in any case. This was the economic situation of commoner women in the mid-sixteenth century, and it proceeded to get worse.

The spread of the capitalist system across western Europe during the sixteenth century markedly affected women's work and was a direct factor in the spread of witch accusations. Heidi Hartmann argues that capitalism grew on top of patriarchy and that the two became "inextricably intertwined."[20] Early capitalism made the poor poorer because, in seeking the large pool of cheap labor that it required, it displaced farm families from their smallholdings, forcing them to become wage laborers. But it was men who had previously been the chief occasional wage earners; though they lost their land and independence to wealthy capitalist farmers, poor men still found work for wages. But women, who had supported themselves (and often their families) from their gardens and dairies, lost their main source of income, and they could not compete with men for paid jobs.[21] These were the conditions that plunged many single women, formerly self-supporting, into poverty in the period 1550 to 1700. The economic situation accounts for the alarming increase in female beggars in western Europe, who so discomfited their better-off neighbors that the neighbors accused them of witchcraft in order to get rid of them.[22]

Economics must be considered as a motive in any account of these persecutions. Obvious examples are the effort to gain a neighbor's property by destroying her through labeling her a witch or the profit made by innkeepers when public executions drew huge crowds, but more complex motives were also at work. Boyer and Nissenbaum found in their study of the Salem outbreak that rivalry over land had caused Salem village to divide into factions, one of which backed its young girls' sorcery accusations against the women of the other faction.[23] They see the girls' attack on neighboring women as a substitute for an attack on the hated stepmother in their own family whom they dared not attack. I suggest that the substitution was wives for the powerful husbands of the rival group, whom the men dared not attack for different reasons. This projection of attack onto the more vulnerable wives rather than their powerful husbands occurred also in Norway, Poland, and Germany.

Though economic motives are important in many trials, they seem to have played an inordinate role in New England. Carol Karlsen analyzed the social and financial destruction of a well-to-do widow of Wethersfield, Katherine Harrison, who was singled out by her neighbors as a witch not only because she owned valuable land but also because she did not remarry; that is, because, in spite of having no sons and, apparently, no brothers, she chose to take charge of her lands herself. Nearby farmers showed her what they thought of this affront to Puritan patriarchy by beating her oxen, boring a hole into the side of her cow, killing her heifer, breaking the back of her steer, destroying her corn crop, and cutting down her hops. The court apparently refused to protect her, and even gave her a heavy fine. Already suspect as a fortune-teller and healer, she was driven out of Wethersfield as a witch. The final disposition of her property is not known, but it is clear that Harrison was not allowed to enjoy it.[24] The point had been made: land was to be inherited and controlled by males.

These New England farmers and their European counterparts were not yet capitalists, for all their greed over land, but they had ceased to be medieval peasants. They were a transitional class, living under the strain of a rapidly changing economy that challenged their religious beliefs about what one owed to one's neighbor. Thus they lived with a sometimes unbearable amount of inner conflict and guilt over their growing ambitions.[25] Witch accusations, with their clear-cut demarcation between who was good and who evil, and who was master and who the subordinate sex, reassured these confused souls, while at the same time enabling them to increase their wealth.

Hand in hand with the greater municipal economic regulation of the sixteenth century was the effort of Europe's monarchies to regulate the behavior of their citizens; the period 1550 to 1650 saw the maximum reform effort.[26] This interference, whether as taxation, market regulation, military conscription, or charges of immorality, was hotly resisted by the common people, whereas some of the wealthier members of villages and towns identified with the government and helped it to enforce the new codes.

These governmental changes or reforms struck especially hard at women, as intervention in their sexual lives (see chapters 6 and 7) and as limitations on their economic roles. Martha Howell has shown how, through political moves and changes in municipal law, women producers in Cologne, some of whom had held high-status jobs, were effectively forced out of guilds by the early sixteenth century. In Leiden during the same century, women faced a diminishing range of high-status jobs, as "trades" were converted into "crafts"; having been banned from craft guilds, women were now confined to lower-paying jobs. Another line of attack was to impose fixed hours for work or training, or to require long journeys in order to trade, none of which women could take on in light of their domestic duties. Howell concludes that "when city governments imposed formal work rules on craft production or trade that conflicted with women's obligations to their families. . . . women could no longer participate." Women were thus forced out of market production—and forced into low-paying marginal work.[27]

Looking more broadly across the German lands, Jean Quataert has observed that by the middle of the seventeenth century, "the removal of single women from independent participation in the guilds and [their] relegation, ideally, to service and household activities" was complete.[28] But household *production for market* had just been forbidden by law! Women were confined to the household just as homes were declared out-of-bounds for producing consumer goods. Bearing in mind that the population of single women was at an all-time high and that women were much more likely to remain single than men, one can see that unbearable economic pressure was being applied to the *femme sole*.

Throughout the sixteenth century, restrictions on women's work had been increasing: London women, for example, participated less in the economy after about 1500, when there was a concerted effort to exclude single women from guilds and livery companies, and by 1700 they were found only in the traditional female trades.[29] Similar pressures were being experienced by German women: widows of master craftsmen were no longer allowed to continue their husbands' work; all widows and unmarried women had to have male guardians; women healers were forced out of the informal areas of medical practice.[30]

In the life of Anna Pappenheimer, a Bavarian wife, mother, and professional beggar, we see clearly the connection between poverty, witchcraft persecution, and the interference of the state. Anna's life was lived far below the level of most of the craftswomen we have been discussing.[31] As the daughter of a grave digger and the wife of an itinerant privy cleaner, she was not only lower-class, she was outcast, for these two professions, involving as they did contact with bodily pollution, rendered the Pappenheimers unfit for ordinary society. And yet, Anna had been married for thirty-seven years and had borne seven children, three of whom were still living. Solid, stable elements of affection and need bound this family together.

As vagrants they had no home, wandering in the warm months from town to town to clean latrines, settling in for the winter in a poorhouse. Anna supplemented their income with begging; she had a professional license and knew the tricks of the trade. Her husband, Paulus, and the two grown sons also set up gambling tables at local fairs. That this humble family should become the victims of the most gruesome public execution in the annals of witch trials would have been inexplicable earlier, say in 1500, or as late as 1800. It was perfectly understandable in the Bavaria of 1600, however, and as such it can serve to sum up the economic and political realities that made the witch hunts flourish.

Bavaria, like all the German lands, was by 1600 suffering from alarming overpopulation, causing food shortages, unemployment, and unrest. There had been uprisings, and the young duke needed a dramatic way to show that he was in charge. He had an even more pressing need, namely, an heir. Married for five years, he and his wife had not yet conceived. Devout to a fault, Maximilian believed that the devil had cursed both his land and his marriage bed.

In 1599 he had ordered his spies, who were in every village and town of the duchy, to be especially on guard to discover the presence of witchcraft. When no witches were found, the ducal order was issued more insistently. It was now *necessary* to come up with a witch or two. Who more likely than the outcast Pappenheimers to fall into the trap? When a convicted murderer with a grudge against them named them as witches, they found themselves bound as prisoners and carried by cart to Munich. We will discuss their fate in chapter 7.

Their story brings us full circle, back to the Flower women, mother and daughters, who died at the hands of one of the wealthiest men of England. Witchcraft did indeed have its economic and social bias: almost always, accusers were at least one notch higher in the social order than those they accused. And in the cases we have just mentioned, some of the poorest and most vulnerable people were made to serve as scapegoats for the mighty.

Given that the victims faced their accusers in a legal system now more centralized and less community-oriented than the medieval courts had been, their chance to obtain justice was slim. The gap between rich and poor of the sixteenth century had created "a rich minority who controlled the courts and a poor proletariat who came before them."[32] In the expanding mercantile capitalist world of the 1500s, being poor was an increasing handicap. And women were growing poor at a faster rate than men, just at the time that they faced more intolerance toward the folk magic and folk medicine that had long been their stock-in-trade.

To summarize the factors causing women's economic condition to worsen, we have seen that, increasingly, capitalism caused a specialization in jobs, but that women were denied the apprenticeships and guild membership that would have enabled them to keep up with specialization, while wages for their traditional work declined. Women were also increasingly refused access to resources, loans, and decision-making roles in commerce. As modes of production and finance grew more sophisticated, women were shunted back into the home and to informal, marginal kinds of work. By 1700 the gap between male and female abilities to earn was wide.

But the economic crisis of 1550 to 1700, crucial as it was, did not alone cause the witch hunts. Sweden, Denmark, and the Netherlands, after all, remained prosperous yet persecuted witches. Neither was political centralization a sufficient cause, although government interference in people's lives was a factor in some areas. On the other hand, Hungary is perhaps the prime example of a country divided and torn with internal dissent that nevertheless found time to persecute witches. The search for the factor common to all the areas of Europe where witches were hunted will concern us next.

Witches' Sabbath. Fear of the magical powers of village midwives and healers led to the demonization of women's curative skills. Here, active, powerful, and threatening figures are shown concocting an ointment. Hans Baldung Grien, Strassburg, 1514. Courtesy of Dover Pictorial Archive Series.

CHAPTER SIX

From Healers into Witches

At this day it is indifferent to say in the English tongue, "she is a witch" or "she is a wise woman."

—*Reginald Scot,* Discoverie of Witchcraft

THOUGH WOMEN were not in fact riding broomsticks or having sex with the devil, what were they doing? Judging from their neighbors' reactions, the activities of at least some sixteenth-century women had a beneficent effect on their communities. Through healing, by both spells and potions, delivering babies, performing abortions, predicting the future, advising the lovelorn, cursing, removing curses, making peace between neighbors—the work of the village healer and her urban counterpart covered what we call magic as well as medicine. This work overlapped dangerously with the priest's job as well.

Much of women's power lay in their being perceived as able to manipulate magical forces. Exercising control in this way not only over the domestic world of women but when possible over men, they wielded influence through the "idiom of the supernatural."[1] Denied the ancient role of clergy or the newly emerging one of doctor, women drew on their own networks of information and skills inherited from their mothers to serve as privileged counselors and practitioners.

But power creates fear, and power based on magic can cause panic. The witch hunt records speak eloquently of the fear of the wise women that developed, especially in men. The role of healer, long respected and even seen as essential, became suspect. Believing that some women were powerful enough even to threaten male sexuality, some segments of society began to carry out a terrible revenge on the magic-workers whom they suspected of having this control.

But before we analyze this demonizing of women healers, we must document the role of the wise woman in sixteenth-century society. The importance of this role in understanding the persecution of women for witchcraft cannot be overestimated: certain women were suspected of witchcraft, not because they were powerless, but precisely because they were seen to have a great deal of power. Because we know about folk healers mainly from court records in which they were accused of malevolent acts, we do not have accounts of healers perceived entirely as beneficent. One glimpses the positive aspects of their work, however, in their trial records.

At Nancy in Lorraine around 1580, according to the witch hunter Nicolas Remy, "a witch named Thenotte" was much in demand as a healer.[2] Called in by a neighboring woman who was ill, Thenotte diagnosed that the disease had been sent by Saint Fiacre, who must be appeased by gifts and a pilgrimage to his shrine. She offered to undertake this journey for a fee. As Remy told it,

> When the price of her services had been settled, she first measured the sick woman cross-wise with a piece of waxed linen, and then folded the linen a certain number of times and placed it in her bosom as if for safety. For the whole of the following night she kept watch before the door of the sick woman's house, and at the break of day set out on her way without ever uttering a word. When she came to the shrine of S. Fiacre she entered and set fire to the linen, and with the wax that dropped from it traced figures in the form of a cross on the steps of the High Altar; and then went out and walked three times round the chapel, the linen meanwhile giving out spluttering and violet coloured flames. . . . And having performed all this, she returned to the town.

Thenotte thus utilized folk magic in a Christian setting in order to heal. Although Remy, who claimed to have sent eight hundred witches to the stake (and I find no reason to doubt him), referred to Thenotte as a witch, he mentions no accusations or trial connected with her. Thenotte, therefore, practiced her remunerative profession unharmed.

From Carlo Ginzburg we learn of an even more successful healer, Lucia, "the witch of Ghiai," but one whose career was already threatened.[3]

When in 1614 one of her clients, Franceschina, was reproved by a judge because she knew "that it was forbidden and a sin to go to such people" as Lucia, Franceschina replied, "I believe she is not a witch, but she punishes witches; and then too I went because many people go to her to have signs made over them, and they even come from beyond the mountains." Lucia was seen as one who could protect from witchcraft, performing counter-magic. Giving an orthodox coloring to her practices, she told Franceschina, "I cannot say [who bewitched you] because the bishop has given me license to make signs over rich and poor without revealing their names, but even though I cannot reveal the names I will give you a clue: you have quarreled with a woman, and she has cast a spell over you." And then Lucia made signs over her, "with two rosaries and two crucifixes which she keeps in a small box, and also with a coral that had been sent to her by the Pope." Lucia too, despite the appellation "witch," practiced as a diviner unharmed, perhaps by claiming connections in high places.

These women, both called witches, in fact functioned in their communities as healers, to which Lucia added the ability to divine who was a witch. Confusing as these professional roles seem to us, the women and men who filled them were essential to their world. Finding one term to encompass their various roles, however, is tricky. The frequent reference in current witchcraft literature to them all as "midwives" is misleading and too narrow. Just in regard to their healing function, women, in addition to serving as gynecologists, practiced also as barbers (chiefly blood-letters), surgeons (mainly bone-setters), physicians (diagnosticians),[4] and apothecaries (herbalists). When we add to these medical roles those of diviner, necromancer, curser, and countermagician, we see the dynamic possibilities for the cunning woman: in a world where neither healing nor therapy were professionalized in our sense of the word, she had the possibility of wielding considerable power. Healer, expert on all matters pertaining to sex, *and* prophetess, she could be labeled "magic-worker," for the basis of her power in all these areas *was perceived to be* the power of magic.[5] The term *healer* alone does not imply for us the magical aspect of the role, yet it is the description most often used in the literature. "Healer-diviner" perhaps best describes the broad range of most of the cunning folk.

Yet it matters what we call these village experts, because all of their roles eventually became suspect of witchery. Prophets, charmers, conjurors, wizards, treasure finders, dowsers, astrologers, exorcists, spell-casters, all who worked through supernatural, magical means were vulnerable to charges of witchcraft and did in fact turn up in trial records. Note how Robert Burton mixed them: "Sorcerers are too common; cunning men, wizards, and white witches, as they call them, in every village, which, if they be sought unto, will help almost all infirmities."[6] Attempts to separate out these magic-workers from, on the one hand, doctors or priests or, on the other, "witches" only forces modern distinctions onto sixteenth-century practices,[7] because they all used magic. An example of its pervasiveness occurred in 1695 at Salem, Massachusetts Bay Colony, when a group of young girls began to show hysterical symptoms; the doctor who examined them considered at length and then pronounced, "The evil hand is upon them."[8]

Priests, although quick to condemn magic used in folk practice, were dependent on magic for much of their own ritual and remedies. Catholics observed the miracle of transubstantiation every time they attended Mass and were offered a variety of magical cures through holy water and saints' bones. It was through the ritual of exorcism, however, that the church brought them closest to the power of the village healer. A dramatic example, found in Boguet's treatise, describes how a priest, in trying to exorcise two demons out of Rollande du Vernois, forced holy water down her throat, tried to feed her consecrated bread, and burned paper with a demon's name on it over an incensed fire.[9] In the diocese of Modena, priests performed Masses and baptisms over magical objects, such as magnets and potions, that both laity and clergy then used for love magic.[10]

Popes were not immune from dependency on magic: when Pope John XXII feared he was being poisoned, he procured a magic snakeskin to detect poison in his food and drink.[11] When Pope Urban VIII was cursed by the Spanish ambassador, he ordered an exorcism at the Vatican with bell, book, and candle, presided over by the hermeticist and priest Tommaso Campanella; the exorcism apparently succeeded, for the pope survived.[12] Urban also used Campanella to ward off the evil effects of eclipses.[13]

Many Protestant clergy carried on successful healer-diviner practices; one Anglican clergyman, Richard Napier, working as a therapist and healer, saw in his lifetime about sixty thousand patients, over five hundred of whom believed they were bewitched and twenty-seven of whom he confirmed as such.[14] Some Scottish clergy, too, practiced magic, believing they could clear the devil from church by sprinkling holy water and ringing the bells.[15]

The churches' attitude toward folk healers was rent with ambivalence. Clergy themselves turned to diviners: the churchwardens of Thatcham in England inquired of a cunning woman to learn who had stolen their communion cloth; in Modena in 1559 the Franciscan Girolamo Azzolini turned to a witch during his illness, absolved her *for healing him*, and then recommended her services to his parishioners. Azzolini was himself an exorcist and a witch-finder, but he recognized the limits of his abilities and the superior power of this witch.[16]

Unfazed by their own complicity in relying on magic, the churches still insisted on attacking folk healers. These latter were in fact the priests' competition. Under whatever name, these women and men were looked up to and depended on, as all healers are. But the women had a special edge over the clergy: as the authorities on matters of sex, they asserted what control was possible over fertility, conception, successful pregnancy, and safe childbirth.[17] They cured male impotence and female infertility, performed abortions, provided contraceptives, and advised on problems of nursing, thus affecting the birth rate, a power that the churches were determined to wrest from them.[18]

A classic case of this professional jealousy was recorded in the *Malleus Maleficarum:* having described how a midwife had killed more than forty children "by sticking a needle through the crowns of their heads into their brains, as they came out from the womb," the authors then described what was to them an even worse crime: "For when they do not kill the child, they blasphemously offer it to the devil in this manner. As soon as the child is born, the midwife, if the mother is not herself a witch, carries it out of the room on the pretext of warming it, raises it up, and offers it to the Prince of Devils, that is Lucifer, and to all the devils. And this is done by the kitchen fire."[19] The midwife's role was interpreted as a crime because of professional jealousy; the midwife usurped the role of the parish priest. Because of her favored position as female healer, she was able to seize the child first and "baptize" it in the name of the devil, while the priest ran from the rectory, arriving too late.

A deep male jealousy pervades this story, fed by the exclusion of all men (including fathers) from the birthing room.[20] Left to imagine what went on inside, they sometimes responded with wild imaginings, as the authors of the *Malleus* did. Male fear runs through the *Malleus,* culminating in descriptions of how a witch can cause a man to become impotent or to lose his genitals; a particularly lewd story describes where the village priest lost his penis.[21]

There was more of a "woman's world" in the sixteenth century than today,[22] and part of the female healer's power lay in that fact. Although well-to-do urban wives consulted male physicians as well as cunning women,[23] most women turned to female healers by necessity as well as by choice. As there were few doctors in rural Europe until the nineteenth century, village healers provided the medical care. They possessed a fund of knowledge about cures handed down from generation to generation, constantly improved by the empirical methods of observation, trial, and evaluation. Their work consisted mainly of prescribing herbal cures, practicing midwifery, and performing rituals of divination and healing.

Many of the herbal remedies developed by woman healers still have their place in modern pharmacology.[24] The village wise woman used ergot to relieve labor pain and to hasten labor, and belladonna to inhibit miscarriage. Digitalis is said to have been discovered by an English witch.[25]

In addition to empirical methods, these women depended also on rituals based on magic. Incantations, the wearing of amulets, and the repeating of charms were universal practices. In order for herbs to be efficacious, as one gathered them one must say five Lord's Prayers, five Hail Mary's, and the Creed. Faith in verbal formulae was strong; one Goodwife Veazy, expert in the cure of canker-worm, intoned this supplication three times: "In the name of God I begin and in the name of God I do end. Thou canker-worm begone from hence, in the name of the Father, of the Son, and of the Holy Ghost." Afterward she applied a little honey and pepper to the afflicted part. Other magical methods included girdle-measuring (the band would shorten if the patient was bewitched) and boiling eggs in urine.[26]

David Sabean provides a dramatic example of magical healing in describing the drastic cure for an epidemic of foot-and-mouth disease undertaken by a German village in 1796: a group of men sacrificed the communal bull by burying it alive, while the villagers hurried to bring buckets of earth from their yards to pour on the dying animal. When criticized for their cruelty, they said explicitly that the cure would not have worked had it been done any other way (i.e., had they killed the bull with a merciful blow and then buried him). The magic, which is to say the power, lay in the precise ritual technique.[27]

Midwives used magical techniques for childbirth, fertility, and contraception: opening doors or chests to open the womb in prolonged labor, and even arranging for a woman to conceive without the participation of a man—by drinking horse's semen.[28] Wearing amulets containing powders could either enhance or prevent conception; the sorceress Mary Woods gave such a charm to the countess of Essex to enable her to conceive. Pierre Clergue, priest and Don Juan of the village of Montaillou, used an herb wrapped in linen as a contraceptive. When being interrogated by an inquisitor, his mistress Beatrice de Planissoles reminisced that Pierre

> had a long cord which he used to put round my neck while we made love; and this thing or herb at the end of the cord used to hang down between my breasts, as far as the opening of my stomach [vagina]. When the priest wanted to get up and leave the bed, I would take the thing from around my neck and give it back to him. It might happen that he wanted to know me carnally twice or more in a single night; in that case the priest would ask me, before uniting his body with mine, "Where is the herb?"
>
> I was easily able to find it because of the cord round my neck; I would put the "herb" in his hand and then he himself would place it at the opening of my stomach, still with the cord between my breasts.

Pierre may have procured this valuable amulet-pessary from the prostitutes he visited in the town or from a village wise woman. Or as a priest who was also a healer-diviner, perhaps he constructed it himself. Wherever he had acquired it, he knew its value. When Beatrice asked him to leave the herb with her, he refused, because then she might use it to have safe sex with another man! Whatever its power, whether as pessary or magical amulet, it worked: Beatrice, who bore four children by other men, never conceived in the years of her passionate affair with Pierre.[29]

Often, when asked to diagnose illness, cunning women came to the conclusion that the person or animal was bewitched, and used their powers to identify the bewitcher. They were known, in fact, for their ability to be witch finders, what Africans today call witch doctors.[30] Consider the *benandanti* for example: they were not best known for their claim to battle with witches but rather for their ability to recognize witches and to cure those who had been bewitched.[31] Having identified the source of the trouble, some healers worked to reconcile the spell-caster and his or her victim. In Scotland, for instance, when Magdalen Blair was asked what ailed a sick man, she divined that Issobel Bennet ("of ill fame") was the cause. She advised him to "take a grip of [Issobel's] coat tail and drink a pint of ale with her And crave his health from her thrie tymes for the Lords sake and he would be well." We cannot know the outcome of this psychosomatic remedy, because, unfortunately, "he did it not." Magdalen might have been rewarded for her efforts two centuries earlier, but this conversation took place in the mid-seventeenth century; Magdalen was put on trial as a witch, and Issobel was banished.[32]

Other witch finders specialized in preventing persons from becoming witches. When midwife Caterina Domenatta of Monfalcone, Aquileia, delivered a baby feet first, she convinced the parents to let her place the child on a spit and turn it three times over the fire; only this extreme measure could protect it from becoming a witch.[33]

Whether the methods were empirical or bizarre, people made no clear distinction between natural or supernatural means.[34] This fact gave the cunning woman her great range of power. The common people of Europe clung to their folk healers, in preference to priests and doctors, until the nineteenth century. They saw that priests could not help during birth, and that many patients of doctors died. Besides, the cunning woman, with her intimate knowledge of her neighbors, was often an effective therapist, a comforting adviser. And her rituals, placing the sick ones at the center of attention, often enlisting the entire family for support, eased their minds as well as their bodies.[35] When Thenotte kept watch all night outside the sick woman's house, she focused the neighborhood's attention on the patient's suffering, a process of support that might in itself cause healing.

The effect of the healer-diviners on their communities cannot be underestimated.[36] One English healer had forty customers a week;[37] it was said that people traveled twenty to forty miles to consult a witch. Elizabeth Cracklow of Oxfordshire had been "sent for to divers places for the curing of people"; Margaret Neale of Aldeburgh, who healed diseases by prayer, "hath recourse of people to her far and wide."[38] People came "even from beyond the mountains" to consult Lucia of Ghiai. When the need was desperate, healers were sought out even when they were in prison.[39]

One measure of their success was the considerable wealth that some earned: Michele Soppe of the Friuli, who claimed he had healed more than forty persons, "was called to give help almost weekly" and had "earned more than a hundred ducats in this way."[40] The necromancer Anna la Rossa of Udine was said to earn more than two hundred ducats a year; "a great multitude of people" came to see her. Not only were common people loyal to these healers but kings, princes, and archbishops sought them out.[41] In Protestant as well as Catholic lands, in city as well as country, the cunning people held sway.

IT WAS THE VERY nature of their power that, ultimately, did them in. Magic is a two-edged weapon, neutral by nature, capable of being focused either for good or for ill: "she who can cure, can kill" is how people put it,[42] and when they said this, they feared the magic-worker as much as they respected her. As the churches' campaigns against folk healing ("superstition") progressed during the Reformations, this double gift became more dangerous to possess, more likely to be identified with Satan's power and the work of his demons.

Healers had always been vulnerable to this reverse charge. Muchembled has provided us with an early account, in the story of the widow Perrée Pingret.[43] In 1446 in France's Département du Nord people came from afar to consult Perrée, who could provide an ointment to bring back a lover or a ritual to improve a marriage or get rid of a husband. Many consulted her for mental as well as physical healing. Thirty-eight-year-old Catherine Jolie traveled from a neighboring village ostensibly for healing, but her true purpose may have been to get help with her marriage to sixty-year-old Mahieu Crepin. Perrée prepared for her a bath of herbs, a magical remedy still relied on today in various parts of the world.[44] After the bath, Catherine's condition improved, but her husband turned black; now Perrée was suspected of sorcery. She was also accused of killing a married woman in her village and her own daughter-in-law. This successful healer was tried on charges of witchcraft; the outcome is not known.

Muchembled observes that the healer was more likely to be perceived as a witch by her neighbors, whereas people from outside the community would see her gifts as beneficent: "One always goes to a stranger to have a spell lifted"—at least in the Nord. This information reinforces Thomas's and Macfarlane's theory that most witchcraft outbreaks were caused by village tensions, that people accused their neighbors of sorcery while seeking the advice of the magic-worker who lived a few villages away.

Not only the healer-diviners, but also their followers, believed that what they were doing was good and necessary. When women named Sibillia and Pierina were interrogated by the Milanese Inquisition between 1384 and 1390, having already been tried by the secular court, they told them that they went every Thursday night to a meeting presided over by a Signora Oriente, to whom they paid homage. There they feasted on every sort of animal except the ass, because it was associated with Jesus, and afterward Oriente resurrected all the animals, bringing them back to life with her magic wand. She led her followers at night to break into the houses of the rich, where they stole food and drink, taking care to spare the homes of the poor, whom they blessed. She taught her followers to divine the future[45] and promised to receive them in paradise.[46]

In trying these women, the Inquisition had stumbled across, not the usual heretics, but members of an old fertility cult (hence the reverence for animals) who rode out at night on the "wild ride," dedicated elsewhere to the goddess Diana but centered here on a living woman, "Oriente." This particular group also had a touch of Robin Hood about it, robbing the rich while respecting the poor, an influence that Jeffrey Burton Russell speculates may have come from the Fraticelli or other fringe religious groups who practiced holy poverty. I suggest still another derivation: when Pierina witnessed that Oriente ruled the society as Christ ruled the world, she revealed a cult centered around a female leader seen as divine. Her claim was reminiscent of the Guglielmites, an earlier Milanese cult whose members believed that their female leader was a Christ figure.[47]

What matters most here, however, is Sibillia and Pierina's claim that what they did at Oriente's meetings was not a sin. The Inquisition disagreed, and sentenced them to wear two red crosses as penance. Brought to court again six years later, Sibillia again maintained that she had not confessed her actions because they were not sinful. This time the Inquisition condemned her of diabolism, and she was burned to death.[48] That this cult, remnant of a folk fertility rite and expression of the growing autonomy of Milanese women in matters of religion, did not conflict in Sibillia's mind with her Christian faith is suggestive of how little orthodox teachings had affected the laity of the late Middle Ages, even those living in a city with a powerful Catholic structure.

The case of Chiara Signorini, taken from Italian inquisitional records, illustrates well that people both feared yet depended on the magic-workers.[49] Chiara and her husband, tenant farmers near Modena, already enjoyed "a poor reputation as far as magical arts and witchcraft were concerned," when they were thrown off a plot of land belonging to the estate of Lady Margherita Pazzani. They had in fact been evicted before, by other masters, out of fear of the spells they cast, and were sinking deeper into poverty.

Yet when Lady Margherita became seriously ill, her relatives *turned to Chiara* to cure her, that is, to lift the spell. They, and later Margherita herself, asked the very person who they believed had caused Margherita's paralysis to heal her and promised the magic-worker land and goods if she succeeded. Chiara did indeed pray for and heal the lady, but when the promised goods were not delivered, she cursed Margherita again, and the paralysis returned.

Arrested in 1519 by order of the inquisitional vicar, she straightaway admitted that she had the power to place or take away spells, but that this gift came from God, through prayer. Chiara then grabbed the offensive by telling the court that she was visited often by the Virgin Mary, who promised to carry out vengeance on Chiara's enemies.[50] She gave her soul and body to this beautiful lady in white, whom she worshiped by "kissing her outstretched arms all the way to the neck with great reverence and happiness, and felt her to be as soft as silk and very warm."

The inquisitor seized on this all too materialistic, unangelic vision and tried to twist it into an admission of demon worship. Subtly his questions set a trap that Chiara slipped into, even describing how she offered her firstborn baby, "raising her child up in her arms and offering it to Our Lady, surrendering its soul and body"[51]—exactly as witch-midwives were reported to offer the babies they delivered to the devil.

Already by 1519 this was seen by the courts as devil talk, as dangerous, heretical doctrine. Why would Chiara risk using the very language of witchcraft in such a setting? She probably had no other religious vocabulary to call on. Everyone knew that she never attended mass; Chiara's religion was folk religion, in which one bargained with God or the saints or, in this case, with the Virgin, promising to worship them if they would do favors, take revenge on enemies, make amends for injustices suffered. Her only religious instruction had come from an old woman who had taught her spells to cure sick livestock. She insisted (rashly) that the Virgin always did all that she asked. Clearly, Chiara did not know the language of her ecclesiastical judges, did not know how her words sounded to them. She could not hope to exonerate herself with such talk.

Because Chiara's drama was played out in an inquisitional court, there was another, final act: the use of torture, in this case, the strappado. Chiara was hoisted up by a rope, probably with weights attached to her feet, then dropped so suddenly that her joints might be dislocated. This method usually brought results, and Chiara was no exception. Soon she confessed to worshiping, not the Virgin, but the devil and being aided in *maleficium* by him. But as soon as she was released from the strappado, she took it all back.[52] With repeated torture they wore her down; although she denied to the end that she had attended the sabbat, still, her admission that the devil appeared to her in prison was enough to condemn her. In penitence she agreed never to call on the devil again.

Had Chiara been in a German court she would surely have been sentenced to death. Given the leniency of the Italian Inquisition in regard to punishment, however, she was sentenced to life imprisonment, prison being the Modena hospital for the poor.

It is believable that this passionate, outspoken, desperate woman might have called on not only the beautiful lady in white but also the devil. Hounded by poverty and repeatedly tricked by the wealthy families she worked for, she may have done as she finally admitted, "called upon the Devil in her despair." Had Chiara had the guidance of a priest, she might have used her magical gifts (seeing visions, hearing voices) to establish herself as an orthodox mystic. But the curses and cures that she dealt in were going out of style.

Throughout the account one senses a proud, imaginative soul, but one unable to deal with the inquisitor's subtleties—or with his demonology. Attend the sabbat, indeed! Chiara's devil was no Prince of Darkness presiding over a great orgy but came to her in the form of a twelve-year-old boy. In light of the newly emerging theology of devil worship, Chiara's folk religion of cures and countercurses looked like heresy and idolatry.

Other sixteenth-century witch trials document the growing suspicion of magic-workers. We saw that many persons whom Walpurga Hausmänin had befriended or attended as midwife turned on her later as the cause of their misfortune. Marguerite Peigne had cured some of her neighbors in Correnol, Switzerland, with herbs from her garden; it was *for this fact* (and the suspicion of hail-making) that she was convicted of witchcraft and banished within her home.[53] Isobel Young's magic had cured some of her Scottish neighbors, but this did not prevent nineteen of them from crying her out a witch; Isobel was hanged and burned. The Bavarian shepherd Chonradt Stocklin had cured men and animals who had been stricken by witches, yet his neighbors turned on him, burning him as a witch in 1586.[54] That such cases were rare before 1550 indicates a worsening in attitude toward healers, a new willingness of communities to turn against their magic-workers.

But one need not have been a healer or a witch finder to draw either the expectation of harming or, then, of curing. One quarrelsome Scottish woman, Elspeth Thomson, apparently built a fearsome reputation just by cursing.[55] Elspeth had a troubled relation with her husband's large family, and it is clear that they were afraid of her. When her sister-in-law's breast milk failed, she suspected Elspeth and therefore asked her to pray for her (that is, to lift the spell); Elspeth finally agreed, and all went well. When her brother-in-law Donald refused to cut peats for her, she retaliated by "getting the sight she desired of him" (putting a curse or possibly the evil eye on him); Donald was reported to say "that as ever before he was still feared for her and that they still discorded and he blamed her for all evil that befell him." When

Donald soon sickened and died, Elspeth's guilt was tested: she was made to touch the corpse, and "immediatle . . . the blood rushed forth at his nose, navel and ears and his corpse bled all the way to the burial place." Dire evidence was fast closing in around her.

Elspeth tried to be neighborly to other family members, offering her daughter as servant to one. But this gesture was refused, and the family in fear tried to shut her out; she was not invited to the birth or baptism of a niece (for fear she would hex the infant), and her own husband claimed that she was on friendly terms with the devil. Ultimately in 1671, when neighbors joined her affinal relatives (relatives by marriage) in accusing her of witchcraft, Elspeth was condemned and hanged.

Elspeth's position as an in-law in a large family was precarious to begin with—she seems to have had no blood relatives to stand up for her, and Larner speculates that she may have been an outsider to the village as well. The loneliness behind her anger over not being invited to the niece's birth and baptism is almost palpable. Yet loneliness and isolation do not necessarily lead to cursing. Somewhere Elspeth had learned the power of particular angry words and used them to lash back when she was hurt. For a woman to be outspoken and aggressive was not acceptable in Scotland's patriarchal society.

The record does not specify at just what point this lamentable state of affairs slipped over into a charge of witchcraft, but the situation was ripe for it: her very existence threatened the family. Yet not all the power lay with the accusers and the courts. Elspeth herself had power; her in-laws lived with a fear so strong that it might have caused the illnesses that they then blamed on her. When witch beliefs became strong enough, they locked a community into a self-fulfilling syndrome; one feared a person, one became sick with fear, thus one knew that that person was indeed a witch.

As for Elspeth's image of herself, whether she saw herself as a witch, Keith Thomas's observation is apropos: "some at least of the witches felt genuine hatred for those around them. Although their resort to cursing and banning was a substitute for real action, they may well have persuaded themselves that an access [to] supernatural power was helping their curses to take effect."[56] Like Chiara, Elspeth had no access to "real action"—legal counsel, protection by her natal family, or the support of the church. Again like Chiara, she protected herself with the only weapons she knew.

In some cases the fear of witchcraft became so great that it required neither cursers nor quarrelsome in-laws to galvanize a community. Thirteen-year-old Anna Catherina Weissenbuhler, an abandoned servant girl, seems an unlikely person to turn three Württemberg villages upside down, but she did so in 1683, simply by claiming that she associated with witches.[57] She blamed a housewife in Gerlingen, one Madalena, who "had taken her often to the witches' dance by day and by night"; there she saw the devil, who "had a goat's foot, was completely black, and was not like a human." Like so many young girls, from Sweden to Salem, she accused an older woman. Madalena was known to be "an old nasty wife with a bad reputation."

Anna Catherina spoke freely about these contacts, perhaps even boasted of them to other children, thereby causing "a great scandal in the town and its territory." What people feared most was that she would contaminate others, would convert them to a belief in or even the practice of demon worship.

People soon rallied to defend their families against her. Turned out of the home where she worked, she was taken under the care of the municipal judge, who sent her to live with and be instructed by the schoolmaster. He soon wanted to be rid of her (parents threatened to remove their children from the school because of her), forbade her to speak to other children, ordered her to sit at a table alone. Soon his wife moved Anna Catherina's bed out of her parlor and into the infirmary, where she was the solitary occupant. The wife said she would get rid of her, even if they sent her to jail for doing so. Anna's own relatives in other villages refused to care for her. She had harmed no one (they said that she had stroked a cat that then became lame, and five hens on which she spat dropped dead, but she had caused no human injury), but she had frightened everyone just by talking about witches, by indicating a familiarity with them.[58]

Anna Catherina's isolation was even sharper than Elspeth Thomson's, for she was rejected by entire communities and was only a young teenager. Unlike the authorities elsewhere, who believed young girls' accusations against older women, the pastors of Gerlingen did not buy Anna's story about being taken to the sabbat; instead they had her searched for the devil's mark, which was found, thus proving that she, not the older woman, was the witch. Anna fell silent, refusing to answer her interrogator's questions any longer (her fate is not known). Sabean commented on her case, "It is not that weak, marginal people are witches but only that in a contest in which magic plays a role, the powerful win."[59] Anna was strong in her ability to panic others, but the very belief in magic that the village elders held gave them the power finally to silence her.

Increasingly, the healer could not win: when an herbalist in Lorraine doctored a man with a potion and his genitals disappeared, the lord of the land ordered her to restore them. She obliged with another, successful herb, but this act of healing was taken as proof positive of her witchery and she was put to death.[60]

Remy provided a classic story of this kind of betrayal of healers in the complex case of Nicolaea Stephana, which also shows how entire families of healers were destroyed.[61]

Nicolaea, a plague-ridder, claimed that she had learned that art from one Matthieu Amants, who had raped her and made her pregnant as payment for his instruction. Matthieu had recently been convicted as a witch (August 1587), when Nicolaea was hired to rid the castle of Dommartin of plague. Working efficiently, she quickly purged the buildings and was paid and dismissed. But Nicolaea hung around, a fatal mistake as it turned out. When the castellan's wife became ill, suspicion fell, of course, on the magic-worker and healer Nicolaea, who was threatened with beatings unless she healed the woman. She was faced with a quandary: if she succeeded, she proved that she had the power of a witch, for "such sicknesses can hardly be cured or assuaged except by the witch who caused them"; if the woman died, she would be blamed for her death. Given this no-win situation, Nicolaea vacillated.

Meanwhile her son, being held with her, realizing the danger they were in, tried to escape but was caught. He then turned on his mother, calling her a fraud and advising the castellan's men to beat her. As Remy retold it, "two brawny peasants did not cease to hammer and kick and pound and shake her, and finally to drag her to the fire, until she gave her promise to heal the woman at that very hour."[62]

The authorities were not finished with Nicolaea or her son. Allowing her to leave, they seized her at the castle gate and imprisoned her. Interrogated by a judge (Remy?) who had already "inquired into her life and behavior," she confessed to having made the woman ill. And although she had healed her victim, still she was put to death; she and her son were burned together at the stake.

This case illustrates the cat-and-mouse game played by a judge with a peasant woman; probably from the time she was associated with Matthieu Amants, she was under suspicion. From then on, no matter how well she served her community, ridding it of plague and curing the castellan's wife, she was doomed, no matter what she did. It also shows the sexual bind of a woman who had been raped: although she was victim in that act, still it was she who bore the onus of the illegitimate birth that resulted from it, in a time that was beginning to punish out-of-wedlock births.

Often when the healer herself was named as the bewitcher it was up to her to lift the spell. The extreme danger of this process is illustrated in the case of Reyne Percheval. When the entire household of alderman Jean Parmentier was bewitched, they suspected their neighboring healer Reyne, who gave them a potion to drink that would lift the spell, with strict instructions not to imbibe it in their own home. They complied, but as Jean began to drink it he fell in a faint; his wife screamed, and Reyne came running. Struggling to help, Reyne was now taken for a witch for sure. Coming to, Jean forbade Reyne to come nearer and threw a burning ember in her face. His wife joined in, beating Reyne with the embers, but the healer made no attempt to defend herself. Reyne was brought to trial for witchcraft.

The life of the Scottish midwife Margaret Lang demonstrates the way in which medical skill and spiritual gifts mixed in one woman's life, and what a dangerous mix it was. Margaret lived in the Scottish village of Erskine near Paisley, was married, and had a grown daughter.[63] Known for her piety, she would walk miles to attend communion services in the neighboring villages, not satisfied with the annual eucharist offered in each parish. But Margaret was more than pious, she was an ecstatic. After she had been at prayer, she would throw stools about the house in a frenzy and "raged as if she were possessed," and when she gave witness to her faith, she was said to speak "like an angel."[64] She had offered to enable a neighbor to see the woman's dead mother and sister, showing that she practiced necromancy, and she was clairvoyant, correctly prophesying her own violent death.

Margaret earned her living as a midwife who was seen as "esteemed" and "sagacious and exact in her business," and who might have managed safely to continue her double role as healer and charismatic had not the young daughter of the local laird begun to have fits. While possessed, Christian Shaw accused Margaret and two dozen others of bewitching her and of conspiring with the devil to kill her. The year was 1697; by that time witch accusations in Scotland had a very long history and were, in fact, diminishing, but this story shows that they could still cause panic in a community. Eleven-year-old Christian could have modeled her accusations on a number of already famous bewitchings of children by older women: the Fairfax children in Yorkshire, Grace Sowerbutts in Lancastershire, the Pacy girls at Bury St. Edmunds, the demented girls of Salem in New England, Loyse Maillat a century before in Franche-Comté.[65] Christian did not require originality to send seven adults to the gallows, for her society was ready to believe children against adults, especially against mature women.

Once Christian had named Margaret—"Pinched Maggie," she called her—others came forward to accuse her. They claimed that she had been present at witch gatherings at Kilmalcolm and in the orchard of Christian Shaw's manor house. Because of similar testimony given independently by witnesses, it seems clear that *something* was going on at the Shaws' and that most of the accused (all working-class folk) had met at nocturnal gatherings. Whether they met to plot against persons representing the gentry like Christian Shaw or for their own entertainment, mainly sexual, is impossible to say, but Margaret and the other accused persons were a fellowship. They practiced magic, using talents that the church not only denied recognition but condemned.

But there were even more damaging charges against Margaret, that she had spoken to James Millar's child on the day the child died and had caused the death of a young servant woman. In court, Margaret gave eloquent speeches in self-defense, "which neither divine, nor lawyer, could reasonably mend"; her very eloquence, however, was looked upon as one of the strongest proofs of her guilt.[66] Despite a full denial of dealings with the devil, Margaret was condemned to be hanged, then burned. The tragedy did not end there, however: Margaret's daughter was soon implicated and arrested. Several years later she still languished in prison; her fate is not known.

On her way to the gallows Margaret made an unexpected confession: that long ago she had committed the sin of "unnatural lust."[67] We are left to imagine what this transgression was: fornication, lesbianism, masturbation? In any case, Margaret admitted that out of guilt over it she had accepted a pact with the devil. After the executions, she was singled out from the other victims to be called "that great impostor . . . a great masterpiece of the Devil."[68] Perhaps because she had been respected as a midwife and churchwoman, her apostasy cut deeper than most.

It is clear from these accounts that the healers thought of themselves as doing good, but this point needs to be made more fully. In showing how Remy and other witch hunters forced the label of black magic onto the practitioners of white magic, Delcambre explained that the witches "really thought they were endowed with divine gifts, and those who consulted them shared this opinion."[69] Many, such as Maria Medica of Brescia and Lucia of Ghiai, healed with holy oil, orthodox prayers, rosaries, and crucifixes; remember, Lucia even used a piece of coral sent her by the pope. Joan Tyrry of Somerset protested that "her doings in healing of man and beast, by the power of God taught to her by the . . . fairies, be both godly and good." Joan Warden of Cambridgeshire, when charged with being a cunning woman, protested that "she doth not use any charms, but that she doth use ointments and herbs to cure many diseases."[70]

The *benandante* and necromancer Florida Basili affirmed, "If it wasn't for us benandanti, witches would devour children even in their cradles." Many of her neighbors admired her for being able to talk with the dead, but eventually they reported her to their confessors and even accused her of having the evil eye—that is, of being a witch who dries up mothers' milk and *who eats little children.* Here we see the reversal, from one who saves to one who destroys. Other *benandanti* too had boasted of how they protected their communities and the crops. But *benandanti* were compromised from the start: their society believed both that children born with a caul were condemned to become witches *and* that these same children were destined to be *benandanti,* that is, to fight against witches.[71] Given this dichotomy, the *benandante* walked a fine line, increasingly forced to protest his or her innocence and good intentions.

Perhaps Margery Skelton of Essex summed it up: when accused of witchcraft she maintained that what she had in fact done "with praying of her prayers" was that she had healed six persons.[72]

The frequent mention of the cunning women's prayers points up how closely these women pressed into the priests' territory. No doubt some of these women had spiritual gifts that would have led them into the priesthood—if they had been allowed in. We must see in many of these careers of women healers and prophets the frustration of women who could have accomplished more if they had had institutional backing.[73]

A further proof of this point is found in the number of visionary women who gave sermons, although preaching was strictly forbidden to women except in a few of the radical Protestant sects.[74] Our examples are all from bewitched women, those who engaged in the reverse side of magic, claiming that they were its victims, but who nonetheless used the experience of magical possession to gain attention and authority in their society. Young Christian Shaw is an example, preaching to crowds in her living room while claiming to be bewitched by Margaret Lang. The nun Louise Capeau, at Aix-en-Provence in 1611, while possessed by the devil Verrine, preached every day in the grotto of Saint Baume; her sermons on the Virgin Mary and the imminence of the Day of Judgment were so effective that one hearer claimed God was converting "soules by the Divell!" The teenaged French demoniac Nicole Obry was the conduit through whom the demon Beelzebub spoke, attacking Protestants at the cathedral of Laon.[75]

It was a terrible irony for the healers when, instead of being supported, they began to be attacked. The noted Puritan divine William Perkins of Cambridge was convinced that *all* the works of wise men or wise women were of the devil. Whether the patient was healed or cursed, it mattered not; they must be punished, "because they deny God, and are confederates with Satan." It was the element of magic that Perkins condemned: "all Diviners, Charmers, Juglers, all Wizards, commonly called wise men and wise women; yea, whosoever doe any thing (knowing what they doe) which cannot be effected by nature or art." And it was the successful healer whom he feared most, because people would be persuaded by her: "but it were a thousand times better for the land, if all Witches, *but especially the blessing Witch* might suffer death."[76]

Though both the public and the church were uneasy about these cases of possession, the work of wise women was mostly seen as good and as essential to their world. Lacking doctors or therapists, villagers and the urban poor depended on them in a crisis of life and death. Many women had taken up the practice of magic because it supported them and gave them standing and power in their communities. As the church's and the state's power to intervene in daily life grew, however, the role of *sage-femme* became riskier; always suspect because of the double-edged nature of magical power and the general suspicion of women, cunning women were now hounded by the authorities. Reginald Scot told about a male juggler at Brandon who performed transferred magic and won fame for it. Scot observed that if an old woman had done it, she would have been burned for a witch.[77] It is this change from sought-after healer to hunted witch that is important to our story.

The torture of Christine Böffgen at Rheinbach, 1631. A well-to-do widow, she was tortured until she died; her property went to the court. From Hermann Löher's *Hochnötige Klage.* Courtesy of the Division of Rare and Manuscript Collections, Carl A. Kroch Library, Cornell University.

CHAPTER SEVEN

Controlling Women's Bodies

Violence and Sadism

We find . . . on her secret parts, growing within the lip of the same, a loose piece of skin and when pulled it is near an inch long [and] somewhat in form of the finger of a glove flattened.

***—Committee searching the body of Mercy Disborough*[1]**

THE MARK in the form of a teat, from which animal familiars or demons would suck, might be found anywhere on a woman's body. The English, whether in Old or New England, were especially adept at finding it. Though men also were accused of having suspicious teats, the very concept of the devil's teat is based on the female function of providing breast milk; it is an inversion of a natural female function, a parody turned into a deadly jest. One woman had seven imps but only five teats and complained that they fought over her like a litter of pups when they fed.

When Margaret Jones, a Boston midwife, healer and cunning woman, was accused in 1648 of having "an apparent teat in her secret parts," her friend explained that it was a tear left over from a difficult childbirth.[2] No doubt this cause, or a swollen clitoris, explained these cases. But Matthew Hopkins, the fanatical witch hunter of Essex, England, would not take child-bearing or hemorrhoids as an excuse, pointing out that the marks "are in the contrary part."[3] Hopkins knew his female anatomy and may have witnessed a number of examinations.

In Scotland the searcher, called the witch pricker, was always male. When two Scottish women wanted to join this lucrative profession they had to disguise themselves as men, "Mr. Dickson" and "Mr. Peterson." The pricker would know a witch because a true devil's mark would have no feeling or blood when stabbed. A contemporary observed that many innocent women were so overcome with shame and fear at having their bodies probed by a strange man that they became numb and could feel nothing, thus appearing guilty.[4] Women's genitals were routinely searched.

These widespread practices terrorized women. When in 1649 the people of Newcastle-upon-Tyne hired a well-known Scottish pricker to rid their town of witches, promising him twenty shillings for every woman he condemned, they set a potential trap for all the women of the town: "the magistrates sent their bellman through the town, ringing the bell, and crying, all people that would bring in any complaint against any woman for a witch, they should be sent for and tried by the person appointed. Thirty women were brought into the Town Hall and stript, and then openly had pins thrust into their bodies."[5]

Most of them were found guilty.

When "a personable and good-like woman" was defended by one of the local gentry, the pricker argued that, having been accused, she must be tried anyway:

> . . . and presently in sight of all the people, [he] laid her body naked to the waste, with her cloaths over her head, by which fright and shame, all her blood contracted into one part of her body, and then he ran a pin into her thigh, and then suddenly let her coats [petticoats?] fall, and then demanded whether she had nothing of his in her body but [yet] did not bleed, but she being amazed replied little, then he put his hand up her coats, and pulled out the pin and set her aside as a guilty person, and child of the Devil, and fell to try others whom he made guilty.[6]

Public events such as this, in which male magistrates watched a male searcher strip a "good-like" woman, frightening her speechless while feeling her body and applying an unrational "test" as to her innocence or guilt as a witch, established an important point about how women were viewed in early modern society: that women by nature, through their bodies, were susceptible to seduction by the devil, and that they must be controlled and if necessary punished by men.[7] Scenes like this took place also in the German, Swiss, and French lands and were brought by English colonists to New England. The searcher's obscene question, "whether she had nothing of his in her body," expresses the rapelike atmosphere. But the possible outcome (the penalty for a conviction of witchcraft was death) was more dire even than rape, and flaunted the power of these men over the very lives of the women whom they abused.

Though it is essential to pursue, as we have, what power women exercised in early modern Europe, as workers, healers, even as witches, a study of women's power will not take us to the heart of the witchcraze. In matters involving violence, there is no complementarity, there is only "power over." Women were indeed active contributors to European society, but once labeled as witches, they became victims, vulnerable to severe persecution.

Not wanting to restrict women to the role of victim, yet acknowledging the imbalance of power in a male-dominant society, Lois Banner asks how "does one then analyze the witchcraft persecutions of the seventeenth century, the greatest explosion of patriarchal power in the European experience?"[8] How else than by accepting that in this instance women were victimized and by accusing those who were in power? To be more specific, I would say that it is only by learning what happened to the bodies of the accused and naming the agents of their torment, by "acknowledging the imbalance of power in a male-dominant society," that we can move ahead in analyzing this particular "explosion of patriarchal power."

Because searching and pricking were carried out on jailed prisoners, that is, on helpless victims, they must be considered a form of torture. Regular judicial torture, as we have seen, was used everywhere except England and was taken to ferocious limits. In the Pas-de-Calais in 1573, for example, one "Nisette," married to her fourth husband and convicted of witchcraft, was ordered to be flogged and banished, *after* having her head flamed with a *chapeau d'étoupe* (a burning circle of flax or hemp).[9]

Torture very often had its sexual angles. Performed on women by men, legal torture permitted sadistic experimentation and gratuitous sexual advances. When the executioner Jehan Minart of Cambrai prepared the already condemned Aldegonde de Rue for the stake, he examined her interior parts, mouth, and "*parties honteuses*" (shameful parts). When a woman was whipped, she had to be stripped to the waist (as Eunice Cole was), her breasts bared to the public. To try to force a confession, a priest applied hot fat repeatedly to Catherine Boyraionne's eyes and her armpits, the pit of her stomach, her thighs, her elbows, and "*dans sa nature*"—in her vagina. She died in prison, no doubt from injuries.[10]

While a female was imprisoned, she might be raped—the young Lorrainer, Catharina Latomia, not yet pubescent, was raped twice in her cell, and nearly died from it. At Ellwangen, Magdalena Weixler gave the jailer sexual favors in return for a promise to be spared torture but was tortured and executed anyway.[11] When one woman was raped and murdered in jail, blame was placed on the devil. Women, sex, and the devil were constantly mixed in with witch lore. Judges in northern France, for example, forced the accused to admit giving the devil "*un poil de ses parties honteuse*" (a pubic hair).[12] Parallels between laws on witchcraft and rape have been pointed out by G. Geis, who notes that both work against women. In rape cases, the accuser (the woman) finds it difficult to prove her allegations, because the very law suspects her of having invited the assault; in witchcraft, the defendant (the woman) must prove that there is no causal connection between her action (cursing, attempted healing, etc.) and the misfortune she is charged with—but the court is operating on a belief in that causality.[13] In either case, rape or witchcraft, the law puts women on the defensive.

It appears that jailers, prickers, executioners, and judges, all could take their sadistic pleasure with female prisoners. And so could respectable ministers and judges. At a public session in New England, Cotton Mather, while working to control a seventeen-year-old girl possessed of demons, uncovered her breasts and fondled them.[14] Women's thoughts, even the most intimate, were made public. The prurient interest priests took in possessed women's bodies and sexual fantasies while exorcising these women was demonstrated clearly at the public exorcisms of Sister Jeanne of the Angels at Loudun and of Elisabeth de Ranfaing at Nancy. Judges at Sugny, Luxembourg, asked female suspects not only about their sexual activity with the devil but about their sexual activity with their husbands and lovers as well.[15]

These men took advantage of positions of authority to indulge in pornography sessions, thus revealing that they wanted more from witch hunting than the conviction of witches: namely, unchallengeable sexual power over women. In reflecting on the sexual abuse of female prisoners in the twentieth century, Susan Brownmiller asks "whether sadistic torture leads by its own logic to the infliction of sexual pain, or whether the motive of eliciting . . . information is merely a pretext for the commission of hostile sexual acts."[16] In the witch hunts, the policy of forcing a witch's confession may have been a cover for making a socially approved assault on her body. Moreover, the basic fact of having total juridical power over women may have fanned the propensity for violence. Because women had never before been prisoners in large numbers, men for the first time now had unrestricted access to them; given the low opinion of women in European society, there was little social pressure to restrain the court officials from taking their pleasure with the victims.

The popular appeal of sexually related torture went beyond the courtroom and jail house. All executions for witchcraft were public events and often drew huge crowds. The general sadism that this engendered will be discussed in chapter 8; here I want to look at the sexual aspects of torture, trials, and executions.

THE HEAVY sexual content of witchcraft prosecution in the sixteenth century parallels the well-documented rise in laws restraining sexual conduct. Among the legal charges on which a person could be brought up, sex-connected crimes—that is, adultery, bearing illegitimate children, abortion, infanticide, and incest—figured large, increasingly so as the two Reformations progressed. Women were more often and more severely punished than men for these crimes. The only sexual crime for which men were punished more often than women was sodomy, sometimes combined with a charge of witchcraft as well.[17] Witchcraft, too, was often sex-related, and charges for all these crimes rose and fell together; the seventeenth century saw a peak of prosecution for abortion, infanticide, *and* witchcraft.

Consider what this meant for the unwed mother in Nuremberg.[18] If suspected of killing her newborn, she was arrested, brought to the prison in chains, her breasts examined for milk. Then the midwife was dispatched to find the baby's body, which was brought back to the mother, no matter how long it may have been dead, to shock her into confessing. Between 1576 and 1617, nineteen women were subjected to this brutal routine, then drowned or beheaded. Women's punishment became more severe in Nuremberg as the sixteenth century progressed: formerly, pregnant prisoners had not been tortured, but now they were no longer spared. Nuremberg was remarkable for a south German city in that it had no executions for witchcraft. This fact did not mean, however, that it tolerated deviant sexual behavior in women or treated them humanely when they were desperate.

In other areas of Europe as well, charges of sex crimes and witchcraft often overlapped: Elizabeth Codwell of Essex, for example, guilty of murdering her bastard child, suspect as a witch, and pregnant with her second bastard, was reprieved from hanging until one month after the child's birth and was then put to death. In Luxembourg, the daughter of a poor manual worker at Santweiler was executed for sorcery and for killing her child. As we have seen, the word *witch* in Luxembourg was associated with *putain* and *ribaude*, meaning "whore." In New England at Salem, George Jacobs called his servant Sarah Churchill (one of the young accusers) a "bitch witch,"[19] combining sexual and demonic sins in one succinct phrase.

When suspicion of abortion or fornication lay in her background, the accused witch stood little chance.[20] When brought to trial in New England, Alice Lake utterly denied that she had practiced witchcraft but confessed that as a single woman she had sinned, become pregnant, and tried to abort the fetus. Although she failed, "yet she was a murderer in the sight of God [and herself] for her endeavors." This admission of attempted abortion was sufficient to condemn her of witchcraft, and Alice was executed, leaving four small children. Like Margaret Lang, she was no witch—but under the extreme pressure of conviction for witchcraft, she broke down and confessed an old sexual sin.

The greatest sexual sin apparently was birth control, whether as contraception or abortion. The sorcery that one woman was accused of was teaching two young women how not to get pregnant. In Hamburg a woman was burned to death because she taught young women how to use abortifacients, and at Zwickau, another female was burned with her books and instruments because she aborted the fruit of the womb "*durch ihre falsche Art*" (through her treacherous method). Midwives were taunted, "How many children have you destroyed? How many pregnant women? How many mothers lying-in?" At Würzburg, where several hundred people were put to death in two years (1627–29), a midwife was blamed for the entire disorder.[21]

This attack on birth control and abortion might be seen as a protection of the fetus, if the authorities had shown a corresponding respect for pregnancy, birth, or infancy. They did not. When Alison Legrand was arrested for witchcraft, although she protested that she was pregnant, she was twice submitted to the ordeal of water ("ducking"). Although proven innocent, she miscarried. Though courts sometimes let a pregnant prisoner go, often they did not, forcing the gravid woman to give birth under harsh conditions. Sometimes the infant died, as did Sarah Goode's newborn in Salem jail; in other cases, the new mother was tortured and executed anyway (Jehanne de Monchecourt in northern France, 1610); in a few cases the pregnant woman, denied a stay, was executed with the fetus (for example, Elizabeth Lowys, England).[22] Children were pressured to give evidence against their parents and to witness their parents' executions. Children as young as three were imprisoned and as young as eight were executed as witches. The society that hunted witches could not claim to be pro-fetus or pro-child.[23]

So concerned were the French about abortion and infanticide that in 1556 the Parlement passed an extraordinary edict: every expectant mother must register her pregnancy and have a witness to the birth. If she did not, and the infant died, she was liable for the death sentence on a murder charge. This unprecedented intrusion by the state into the act of childbirth made infanticide into a *crimen exceptum*,[24] in the words of Edward Peters "the crime so dangerous to the civil community that the very accusation acted to suspend traditional procedural protection to the defendant, and opened the way for the most ruthless and thorough kind of prosecution, undertaken to protect the state from its most dangerous enemies."[25] Not even witchcraft was a *crimen exceptum* in France, but infanticide was.

All these charges were based on the actual activities of women. They were distortions, a dangerous twisting of the truth, but they were reactions to what women did in order to control their fertility. An even more dangerous projection onto women, however, came from fantasy, not fact, from the sexual fantasies of inquisitors and secular judges about what went on at the "sabbat." In trial records from everywhere in Europe (except England and Russia) we learn that women were believed to have an erotic propensity for devil worship.

Consider the case of a healer named Matteuccia of Todi, Italy, who was brought before the Inquisition for prescribing a contraceptive for the concubine of a local priest and for dispensing love potions. Admitting at first only to using herbal remedies, by the time the inquisitor finished with her she had confessed to anointing herself with an unguent made with the fat of babies in order to invoke demons and be transported to the sabbat.[26]

Moving further into the realm of judicial fantasy, we find women accused of flying to the sabbat on phallic broomsticks, being seduced by demon lovers, joining in orgiastic dances, kissing the devil's ass, copulating indiscriminately with men, other women, relatives, demons, or the devil himself, and giving birth to demon children.[27] Women were believed capable of these acts because of three qualities: being hypersexed, weak-willed, and given to melancholy. The devil could seduce a woman to his service when she was horny, or melancholy (because she was broke or had been deserted by her man), or simply because she lacked character. The classic statement from the *Malleus Maleficarum*, "all witchcraft comes from carnal lust, which is in women insatiable," summed up the widespread belief that women were by nature oversexed, wicked, and therefore dangerous to men. It is not surprising that many demonologists stressed the witch's ability to render a man impotent, even to cause his genitals to disappear,[28] for the witchcraze took place during a period when women were perceived as sexually omnivorous.

In these proscriptions we find that the most disgusting part of women's disgusting bodies was their menstrual blood. When Stevenote de Audebert showed the witch hunter Pierre de Lancre her pact with Satan written in menstrual blood, he was horrified to look at it. But not too horrified; his fascination overcame his disgust. One must ask why she showed it to the man who boasted he had tortured some six hundred persons, and who put to death eighty, in a brief four-month tour of southwestern France. It is likely that Stevenote was proud of this document. At any rate, showing it to de Lancre was her undoing, for she was burned at the stake.[29]

Early modern people were not casual about menstrual blood.[30] Calling menstruation a "sickness,"a "monthly disease or infirmity," or using the poetic term "the flowers," they referred to the flow as excrement, a "Monthly flux of Excrementitious and Unprofitable Blood,"[31] an impurity with a loathsome smell. They understood the flow to be proof of the inferiority of women's bodies compared to men's: men used all their blood, whereas women had a superfluity. If her period was blocked, this impure excess would trouble her brain, causing melancholy and even suicide. The foulest object that a seventeenth-century person could name was "a menstrous rag." Beyond this disgust over a natural function of the female body, however, lay a fear of its power. Menstrual blood was believed to have magical effects, bewitching a lover, serving as an aphrodisiac, assisting in conception; an extreme fear was that intercourse during menstruation would kill the man. Here we see a clear example of the no-win position of women in that society: they were inferior and yet dangerous, disgusting and yet powerful, and it was their bodies that chiefly made them so.

Larner suggested that it was in the era of the witch hunts that "the evil effects of the menstrual fluid [were shifted] from the menstrual blood to the woman herself." From this shift it was only one step to perceiving a woman as having by nature the characteristics of a witch. Larner believed that "this shift reflects an intensified misogyny in this period."[32]

Women were seen as overassertive sexually, even to the point of wanting to be raped, a belief widely held in the medieval period. The later idea that women wanted the devil to seduce them was based on the medieval literary formula in which women seek and enjoy rape.[33] From the Pays Basque came the saying, "*Un coq suffit a dix poules, mais dix hommes ne suffisent pas a une femme*" (One cock is enough for ten hens, but ten men are not enough for one woman). About French beliefs in general, Martine Segalen concluded, "Of all the maleficent powers which a man is led to fear in his wife, the most redoubtable are her sexual appetites, which threaten to subjugate him to her power."[34]

Old women especially were seen as oversexed. Much of the basis for legends of demon lovers stemmed from the belief that women were sexually insatiable and could not be satisfied by mere mortal men; widows were, of course, seen as all the needier. In his study of myths about widows, Charles Carlton concluded that "in the sixteenth and seventeenth centuries [men] felt that widows, once their husbands had whetted their sexual appetites, were all potential nymphomaniacs, rather like Chaucer's Wife of Bath." Carlton quoted Nathaniel Smith in 1669, "He that would woo a maid must fiegn, lie, or flatter, but he that woos a widow must down his breeches and at her."[35] Noting the fear that men expressed of these oversexed women, Carlton asked if these anxieties might help explain why widows were frequently accused of witchcraft. Surely he is correct in deciding that "men were afraid of widows because they did not fit into the age's concept of a hierarchical cosmic order. Being without a man to guide them they were, so to speak, a weak link in the great chain of being."[36]

Yet this projection of a supersexuality onto older women conflicted with the church's teaching that sex was only for purposes of procreation. Postmenopausal sexual activity was, in that light, inappropriate and illicit in any case.[37] There were thus many reasons for objecting to an older woman who was sexually active.

Old people, and old women especially, were hated for the way they looked. In an age that worshiped outward beauty and equated it with inward virtue, an ugly old woman was seen as evil, and therefore as a witch. An observer of the witch hunt in Essex wrote that suspicion fell on "every old woman with a wrinkled face, a furred brow, a hairy lip, a squint eye, a squeaking voice, or a scolding tongue . . . a Dog or Cat by her side."[38] Bizarre sexuality was attributed to these women, such as Temperance Lloyd, who when searched was found to have two teats in her "secret parts." Poor, addled old Temperance confessed that a Black Man had sucked on them. She was hanged.[39]

Having begun this discussion of the connection between women's sexuality and witchcraft with comments on the victimization of women, it is important also to take a broader view of early modern women's sexual lives. Putting aside the myths about their sexual insatiability and their demon lovers, what *were* women doing sexually? One thing seems clear: they were asserting themselves more and taking more responsibility for their sex lives than women have since, until very recently.[40] Because premarital sex was the norm and premarital pregnancy not condemned until the seventeenth century, young women and men were freer to learn about themselves sexually, to experiment sexually, and to try out partners than they would be again until the 1960s.

I can find no evidence of how premodern women felt during intercourse except Chaucer's exquisite description of the Wife of Bath, who so loved "the tickle in her root"—and this observation was written by a man. But given the witch hunters' obsession with sex, it is not surprising to find detailed descriptions of what it was like to have sex with the devil. There was an almost universal assertion by women on trial for witchcraft that the devil's touch was cold and disagreeable. Boguet, for example, quoted a suspected witch as saying that the devil's "semen was very cold," and "that she had several times taken in her hand the member of the Demon [which] was as cold as ice."[41] Given the frequency with which witness like this turns up in the records, one might conclude that sexual attraction was not the channel through which the devil won women over. But by contrast there is the testimony of fifty-seven-year-old Suzanne Gaudry that she "took contentment and nothing else" when having sex with her demon familiar, Petit Grinniou. That Susanne enjoyed sex with her demon cannot have helped her case; she was burned at the stake in 1652.[42] At any rate, it is possible that women did enjoy sex more[43] before the Reformations regulated sex and nineteenth-century bourgeois attitudes imposed more passive views of women's sexuality.

Furthermore, women were encouraging their young daughters to take lovers, were arranging this for them, and not, apparently, with marriage yet in mind; the intention must have been to supervise their sexual initiation. Stories that recur in court confessions, from Scotland, England, and France, indicate that children's first sexual experiences were arranged for them, as is still done in some non-Western societies. Elizabeth Anderson may have been a bit precocious at thirteen, but she was expected to go out with the "little dark man" whom her grandmother introduced her to and urged her to hold hands with. In Lorraine, Dominique Fallvasa testified that "although she was not yet of an age to do after the kind of women, she was sent by her mother into a thick wood where she would find a handsome young man whom she would easily be able to love." The story continued:

> She was gathering rushes for binding up the vines with her mother, and they lay down on the ground to rest themselves. . . . Her mother began to warn her not to be afraid if she saw something unusual, for there would be no danger in it; and. . . . There suddenly appeared one in human form who seemed like a shoemaker . . . [who] made her swear an oath to him, and marked her upon the brow with his nail in sign of her new allegiance, and finally defiled her before the eyes of her mother. And the mother in her turn gave herself to him in sight of her daughter. They then joined hands and danced for awhile.

Boys might receive the same treatment: Erik Hennezel's parents gave him a woman whom he madly loved and "at once and greedily wallowed in carnal bestiality with her."[44] At his trial he identified her as a succuba. That all of these stories when told in court end in disappointment, as the lover vanishes into the air or turns into a demon, does not invalidate the glimpse they give us of sexual initiation among peasants. Whether the parents arranged this in order for the child to have a "proper" (i.e., nontraumatic) first encounter with sex, or in order to make money, or to lure a lover for themselves (as in Dominique's mother's case), we cannot know. But the stories indicate that among peasants virginity held no value for marriage, and that initiation took place very young.

And women were loving women; evidence is scant but suggestive. Aside from the myth about the sabbat, that its devotees had sex indiscriminately, males with males, females with females, I can find only four cases of lesbianism, two clear, the other two uncertain, in witch trial records.[45] One of the former is one of the celebrated cases of demonic possession that seized French nuns. In the earlier convent cases at Marseilles, Loudun, and Louviers, when nuns became bewitched they blamed priests, usually their confessors, for seducing and bewitching them, claiming the priests were really servants of the devil. Several prominent priests were burned at the stake on these charges.[46] At Auxonne, however, the nuns accused not their priest but their mother superior. This public charge of lesbianism in a convent created an even greater scandal than the notorious cases mentioned above. The Parlement of Dijon took up the charges, could not handle them, and dismissed the case.[47] But these dramatic convent cases, fueled as they were by sexual repression, do not make an adequate basis for understanding either heterosexual or homosexual sex of the period.

A second case comes from ecclesiastical court records in Pescia, Tuscany, 1619 to 1623.[48] Benedetta Carlini, the young and gifted abbess of the Théatine convent there, experienced trances in which Jesus praised her, gave her the stigmata, and exchanged his heart for hers. Benedetta put on a public marriage between her and Jesus, and led a public processional to ensure that Pescia would be spared the plague. After a careful investigation, the authorities gave their approval to her ecstasies.

A second investigation, however, provoked by the papal nuncio, revealed another side to Benedetta's spiritual life: the nun who was her companion reported that Benedetta, while possessed by a male angel named Splenditello, had forced her to have sex with her, a relationship that lasted for several years. This astonishing revelation raised more questions than the investigators could handle. Was Benedetta responsible for her actions? She was, after all, in trance each time she seduced the nun. Was she committing heterosexual or homosexual acts? The two bodies involved were both female, but Benedetta spoke and even looked like a young male while she was possessed. To further confuse the picture, Benedetta was known to flirt with priests at the gate where the life of the nuns touched that of the outside world, and she had entered a mystical marriage with Jesus. Was she a witch with a demon lover (her "Jesus"), or was she bewitched, the innocent victim of someone else's sorcery? Not knowing what to make of the charges, the commission eventually concluded that her "voices" were demonic but passed no sentence on the charge of lesbianism. Benedetta was sentenced to life imprisonment within the convent. After all, because she had a following in the town, she was a potential threat to law and order there. As for her lesbianism, Benedetta could have been burned at the stake as a sodomite. There were a few precedents in Europe—five, to be exact, in the criminal records—of the death sentence for female sodomites.[49]

Another case, less clear, is found in the trial of Elizabeth Bennet of Essex. Accused by William Bonner of being "lovers and familiar friendes" with his wife, whom Elizabeth had made very ill (or possibly had killed), Elizabeth was hanged as a witch. Granted that she was accused of many other crimes, including being an "olde trot, old whore, and other lewde speeches," still it seems likely that sexual deviance was a basic charge.[50]

The final case, harder still to define, is that of Margaret Lang, the Scottish midwife and ecstatic discussed in chapter 6. Accused by an eleven-year-old girl of bewitching her, Lang was tried, convicted, and sentenced to be hanged. At the gallows she confessed that when she was young she had committed the "unnatural sin," a fact she felt so guilty about that she made a pact with the devil over it. The only other time I have come across this phrase is in the trial of Marguerite Douyn, a French servant girl accused of "having unnatural sex with her master." Because this was heterosexual sex, the charge apparently related to the physical positions.[51] So the nature of Margaret Lang's sin, called by a contemporary her "unnatural lust, which is known to some of your number," remains uncertain. Her case shows how difficult it is to write about sexual history.

Beyond the possibility that early modern women did enjoy and were more assertive about sex than women in a later period, there is one more sexual factor that must be raised: in the early modern period, married women were almost continuously pregnant or nursing—and it was hard on them. Furthermore, almost half their children died before they were five. When the Scotswoman Bessie Dunlop surrendered herself to Satan, she was just up from an excruciating childbirth and hurrying across the moor seeking help for what she feared was her husband's fatal illness; in short, the devil got her while she was down. As the instruments of torture were being prepared at Barbe Gilet's trial in Lorraine in 1587, she calmly told her jailers to stop; she would confess, not in order to spare herself torture (which she claimed she could have endured) but in order to seize her opportunity for death—so that "the four young children which still survive of the many that I have borne" would not be raised by her, in the service of the devil. Her death would free them; she would sacrifice herself for them.[52] Barbe had borne and lost many children and been hounded by the devil all the while. No wonder that she was ready to quit this life.

It is important to review the many ways that having a woman's body made a difference during the witch hunt. First, the distinctively female external parts of the body—breasts and labia—were the model for the devil's teat, a sure sign of guilt, and the female function of nursing was the basis for the myth of imps and familiars, who sucked on witches. Some of the most basic and negative imagery of witch lore was thus taken from female anatomy.

Birth control, abortion, and infanticide, all seen as heinous crimes and all the almost exclusive practice of women, were connected with witchcraft and thus compounded its offensiveness. Homosexuality was being increasingly persecuted, and lesbianism may have been connected with demonism, although it is impossible to say on the basis of a few cases.

That women were seen as more strongly sexed and of weaker character than men were crucial points, becoming the basis for the interpretation of the sabbat as a sexual orgy and for the belief that it was inevitable, hence "natural," for women to be seduced by Satan. This view of female sexuality both expressed and intensified men's sexual fright of women. Applied to old women, it made them grotesque and physically repellent. All women without men were seen as especially vulnerable to the devil.

Mother-daughter pairs were especially suspect, and many were burned or hanged together. A mother-daughter pair was buried alive for sorcery in Cologne, and a number of three-generation groups of female victims are known, as well as mother-son pairs. These accusations confirm a belief both in the hereditary nature of witchcraft through the mother and contamination through nurture. They underline the tension already evident in the huge number of accusations made by girls against older women, a tension exposing the desire of females as well as males to "kill the mother."

Finally, the authority figures in witch trials were entirely male. The majority of accusers,[53] the ministers, priests, constables, jailers, judges, doctors, prickers, torturers, jurors, and executioners, and the courts of appeal as well, were 100 percent male. This all-male establishment paid off: as we have seen, 80 percent of those accused and 85 percent of those executed by it were female. As for the appeal process, few women attempted it: in France, 50 percent of the appeals to Parlement were by men, although only 20 percent of the accused were male.[54] The power of the courts trying witches, operating as they were under an extraordinary dispensation from normal legal procedure, gave these men exceptional power over women, and many of them used it to carry out sadistic sexual practices on the victims. Therefore when women asserted themselves, challenging this patriarchal system in any way, they were punished. It was apt that the Scotswoman Margaret Lister was described in her indictment as "a witch, a charmer, and a libber," "libber" meaning then what it means today.[55] That historians in the past could have ignored the blatant gender oppression of the witch persecutions and that some in the present continue to blame the victims, is as extraordinary as the historical facts themselves.

We have seen that by the witch hunt European women as a group were criminalized for the first time.[56] Their vulnerability to mass persecution was proven, their alleged propensity for evil dramatized. Although the oppression of European women had a long history before the sixteenth century, it "came into its own" then. The lengths to which men in power would go in order to control women became more violent, more public, and more organized.

THE ULTIMATE form of torture was to be burned alive, and the most horrifying symbol of some men's power over all women and over some other men was public execution at the stake. That this ferocious type of punishment was commonly carried out on witches added to the sadistic nature of their treatment, compounding the sexual torture that many had already been subjected to.

That this torture was carried out in the presence of large crowds often numbering in the thousands gave it a ritual meaning beyond that of simple punishment. As a public purging of evil, it declared that the land was rid of demonic enemies and that not a trace of their hated presence remained. Once the condemned had been reduced to ashes, those very ashes would be thrown to the wind or scattered over moving water. But public witch executions were more even than a purging: they affirmed that the ruler who ordered them was godly, and even more important, that his power was greater than the forces of evil.[57] The fate of a poor German family illustrates this point.

Anna Pappenheimer, who was fifty-nine in 1600, was, as we have seen, the daughter of a grave digger, an outcast group in Germany at that time.[58] Marriage opportunities for outcast women being few, Anna had seized the chance to marry Paulus Pappenheimer, an itinerant privy cleaner, also a member of the underclass. In addition to being suspect as outcasts and as wanderers, the Pappenheimers were Lutherans in a Catholic land, the duchy of Bavaria.

But Anna had several things going for her. By the time she emerged into the historical record in 1600 she had been married for thirty-seven years, had borne seven children of whom three sons survived, and had despite constant poverty kept the family together. A respectable woman, one might think.

The Bavarian government thought otherwise. Its young duke, Maximilian, after an intensive Jesuit education, had become concerned about witchcraft in his duchy. As a teenager he had witnessed the trial of several women for witchcraft. Now, worried about unrest among his barons and city oligarchs and a rise in highway robbery and vandalism, he searched for a way to demonstrate his power. Already concerned that witches might have put a curse on him (his wife had not been able to conceive), he called for a witch hunt. His theological advisers, threatened by the new Protestant movement, were eager to cooperate with him in every way. It was not enough that the Bavarian Council of State was already legislating about almost every aspect of its citizens' lives: "against the marriage of young Catholics into Protestant communities, against the sale of non-Catholic books, against mixed bathing, against dancing in the evenings, against extravagant weddings, against fortune-telling and superstition, against vagrancy and highway robbery."[59] Even though Bavaria was filled with ducal spies, still people did not obey these rules. What was needed, the duke decided, was a show trial, a public spectacle that would make it clear to all his subjects, high and low, who was in charge in Bavaria.

When the Pappenheimers, already seen as polluters of society, were named as witches by a condemned criminal, they were duly arrested and brought to Munich. Held in separate cells, they were questioned repeatedly but would not admit to sorcery. Tortured with the strappado, however, they began to break. Anna finally confessed to flying on a piece of wood to meet the devil, having sex with her demon lover, murdering children in order to make an ointment from their bodies, making a demonic powder from dead children's hands. The ointment and powder, she admitted, were used to carry out murder. After a long, well-publicized trial, the entire Pappenheimer family was convicted of witchcraft.

The execution of the four adult Pappenheimers drew a crowd of thousands from the surrounding countryside. First, they were stripped so that their flesh could be torn off by red-hot pincers. Then Anna's breasts were cut off. The bloody breasts were forced into her mouth and then into the mouths of her two grown sons. (This had not been the custom until Duke Maximilian's time.) A contemporary torture manual recorded that "the female breasts are extremely sensitive, on account of the refinement of the veins."[60] This fiendish punishment was thus used as a particular torment to women. But it was more than physical torture: by rubbing the severed breasts around her sons' lips, the executioner made a hideous parody of her role as mother and nurse, imposing an extreme humiliation on her.

Now a procession formed, over half a mile long, led by a municipal official carrying a large crucifix. Legal officers wearing red and blue tunics, the four Kings of the Night representing the four quarters of the city, the ducal chief justice, and a crowd of clergy helped to fill the ranks. Church bells pealed to celebrate this triumph of Christianity over Satan; the crowd sang hymns; vendors hawked pamphlets describing the sins of the victims.

Meanwhile, Anna's chest cavity bled. As the carts lurched along, the injured prisoners were in agony. Nonetheless, they were forced at one point to get down from the carts and kneel before a cross, to confess their sins. Then they were offered wine to drink, a strangely humane act in the midst of this barbaric ritual.

One can hope that between the wine and loss of blood, the Pappenheimers were losing consciousness. They had not been granted the "privilege" of being strangled before being burned, but in keeping with the extreme brutality of these proceedings, they would be forced to endure the very flames.

Further torments awaited Paulus. A heavy iron wheel was dropped on his arms until the bones snapped. Despite the fact that it was Anna who was the witch, not he, she was spared the wheel, because it was never used on women. Then Paulus was impaled on a stick driven up through his anus. By this brutish parody of anal intercourse, he received not only intense physical torture but also was branded a sodomite; again, as with Anna, he was subjected to a humiliation that canceled out what his life had really been.

The four Pappenheimers were then tied to the stakes, the brushwood pyres were set aflame, and they were burned to death. Their eleven-year-old son was forced to watch the dying agonies of his parents and brothers. We know that Anna was still alive when the flames leapt up around her, for Hansel cried out, "My mother is squirming!" The boy was executed three months later.[61]

After the Pappenheimers' show trial, there was less unrest in Duke Maximilian's lands. But even this fact did not ease the pressure on suspects: as late as 1631 there were still large numbers of accused witches in his prisons.[62]

The Pappenheimer case can serve as an introduction to how the sixteenth- and seventeenth-century state intervened in the lives of individuals, women especially, using sexual references to underline the state's absolute rejection of certain persons. How the growing power of the state also changed gender relations within European society fundamentally will be examined next.

Ein erschröckliche geschicht / so zu Derneburg in der Graff-
schafft Reinstein- am Hartz gelegen- von dreyen Zauberin- unnd zwayen

The burning of three witches at Derneburg, Harz, in October 1555, as documented in a broadside newsletter. Public tortures and executions of witches officially conveyed strong messages about the expectations and limits of women in society. Courtesy of Dover Pictorial Archive Series.

CHAPTER EIGHT

Keeping Women in Their Place

IN THEIR ground-breaking reperiodization of European history as women's history, Bonnie Anderson and Judith Zinsser conclude that "the unequal relationship between women and men, present at the beginnings of history in Europe, intensified as time went on. The early nineteenth century marked the nadir of European women's options and possibilities." Noting, as we also have done, that centralizing of government and religion lessened women's opportunities, Anderson and Zinsser sum up the problem for women as follows:

> The centuries from the Renaissance through the Enlightenment broadened the possibilities for men, giving more men access to education and choices in occupation. They did the opposite for women. New national law codes denied women control of their property and earnings, gave primary authority within the family to the husband alone, outlawed any efforts by women to control their fertility, and barred women from higher education and professional training.[1]

Though all these factors are important, they still do not fully explain why women's lives were more restricted in the early 1800s than ever before or since. Elsewhere the authors observed, "The witchcraft persecutions remain the most hideous example of misogyny in European history,"[2] but they did not factor in the hunting of women as witches when explaining why the early modern centuries were good for men but disastrous for women. I will argue that the witch hunts played a key role in this decline of women's status.[3]

Anderson and Zinsser also overlooked a second cause of women's extraordinary subordination, namely, the increasing power that European men were claiming over the world. I will posit that as their control over other peoples spread through imperialism, European men exerted more control over their own women.

Before we look at the way imperialism, colonialism, and misogyny reinforced one another, however, we must turn back to the witch hunts and examine their effect on the era that produced them. What difference did it make to women that they were for the first time criminalized as a group? Or that they were hunted out primarily *because they were women?* And as for men, what effect did having this power exert on them?

IN MUCH of western Europe in the peak years of the craze, any woman might have felt like a hunted animal. When we narrow the focus from the national level to that of village or town, we see the real horror of this period for women. In an attack that ultimately cut across lines of age, class, and income, women found themselves alone. With few exceptions, their families did not speak up for them out of fear and, in some cases, turned against them. Accused by their neighbors or named under duress by their friends, usually they faced the court without any support. Faced with legal procedures they did not understand and threatened with torture, they struggled to say what they thought the judges wanted to hear. But many were not let go,[4] and the hopelessness of the voices that speak through the trial records from prison underlines the fact that they realized there was no way out for them.

Women thus learned to live with a fear far greater even than our current dread of rape and assault.[5] If a woman could be cried out a witch for telling someone's fortune or speaking back to a neighbor, well then, one had better stay to oneself, mind one's business—and obey one's husband. Women learned especially not to trust other women, for what woman might not be called up before the judge and start blabbing?

The sociologist Carole Sheffield maintains, "Sexual terrorism is the system by which males frighten, and by frightening, dominate and control females."[6] We have dealt with a variety of ways this was done: by rape, body searches, verbal smears, torture. The chief sixteenth-century device for teaching both sexes about men's ultimate control over women, however, was the public execution of witches. Strangely, little can be found in the trial records or eyewitness accounts about the culmination of the trials: the carrying out of the death sentence is seldom described, and almost never in detail.[7] The most complete execution accounts we have are of the Renfrewshire executions in Scotland, the burning of the Pappenheimers, the hangings at Salem, the executions of several well-known priests in France, and the *auto-da-fé* at Logroño, Spain—and even this last falls silent over the actual deaths. Even more strange is the silence on this subject of some of the major witch hunters—Remy, Boguet, de Lancre, Kramer, and Sprenger. Had they no stomach for seeing their projects through to the end?

The near silence of the records about this crucial element (crucial certainly for the victim, but also for the crowd) requires us to reconstruct. What did a woman standing in the crowd outside Munich see, think, feel, as she watched Anna Pappenheimer's arms burned with hot tongs, her breasts cut off, her body burned alive? What were the messages of this savage scene, one that the onlookers knew occurred thousands of times, in one version or another? For all of the onlookers a major message was that the power of the devil, for that moment and in that place, was overcome, and that the Catholic church and the government of Duke Maximilian were safely in charge of Bavaria. But for the female onlookers there were other messages, for everyone knew that, even though men also might be condemned, witchcraft was quintessentially the crime of women. To examine this public rite, I will use Tom Driver's categories of ritual in order to analyze what that particular message was for women.[8]

Ritual is display. This execution, through the elaborate procession of ecclesiastical and secular officials, displayed the absolute power of the state over the individual, of the church over Satan *and* the individual, of public law over the private realm of the family. But because the torture that preceded the killing was gratuitous, the prisoners having already confessed and been convicted, it signaled that this ritual displayed something more. Some of the torture was customary, such as gouging the Pappenheimers' flesh with hot tongs; this would sear some of the evil out of them, thereby winning them some small hope of salvation. It would also give the crowd a thrill of horror and warn them not to play around with the law as the Pappenheimers had allegedly done. As for breaking the criminals' bodies on the wheel, that was frequently done in Germany. But mastectomy and being impaled—these were ferocious punishments, which signaled to the crowd that these prisoners were singular; they were wild beasts whose very existence threatened the state of Bavaria.[9]

These were the messages to all. To a woman, however, there was more: cutting off Anna's breasts dewomanized her, said that the most dangerous thing about this evil woman was her sexuality, that her only hope of salvation lay in becoming not a woman. The message to the females in the crowd was, Be not-a-woman yourself; be as invisible about your sexuality and your motherhood as you possibly can. In a century in which men wore codpieces to emphasize and flaunt their genitals, women were being told, It is dangerous to show your breasts; don't even nurse your babies in public.

Ritual needs limits. Being a structure, its form must be limited to be recognizable. By 1600 in south Germany, witch burnings were a familiar event whose components spoke a language that all could understand. At Munich, however, the form of witch execution was pushed to the extreme. Just as ritual requires order, it also tends to push beyond its limits, and when it does so it can become deadly. The Pappenheimer family's execution did not occur late in the witchcraze; people were not yet bored or jaded by the tortures and burnings—if indeed they ever became so. Yet here the planners (the municipal council and Jesuit advisers) broke the boundary of what was required. The "language" of ordinary executions was deemed not sufficient to communicate their message. Thirteen years before in nearby Württemberg, searing her breasts with hot tongs and cutting off her hand had been sufficient to prepare Walpurga Hausmänin for the stake. Except in southern Germany, mastectomy was never before or again used in witch executions, to my knowledge. What fear (of the devil), what hatred (of women), what mad drive for power could have motivated these planners to push their ritual to this extreme?

The woman in the crowd would see Anna being stripped and would know that men had planned this as a pornographic moment, and, no matter how much she feared a witch, she would share Anna's shame. The woman would know that pornography breeds violence and would shiver in fear of what the executioner would do next to the half-naked woman. When he reached for his knife, took one of Anna's breasts in his hand, cut off the flesh, plunged the bloody nipple between her lips, the woman would have felt the knife in her own flesh, would have gagged, wanted to vomit, as much from shame as from horror. She would feel faint from the question pounding in her head: Can our bodies be this evil? Is there no limit to men's hatred of us?

At this point I am tempted to say that the planners were demonic people, deranged by their evil, and to leave it at that. But given the depths of evil in our own century, I have learned that one dare not dismiss evil by calling it madness. The "madman" who has enough sanity to gain power is not insane. The planners of the witch hunts were perfectly sane, yet they planned a ritual that went to an "insane" length. There is also the question of where to lay guilt: between the planners (elite Bavarians) and the torturers (commoners), who is guilty of the Pappenheimers' deaths? Duke Maximilian did not torture Anna, nor did he witness her execution, as far as we know, yet he and the other planners, as well as the executors, are complicit in her death. We can pursue these questions further through the remarkable parallels that exist between this seventeenth-century state interference in civilians' lives and recent state-sponsored lessons in violence from Argentina. According to the analysis of Frank Graziano,[10] the disappearance, torture, and death of over twelve thousand Argentines, mostly students and workers, between 1976 and 1982 was carried out in order to purge that society of internal, invisible enemies, indeed, of enemies manufactured by the government. I observe that, like sixteenth-century witches, the Argentine victims were seen chiefly as ideological opponents of law and order, persons who "spread ideas which are contrary to Western and Christian civilization," who were seen as opponents of God. They too were accused of imaginary crimes, fantasies bred by the Argentine military leaders. Typical victims were described as "disoriented and gloomy students" who played guitars and scribbled graffiti, in other words, marginal types afflicted with "grave moral sickness." Immigrants were also suspect, declared to be "debris," like witches, "not assimilable to our sociability."

Graziano maintained further that the Junta's type of attack marked a change in focus for state oppression: from jailing political groups to torturing individual human bodies, ostensibly to gain information about a communist conspiracy against Argentina. But torturing prisoners did not produce substantive information about threats to Argentine society, for in fact the accused had none. Instead, they were tortured until they accepted a mythological construct in which they became the enemy of the state. The approach was highly ideological. Graziano comments that "like medieval inquisitors, [the torturers] altered the very fabric of reality by scripting roles and making those summoned before them play these preassigned and largely prewritten parts." Parents were tortured in front of children and vice versa; women were raped. The twentieth-century version of the most extreme torture was to throw live prisoners out of airplanes into the sea. More routinely, victims were shot and their bodies incinerated, so that all trace of them was erased.

Throughout, the torturers maintained that they were doing God's will. One *desaparecido* was told, "You are the Antichrist. . . . I'm not a torturer, I'm an inquisitor." Just as Duke Maximilian and his priestly advisers believed that they were saving Bavaria from the devil, so the Junta claimed that it was purging Argentina of godless communism. And like the Bavarians, in order to heighten the punishment for so heinous a crime (and the pleasure, for the guards), the Junta eroticized the violence. Gang rape, necrophilia, castration, and cannibalism were "rated" for their potency to turn the guards on sexually. Always, there was gratuitous violence, the victim being kept alive as long as possible so that the torturer might experience maximum pleasure. And always, the Junta identified itself with Christ (as the savior of Argentina), declaring itself a martyr when it was finally voted out of office.

Throughout both the seventeenth-century material and the Argentine account runs the same connection between reactionary Christian ideology and excessive abuse of prisoners. Graziano concludes that they are not a contradiction but mutually interdependent. By justifying the attack on innocent civilians *in religious terms,* the Junta had already broken with the restraints of law and convention; it had therefore given itself license to go to any extreme of punishment. By declaring a form of "holy war" against these imaginary subversives, the Argentine dictatorship believed that the Argentine people, and indeed the world, would accept whatever it did. Planners and torturers therefore became one force, and it is not possible to declare one guilty without the other. In seventeenth-century terms, this translates as follows: the theoreticians of the witch hunt (rulers, priests, jurists, judges) and the torturers (guards, searchers, executioners) were one force, totally interdependent and therefore both guilty; the argument fits both cases. But though Graziano states that in Argentina the payoff for each group was different (politicoreligious for the former, psychosexual for the latter), I do not find this distinction in the records of witch hunting: here the judge searching for the "truth" about the devil's hold on Christian society appeared to have been as fascinated by the erotic element as the common jail worker.[11]

But the question of the extreme violence of the witch hunt's rituals is not entirely answered by these insights into "divine violence," for these events were deliberately made as public as possible, whereas much of the Junta's work was carried out in secret. We may find further help by considering the nature of sacrifice. Returning to Driver's categories, we find that ritual requires sacrifice. Because rituals are transactions, exchanges between a source of power and persons lacking sufficient power, a propitiation must pass from the weaker to the stronger. In that sense, Anna Pappenheimer, and the one hundred thousand or so other victims of the witch hunt, was an offering. Not an ordinary gift, as a tithe of one's money or crops would be, but a sacrificial offering; that is to say, a gift that was irrevocable, that could not be taken back or replaced. Therefore, Anna had to be killed, not just to rid the earth of her polluting presence, but to establish that the authorities had made an ultimate sacrifice, a human sacrifice, to the Christian god. The woman in the crowd would understand that being female had a perverse value in that society, that women were the preferred sacrifice, that because women symbolized evil more than men, they thus served as its preferred scapegoats when the rulers needed one.

The term *scapegoat* fits condemned witches in some ways, not in others. When a community faced a crisis, as after a hailstorm or during a plague, its leaders *created* a scapegoat(s) to be sacrificed. By condemning women to a ritual violence, the leaders escaped the Christ-role that would dictate that *they* sacrifice themselves in order to remedy the problem. As imaginary culprits, witches were surrogate victims, hence scapegoats.[12]

But the sacrifice is more than an offering: it consists of two actions, the propitiation just described and a transaction whereby the object or the person sacrificed becomes sacred.[13] Here is where the witch persecutions fail as rituals of sacrifice. In death the women are not transformed into saints; they do not qualify as scapegoats, who, no matter how unworthy or even hated they are, gain power through being sacrificed.

By looking at René Girard's definition of a scapegoat we see other ways in which these women did not qualify.[14] On Girard's first count, that of marginality, they do qualify: as women, all were marginal by gender, and many were marginal in other ways, so marginal that no one would avenge them. Further, the fiction of their guilt must be maintained, at no matter what effort. But beyond that, the witches were not treated as traditional scapegoats. Everyone did not take part in the killing of witches (unless being part of the crowd at the executions counts, but that was a passive role). Unlike the bull at Beutelsbach, whom everyone hurried to throw dirt on, the witches were seldom stoned to death or buried alive by crowds. The important next step seldom occurred either; usually there was no celebration following the killings. The banquets and entertainments that followed the numerous executions at Offenburg in southwest Germany stand out in the records as an aberration. Unlike the ritualistic dancing, singing, feasting, and drinking that Girard describes as customarily following a sacrificial death, these executions produced no festivity, no release of tension, no exulting.

In addition, these ritual killings did not bring peace. They did not resolve community hatreds, except at a temporary, superficial level. These deaths were not meant to bring communal peace, but rather to settle scores with the devil. Perhaps they could not bring peace because the victims were not granted a sacred value. Girard's final definition, after all, is that the scapegoat must be deified. But this one lasting "plus" that might come from ritual killing was missing in witch executions. Therefore these burnings and hangings were sheer brutality. These are rituals of nullity, dead ends. Perhaps the extreme forms of torture and suffering they exhibited were required to make up for that lack.

But the way witches were executed can tell us about the peculiar value of certain women to European society, a value strangely mixed between their power and their danger. Let us return to the bull that was sacrificed by the people of Beutelsbach. The villagers claimed that the bull had to be buried alive, had to be killed in that gruesome manner or else its death would not be efficacious. Because the bull was being killed in order to propitiate disease (disease being horrible), its death too must be cruel and agonizing. The majority of executions for witchcraft, too, involved gratuitous suffering—torture, mutilation, or slow death by fire. Some convicted witches were "humanely" strangled, but most suffered needless pain. I conclude that these witches' deaths would not have been efficacious, would not have served their intended purpose, would not have been a true sacrifice like that of the bull, unless they too were preceded by gratuitous pain and mutilation. Because the execution of witches routinely involved torture of some kind, these killings must have been seen as efficacious and as a true sacrifice, and the crime for which they died seen as horrible.

The bull, however, was a very valuable piece of property. As the only bull in Beutelsbach, owned by the community, it was a worthy sacrifice indeed. The same cannot be said for accused witches, the majority of whom were not important members of their communities. Once again, I conclude that the lack of importance of the victims had to be made up for by the severity of their punishment.

Now we come to a harder analogy. The bull, Sabean informs us, was the mediator between the village and the disease. What did Anna mediate? She stood between Bavaria and the devil. But how could she, the polluting one, be the mediator? Only by serving as the carrier of all of Bavaria's sins, by symbolizing all that was unacceptable to that society. Anna the beggar, daughter of a grave digger, wife of a privy cleaner, and now alleged witch, was the perfect candidate to mediate between good and evil. For one matter, by standing for all that was unclean and depraved, Anna was able to make perfectly clear the difference between good and evil. Having done so, had she gained the power to mediate between Bavaria and the devil, to expiate, through being killed, the shortcomings of Bavaria so that the people would not be punished? The record does not claim this. I can only point out the similar dynamic in other sacrifices.

The bull, Sabean continues, stood for the whole collectivity of the village. How could Anna be that for all of Bavaria? Exactly as above, she was "elevated" from her former humble status to the formidable role of state symbol, a convenient representation of Bavaria's transgressions.

But that is about a bull. Why did witch hunters require human sacrifice? A set of beliefs about evil animals could have been worked out instead; the concept of the harmful "familiar" was already a step in that direction. The work of the anthropologist Peggy Sanday may take us further.[15] In describing the treatment of prisoners by a group of Native Americans, involving every conceivable kind of torture, including the slow burning of every inch of the victim's body and cannibalism as well, Sanday records that the Iroquois knew "that the gods preferred human flesh." On this subject, Europeans were more like Native Americans than the Europeans might have suspected. What we would immediately call "savage cruelty" when done by Indians, we have hidden under rubrics of "legal change" or "religious turmoil" when perpetrated by Europeans during the witch hunts.[16] At any rate, acts such as tearing the flesh of the living victim gave an almost sacramental quality to these executions. The fact that it was human flesh made it the ultimate sacrifice, one surely pleasing to the savage God of the sixteenth century.

Because rituals by their nature demand an ultimate act, partial punishments like whipping or banishment do not qualify as ritual sacrifice. The sacrifice must be irreversible—that is, it must kill—and it must offer an irreplaceable gift—that is, a human being—to achieve maximum efficacy. Theoretically in ritual it does not matter so much who is killed, or how, provided that the ultimate act of murder takes place. But in the witch killings the victim had to be a certain sort of person, one perceived as a servant of Satan. This limitation weakened the ritual in the eyes of the community; it opened a gap for doubting, room for arguing that this or that victim may not really have qualified. I believe that this is another reason why witch hunters resorted to gratuitous (in addition to juridical) torture: to make the evil nature of the victims absolutely clear to the crowd. Women, already thought to be evil by nature, were the best choice. What mattered, what made the ritual "work," was simply that they suffered and died.

For the ritual of witch killing demanded that they suffer. Torture has been described as the product of the need to socialize and regulate violence,[17] and no doubt the public torture of witches channeled some of the community's destructiveness. But because each witch killing led to more, I assume that, in the long run, the public torture and killing exacerbated communal brutality rather than lessening it. What exactly did the crowd gain from witnessing such extreme suffering? Though the crowds who flocked to witch executions are never reported to have expressed sympathy for the victims, neither did they send up cheers. They seem to have been silent observers, perhaps assuring themselves that dangerous persons were indeed out of the way. Mainly, they seem to have drunk in the horror. One thing is sure: their large numbers prove that they did not shrink from brutality but rather sought it. They "lived off of" the dying agonies of others, drinking in violence, leaving us no doubt about the capacity of early modern Europeans for brutality and their attachment to it.

Yet there was one extreme that they were not asked to go to: they did not eat the humans whom they sacrificed. Cannibalism was not a part of their ethic and was resorted to by Europeans only in times of extreme famine. Although they were fascinated by cannibalistic practices when they encountered them in the New World, they did not adopt them.[18] Instead, they wanted to see the absolute eradication of the witches' bodies, even down to the scattering of the ashes. Aside from imbibing violence, they did not ingest their enemies the witches, as the Iroquois and Hurons did to one another. Anna's body was a human sacrifice to the Christian God. But in offering her up, the Bavarian authorities acknowledged the potential power of the devil, who had been, in this case, defeated. Society did not invest her flesh with any saving power, nor her ashes, even after they had been purified in the flames. For that reason, this was not a ritual with the power of atonement; it was instead a ritual of revenge. Its power over contemporaries lay in the amount of suffering it caused, in the amount of fear it generated; it did not heal. In fact it was entirely destructive, unless, that is, one considers its teaching function to be a positive one. As a didactic device, the ritual execution of witches succeeded superbly.

To return once more to Driver's categories of ritual, I note that ritual effects transformations, changes that cannot otherwise be brought about. What was the lesson of Anna's death, and what change did it bring about? The woman in the crowd would vow never to go near a magic-worker again, no matter how badly she needed her advice; she would never again trust a midwife, would neither tell nor ask her anything, no matter how urgently she needed her help. Come to think of it, she would guard her lips with her neighbors—because any woman could be a witch, she must not be associated with any of them. The women's subculture of the Middle Ages, which has been much studied, began to dissolve under the terror of witch hunting. The new cult of individualism that cultural historians write about in connection with the sixteenth century was based not only on capitalistic competition or Renaissance idealism; it was, in the case of women, based on fear. In the lands of the witch hunts, women came to fear one another, for their lives.

Another transformation effected by the witch hunts altered community life. Alan Macfarlane and Robert Muchembled have argued that witch accusations developed in order to resolve village tensions.[19] Looked at from the other end of the story, not that of accusation but of public execution, one must question their conclusion. As Erik Midelfort wrote, "If this was social catharsis, it nearly killed the patient."[20] To do Macfarlane justice, he acknowledges that English village life was undergoing change and that the relief that witch accusations brought merely masked those deeper tensions. But surely the reign of terror that was unleashed by the witch hunt *added to* the level of violence in sixteenth- and seventeenth-century Europe. Just as we know that we are brutalized by the violence on television, in the same way that earlier society's tolerance for violence was raised by the public nature of witch executions, and specifically their violence against women. These rituals taught people that "the woman's crime" deserved the most severe punishment possible, that women, who up to that time had seldom been marked publicly as criminals, were capable of doing the ultimate evil.

Finally, ritual seeks conversion. The obvious conversion here was demanded of the victim—that she confess, and thus save her soul while losing her life. But a more far-reaching conversion was being preached: as the woman in the crowd watched Anna's ashes being scattered, she knew that she too was evil. The saying went that "there is something of the witch in every woman." In the moment that Anna stepped up into the cart, she became The Witch, and thereby she became every woman. For the woman watching her, what was changed and transformed by the ritual was her belief about herself. In this highly instructive rite, anyone might learn to fear and obey the rulers of Bavaria; what a woman might additionally learn was that her very nature was demonic. And if someday the authorities came for her, she would at first protest her innocence, but finally she would admit what she had learned to be the truth at Anna's burning: that she too belonged to the devil. She had internalized the message.

We are beginning to trace the dehumanizing effects of this campaign on women. For one matter, women began to fear to speak up for themselves. In England, for example, the seventeenth century saw a decrease in the number of rape accusations brought to court (*not* necessarily in the number of rapes committed), and most of the few men brought to court on the charge were acquitted; rape, then as now, was difficult to prove. The lower accusation and conviction rates began to appear between 1558 and 1599, just after the major witch hunts got under way. The compiler of these statistics, Nazife Bashar, concludes, "Male judges and juries were loath to punish in any way other males for any sexual offense against females. . . . [although they] were quite prepared to send to their deaths members of their own sex for crimes other than rape."[21] No doubt the low conviction rate discouraged women from turning to the courts, because evidence about rape is painful to give even when the court is sympathetic. But we must emphasize the fact (as Bashar does not) that this trend occurred just as women themselves were being indicted for witchcraft. It was no time for women to stir the waters.

Women began to protest less in general. From having, at the end of the Middle Ages, a reputation for being scolds and shrews, bawdy and aggressive, women began to change into the passive, submissive type that symbolized them by the mid-nineteenth century. True, *some* women still dared to act up. Some rioted for bread and took matters into their own hands in the markets. In 1766 at Ashby-de-la-zouch, for example, an old Englishwoman, enraged that a farmer asked two pence too much for his butter, clapped "one hand in the nape of his neck, [and] with the other rubbed a pound of butter all over his face"—an act worthy of any spirited medieval market woman. At Hereford market in 1757 "a female mob," incensed that a badger (a buyer) had tried to buy grain above market price, seized him, "and beating him in a very severe manner, they broke all the windows in his house." But food for their families was not the only need that drove eighteenth-century Englishwomen to riot. On the crucial question of the enclosure of land (farmland being taken over by entrepreneurs for more profitable sheep grazing), women in Staffordshire in 1771 destroyed the fences that enclosed the common near their homes. Arrested and jailed, they were rescued by local citizenry who attacked the jail with stones.[22] Frenchwomen were active in their Revolution,[23] and in both countries a handful of women saw that they must demand their rights.[24] But the times were against them. Throughout the nineteenth century middle- and upper-class women were increasingly forced to be ladies, and female sexuality was perceived as passive. As Judith Walkowitz commented of this period, "There seemed to be no social space or social narrative for independent female desire."[25] Even as the first women's movement was being organized in England and the United States, women elsewhere in Europe were still seen as the potentially dangerous sex that must be controlled—and "control" was what European men had gained a lot of experience at doing.

IF THE SIXTEENTH and seventeenth centuries were a time of declining status for women, they were a brilliant period for some Western men. Never before had they had such an opportunity to exert their power over others. Despite the number of factors that they could *not* change, such as plagues, inflation, and famines, they nonetheless gained control over much of the world's natural resources and wealth, not the least part of which came in the form of human beings. David Brion Davis reports that this "resulted in the enslavement of captives on a scale unmatched in previous human history." The Atlantic slave trade was different not only in magnitude but in the basic attitude of owners toward slaves: the Iberian slave masters, for example, "never looked upon certain classes of slaves as carriers of culture and refinement" or gave some slaves positions of public importance, as other slave-owning societies had done.[26] To Europeans, slaves were exploitable cheap labor and nothing more. Sixteenth-century parallels between the growth of the African slave trade and the violent misogyny of the witch hunts need to be examined.

We need to see the similarities between all women in a patriarchal system and all persons in an unfree status. But first, consider a difference: a free woman would appear to have every advantage, being able to own slaves herself and to benefit from whatever forms of racism and classism her society used to rationalize slavery. A closer look reveals that, in fact, free women and slaves of both sexes fell into many of the same categories in the eyes of early modern European men. Neither had control over what they produced, other than in exceptional circumstances, and their labor could be coerced. Both were seen by the law as children, as fictive minors who could be represented in court only by their masters/husbands. Both could legally be beaten, debased, and humiliated. When mistreated, both were impotent to gain help from others within their group, nor usually could their families help them. Both were caught in a hereditary system. Both were needed as well as rejected. Both could be sold.[27] Under certain conditions defined by their masters/husbands, both could be put to death for being what they were—female, or black. These are ample grounds for considering the two groups together.

Orlando Patterson's definition of slavery can serve for sexism as well: a relationship of power and dominion originating in and sustained by violence.[28] Patterson points out the tremendous symbolic value of the slave for the rest of society: "Without slavery there would have been no freedmen." As for women, I have argued that, without the female witch as the symbol of evil, other Europeans could not have believed themselves to be good or just, that without the conspiracy theory about the devil, neither state nor church could have made as absolute a claim to power.

Patterson observes that a new historical stage of progress always causes an identity confusion, a point especially relevant for this discussion. The sixteenth-century leaders of Western expansion were caught up in unprecedented new challenges, moral as well as economic and political; this produced what Lynn White has called their "Age of Anxiety," one of "the most psychically disturbed periods in human history."[29] To ease their identity crisis, they needed the slave and the witch as never before. It is thus not surprising that, although Europeans had always practiced slavery and the subordination of women, in the sixteenth century they greatly increased their focus on both.

Both slaves and witches are human beings who are no longer treated as such; they are humans whose full humanity is sacrificed, and in that process they become guideposts for a confused society. As subhumans, they are useful beyond their economic role, for only they live on the boundary between good and evil, only they can "cross the boundaries with social and supernatural impunity." Because women were believed capable of serving the devil, they were the humans who could be seen as totally demonic creatures, the evil Other. Because slaves were by definition the most marginalized and alienated of persons, they were seen as "almost beasts in human form."[30] While Western men were carrying out their extraordinary conquest of much of the world, they were foisting off onto other groups the characteristics of evil. Thus most Western men were not forced to ask themselves, Is slavery immoral? Is it wrong to put women to death for witchcraft?

European men were able to assert the absolute power of enslavement over somewhere between eleven million and fifteen million Africans in the three centuries of the Atlantic slave trade.[31] This control was a small matter, however, compared to the opportunity they found in the New World itself (both North and South America), where they encountered a population of about eighty million indigenous people, whom they proceeded to enslave, overwork, and infect until 90 percent of them had died. The Indian population suffered a startling drop from eighty million to about ten million in less than a century, primarily from exposure to European diseases but also from war, forced labor, and overtaxation leading to malnutrition. These seventy million deaths represent the greatest massacre in history.[32] Looking at how "civilized Christian" nations carried out this genocide will tell us much about sixteenth-century Europeans.

Ronald Sanders has argued that Europeans thought of Amerindians and African slaves in the same light as Jews and Moors and treated them accordingly.[33] The Spanish, having expelled their Moors and forcibly converted their Jews in the very year in which they dispatched Columbus on his first voyage, had thus a vivid, active tradition of intolerance and racism to call on in shaping their attitudes toward blacks and Indians. Having long held a relatively humane theory of color differences (that race was explained by climate), in the fifteenth century, Spaniards had begun to change their theory of race. Arguing now that darkness of skin indicated a defect in nature, they developed a new insistence on "purity of blood."[34] Added to that was their extreme intolerance over religion, an absolute insistence on a homogeneous Christian population, on a "purity of faith."

Seeing Indians as "the other" just as they had Jews and Moors, Spanish conquerors labeled the Indians pagans. Cortés called the great Aztec temples *mezquitas* (mosques). Bernal Díaz even thought he saw traces of Jewish influence in Aztec statues and temples and speculated that they had been brought by Jews during the first-century diaspora![35]

Having persecuted the Moslem and Jewish Other back home, the Spanish did not hesitate to do the same to the Americans. One Spaniard observed that they enslaved so many that the Indians "no longer approach their wives, in order not to beget slaves." Another claimed that "the Spanish treat them worse than slaves." The Spanish philosopher Sepulveda called the Mexicans "uncivilized, barbarians, wild beasts." He lumped together Indians, women, and animals, all creatures without a soul of their own. Considered unable to govern themselves, they were identified with savagery and evil. Sepulveda argued that because Indians were vastly inferior to the Spanish, it was just to wage war on them. By the same argument he could have justified the witch hunts, a war on women. Speaking of Indians as cattle, Columbus said, "They have brought me back seven head of women, girls and adults." Tzvetan Todorov concludes that the Spanish saw Indians as "inferior beings, halfway between men and beasts."[36]

Having seen what followed when women accused of witchcraft were declared to be less than human, we can be prepared for the way some of the Spanish went about subjecting these "inferior beings."[37] They cut off the hands, noses, tongues, penises of captives; they cut off women's breasts. They branded slaves' faces with the initials of their owners. They tore children from their mothers' arms to feed them to dogs. They tested the sharpness of their swords by randomly cutting off heads or disemboweling the nearest Indians. They beat female captives to force them to submit sexually. To make a show of their power they burned captives alive at public executions. When Cortés put down the uprising at Panuco, he burned alive all the chiefs, while forcing their sons to watch. Even the most outspoken critic of this fury, Bishop de Las Casas, ordered a disobedient Indian to be burned to death.[38]

Because these strategies were in the spirit of contemporary attacks on witches, one must ask if the *conquistadores* made a connection between evilness in European women and Indian women. A scene recorded by Amerigo Vespucci in 1499 sheds some light.[39] While sailing down the coast of Brazil, his group encountered Indians; these people seemed shy. In order to win them over, the Europeans sent to them a young man, one "who was very brave and agile":

> This young man went among the women, and they all began to touch and feel him, marveling at him extraordinarily. But meanwhile a woman with a great stick in her hand was coming down the hill, and when she arrived where the boy was standing, she gave him such a blow on the back with her stick that he fell dead immediately. In an instant, the other women grabbed him and brought him up the hill, dragging him by the feet. . . . There the

> women still were, tearing the murdered young man to pieces before our eyes. And, holding up the pieces one by one for us to see, they roasted them in a great fire they had made, and ate them.

Adding this story to accounts of Amazon warriors (Columbus believed in them), one gets a picture of fierce females who were bloodthirsty cannibals. Fact and legend combined to create a frightening image. Europeans had long accused heretics and witches of anthropophagy; encountering a culture that actually practiced it must have terrified them. Encountering *women* who practiced it can only have increased the colonists' fear of their own women, already suspect as witches.

Of witches, Sanders observed, "It is not hard to discern connections between the emerging racism of the epoch and the new outburst of antagonism against these shadowed creatures of the night."[40] Witches and Indians were ill fated in sharing a number of characteristics in the eyes of European men: both were thought to worship "demons" and to be cannibalistic and should therefore have a war of extermination fought against them—in the name of Christianity. Both were condescended to as children, yet were feared. Both stood for the Other, for all that Western men believed they were not.

Todorov argues that in 1492 Spain "repudiates its interior Other by triumphing over the Moors in the final battle of Granada and by forcing the Jews to leave its territory; and it discovers the exterior Other, that whole America which will become Latin [because of Spain]."[41] He is right enough that the Spanish believed they had vanquished all internal contradictions from their society by the great expulsions, but he overlooks the fundamental contradiction, the potential impurity that remained: the possibility that their own women might betray them. Until we see the fear that this potentiality bred, we do not fully understand these conquerors.

Pointing out that they were caught between medieval religiosity and modern materialism, Todorov senses the way in which this made them vulnerable and confused. Everywhere they drove the Indians unmercifully in their greed for gold, all the while dreaming of converting them into model Christians. In their confusion (and greed) they became more violent: "Everything occurs as if the Spaniards were finding an intrinsic pleasure in cruelty, in the fact of exerting their power over others, in the demonstration of their capacity to inflict death." Acknowledging that sheer economic greed cannot explain this, Todorov sets up two kinds of societies, "sacrifice societies" and "massacre societies," in order to get at the dynamics of such great violence.[42]

Todorov identifies the Aztecs as an example of a sacrificing society. Their killing is done on their home ground and is done publicly and ritualistically. Victims are chosen individually, for certain reasons, by strict rules: though they must not be from one's own society, neither must they be too alien; they must speak their captor's language and must "assimilate" the captor's ideology while in prison. The murders are done in the name of an official ideology; they are in fact religious murders, and they testify to the strength of the social fabric of that society. These sacrifices are like the deaths caused in Europe by the inquisitions.

Spain and the other colonial powers are examples of massacre societies. They carry out mass killings and do so abroad; colonial wars provide the ideal setting. They thus hide their murders, trying to keep them secret. Victims are chosen indiscriminately and come from groups seen as totally alien; they are identified with animals, and their deaths have no ritual meaning. These murders serve the purpose of indiscriminate extermination; they are savagery for the sake of savagery. They testify to a weak social fabric, to what Patterson labeled identity confusion. They are amoral murders—modern killings, if you will.

Yet Todorov overlooks what else the European colonizers were doing in that century, namely, how they were extending their power at home. While perpetrating massacres abroad, they carried out sacrifice killings at home, public executions supported by official ideology whose victims were individually chosen. Witch executions fit the definition of sacrifice killings in all respects except that the victims were not a little alien; in fact, they were not alien at all but were from the very society that was murdering them. This fact throws into sharp relief how remarkable it was that European society turned on its own women, how unnatural an act that was. It goes far to explain the weird mythology made up in order to turn those women into someone alien. The fantasies of demonic lore were essential to change the woman who lived next door into a creature who could be tortured and burned.

I conclude that ruling-class European men looked at and treated their women basically as they did their African slaves and Indian serfs and as they had treated Jews and heretics before them, namely, with increasing violence. Viewing women as property, husbands became more authoritarian, a role no less oppressive for being disguised as paternalism. Just as slavery produced the myth of the good master, so patriarchy created the myth of the benevolent ruler of the family. Viewing women as dangerous (doesn't the master come to fear the slave?), judges and priests devised a satanic conspiracy theory to punish women who might step out of line. As the sociologist Richard Horsely observed, accusations of witchcraft were "a highly effective means of social control."[43]

These events hold up a mirror to European men of power, and the image reflected is an ugly one, deeply disturbing for the future of any less powerful group whom they might control. Todorov's chilling comment is apt: "The 'barbarity' of the Spaniards has nothing atavistic or bestial about it; it is quite human and heralds the advent of modern times."[44] The advance of democracy that began in the Puritan Revolution and elsewhere may have mitigated some of the most tyrannical aspects of Western power, including encouraging an end to witch hunting.[45] It did not, however, establish full protection for any of these groups. Racism, neocolonialism, and misogyny are still with us.

Epilogue

We have lived with violence so long.
Am I to go on saying
for myself, for her
This is my body,
take and destroy it?

Adrienne Rich, "Natural Resources"

IN 1985 THE GERMAN village of Gelnhausen, a village that had immured witches in its tower, decided to make a tourist attraction of the old "Witches Tower." But on the day that it was to open to the public, a group of women surprised the townsfolk by staging a protest. Dressed in white, they walked around the tower carrying placards with the names of those killed there long ago; the last placard read: "We will remember the *names* of those who died."[1]

This book has been an effort to remember the names of those who died across Europe. So far, few have said, "Yes, these things really happened." And no one has yet said, "They will never dare to happen again."

Appendix A
Early Modern Sources for the Witch Hunts

Evidence for the persecutions comes primarily from four types of sources: court records, accounts of sorcery and accusations (eyewitness or otherwise), witch hunters' manuals, and theoretical polemics by both believers and skeptics.

Trial records are often cursory in the extreme, leaving out names, dates, and verdicts, and many are lost. Even so, they present the basic record. An impressive beginning has been made on finding, editing, and publishing this material, starting with W. G. Soldan's *Geschichte der Hexenprozesse* of 1843.[1] Soldan's was followed by three other basic compilations, Joseph Hansen, *Zauberwahn, Inquisition Und Hexen prozess in Mittelalter* and *Quellen und Untersuchungen zur geschichte des hexenwahns. . .*; Henry C. Lea, *Materials Toward a History of Witchcraft* (although Lea summarizes, his "materials" are highly useful). A cross-cultural compilation including trials from Africa and India appeared in 1974, William Woods's *A Casebook of Witchcraft: Reports, Depositions, Confessions, Trials, and Executions for Witchcraft During Three Hundred Years.* Calendars of court cases, such as Kieckhefer's for pre-1500 Europe and that of Larner, Lee, and McLachlan for Scotland, and discussions of indictments, such as Ewen's for the English Home Counties, give an idea of the scope and types of trials.[2] David Hall published a useful collection of materials on the New England trials, and the standard reference on the Salem trials is available in an edition of 1977.[3]

Two anthologies offer trial accounts and theoretical works: *Witchcraft in Europe, 1100–1700* and *European Witchcraft.*[4] Rossell Hope Robbins's *Encyclopedia of Witchcraft and Demonology* gives an extensive list of cases. The foundation of current witch trial *analysis,* however, lies in the intensive regional archival studies that began to appear in 1945 with Bader's research on Switzerland, some of which contain trial transcripts.[5] A remarkable number of scholars have devoted their research since then to a topic long considered absurd or disgusting, and we now have sound basic publications on a number of witch trials in Germany, the Basque lands, the Friuli of Italy, Luxembourg, the Netherlands, northern France, the Jura including Franche-Comté, Scotland, Essex and the Home Counties in England, Scandinavia, Estonia, Poland, Russia, Hungary, and New England.[6] Though much remains to be done, these publications have opened up a new topic for historians to work on, one that illumines folk culture and popular religion at a point where they intersect with the elite power of courts, churches, and states.

Eyewitness accounts and pamphlets written at the time of the trials furnish more human interest but must be read with caution. When Edward Fairfax wrote about the bewitchment of his children, for instance, he could not have given a disinterested report.[7] Moreover, the alleged witches seldom speak in these records, and the writers came almost always from the elite culture that sat in judgment on the accused. In addition to those listed above, the following accounts were consulted in this study:

Account of trial . . . of six witches at Maidstone at assizes . . . in 1652. London, 1652.

Anderson, Joseph. *Confessions of the Forfar Witches.* Edinburgh, 1661; n.p., 1888.

A True and Impartial Relation of the Informations Against Three Witches, viz., Temperance Lloyd, Mary Trembles, and Susanna Edwards . . . at Exon, Aug. 14, 1682. London, 1682.

Capeau, Louise. Michaëlis, Sébastien. *Histoire admirable de possession et conversion d'une penitente.* Paris, 1613. Translated by W. B., *The Admirable Historie of the Possession and Conversion of a Penitent Woman.* London, 1613.

Essex. *The Witchcraft Papers: Contemporary Records of the Witchcraft Hysteria in Essex, 1560–1700.* Peter Haining, ed. Secaucus, NJ: University Books, 1974.

Fairfax, Edward. *Daemonologia: A Discourse on Witchcraft as It Was Acted in the Family of Mr. Edward Fairfax of Fuyston, Yorkshire, in 1621.* Harrogate: Ackrill Publishers, 1882.

Flower Family. *The Wonderful Discoverie of the Witchcrafts of Margaret and Phillip Flower, daughters of Joan Flower.* London, 1619; New York: Da Capo Press, 1973.

"Harrison, Katherine." In David D. Hall, *Witch-hunting in Seventeenth-Century New England: A Documentary History.*

"Hausmänin, Walpurga." First printed in the Fugger Newsletter, translated in *European Witchcraft,* edited by E. William Monter.

Kyteler, Alice. Ledrede, Richard de. *A Contemporary Narrative of Proceedings Against Dame Alice Kyteler, for Sorcery in 1324.* London, 1843.

Lang, Margaret. *A History of the Witches of Renfrewshire.* 1698; new ed., Paisley: Alexander Gardner, 1877.

N. N., Eichstätt, 1637. Translated in Robbins, *Encyclopedia of Witchcraft and Demonism.*

Pacy girls. Hale, Sir Matthew. *A Tryal of Witches, at the assizes held at Bury St. Edmunds on March 10, 1664.* 1682; London, 1838.

Potts, Thomas, H. *Pott's Discovery of Witches in the county of Lancaster.* London, 1613, 1746; Manchester, 1845.

Salem Witchcraft Papers: Verbatim Transcripts of the Legal Documents, edited by P. Boyer and S. Nissenbaum. New York: Da Capo Press, 1977.

Warboys, the witches of. Richard Boulton, *Complete History of Magic.* London, 1715.

Webster, David, ed. *A Collection of Rare and Curious Tracts.* Edinburgh, 1820.

An indispensable, but again often unreliable, source is the witch hunter's manual. The influence of the classic guide, Kramer and Sprenger's *Malleus Maleficarum* of 1486, is shown in its publication record: six editions before 1500, at least thirteen by 1520, another sixteen by 1669. It was soon translated into German, French, Italian, and English, was intensively quoted in later manuals, and soon spread into civil law.[8] Furthermore, it likely helped to spread the witchcraze to New England, for portions of it were printed in a book belonging to Increase Mather.[9]

Kramer and Sprenger, both important priests in the Dominican order in Germany, lent their prestige to popular beliefs about witchcraft already current: the sorceress's pact with the devil, how unguents are made from the bodies of unbaptized children, why a witch cannot escape from the devil.[10] Most important, the authors juxtaposed virulent antifeminine and antisexual material with witch accusations. Quoting biblical, classical, and medieval sources, they claimed that women are liars, more superstitious than men, more impressionable, wicked-minded, and in need of constant male supervision: "When a woman thinks alone, she thinks evil. . . . Women are intellectually like children." Women's ultimate flaw in the eyes of these two priests, however, was their inordinate carnality. Claiming that witchcraft in fact "comes from carnal lust, which is in women insatiable," the authors blamed witches for causing impotence in men and for seducing them and destroying their souls. In the face of such horrors, the authors praised God for having "preserved the male sex from so great a crime," and no doubt added thanks that as celibates they were less likely to fall into the trap of wicked women.[11]

This document launched the witch persecutions as an attack on women. Until the publication of the *Malleus,* men had been accused as often as women, and the total numbers of victims had been small. Though it is true that the major persecutions did not begin until about seventy years after the publication of the *Malleus* (c. 1560), the fact that the witchcraze attacked women, and especially their sexuality, points to the *Malleus* as an important contributing factor. Subsequent manuals and the polemical literature both quoted the *Malleus* at length.[12] That it had been published with a papal bull commanding the extirpation of all who "have abandoned themselves to devils, incubi and succubi" added greatly to its influence.[13] And that Kramer and Sprenger were appointed inquisitors by the pope, with instructions to the secular powers to assist them, helped them to begin a model witch hunt in the German lands. In Innsbruck Kramer tried fifty-five women and two men for sorcery, invocation of devils, and blasphemy, but was forced by the local bishop to release the accused.

There had been witch hunters' manuals before the *Malleus* (Nider's *Formicarius,* for example, written before 1438) and would be others after, written by both clerical and lay judges. Because by the late 1500s torture was routinely used in Continental witch trials, the accounts became more lurid as time passed. Nicolas Remy, for instance, layman and chief justice of Lorraine, was proud that he had put "over eight hundred" persons to death as witches in fifteen years.[14] Because Remy took careful notes, his reports give us a strong sense of having been present at the interrogations. Though Remy had a well-trained mind and was skeptical of some of the evidence, still he was a man of his century: he never accepted a natural cause for any action, insisting always on a supernatural (i.e., Christian) explanation. Convinced as he was of the danger that witches posed to Christian society, he was merciless to those whom he found guilty, burning one victim with red-hot tongs, then placing him alive on a fire. Before Remy retired, the common people grew so to fear him that some killed themselves in prison rather than face execution. Seventy-five percent of his victims were women.[15]

Yet Remy, who was also a poet, appears an educated, reasoning man, as do the other famous judges. The Burgundian Henri Boguet, chief judge of St. Cloud in Franche-Comté, was a man of the Renaissance who quoted Virgil, Horace, Apuleius. Yet he also quoted the *Malleus* and believed that the devil had sex with witches who had flown through the air to meet him at the sabbat. As for the female sex, Boguet claimed that the devil "knows that women love carnal pleasures, and he means to bind them to his allegiance by such agreeable provocations;[16] but he even-handedly claimed that "male witches are addicted no less," and that the devil obligingly appeared to them as a woman. Because Boguet's grounds for using torture were broad and his methods concise, his manual became the one most used by local parliaments. Boguet tried thirty-five persons, condemned twenty-eight, and allowed four more to die in prison,[17] a death rate of 91 percent.

The most colorful of the French judges was Pierre de Lancre, layman, royal counselor to the Parlement at Bordeaux, and outspoken puritan. Armed with a royal commission to extirpate witchcraft from the region south of Bordeaux, de Lancre spent four months there, interrogating and torturing some six hundred souls. Relying mainly on the evidence of children, he brought over eighty persons to the stake, most of them women. Believing that no punishment was too harsh for this extraordinary crime, he advocated the death penalty even for children. As for women, he established at the start why these creatures between man and brute beasts, fickle shrews, were the devil's special targets.[18] Using misogynistic language identical to that of the Jesuit Martin Del Rio, with whom he had studied witchcraft at a Jesuit seminary, de Lancre declared that women are the imprudent sex, "*imbecille*," who use natural or demonic phenomena in order to perform divinations, who dream passionate dreams, who have a nature "*humide et visquesue*" ("humid and viscous").[19] De Lancre was badly shaken on observing that in Basque churches women performed the "*marguilliere*," which involved carrying the albs and candles to the altar, spreading fresh altar cloths. Not only did they dare to approach the altar, but they did so at dawn and in the evening, that is, when the church was dark, and they were not even married women but young virgins. De Lancre's mind could not rest from thinking of what the priests were doing with these young women in their darkened churches.[20] Even worse, to his way of thinking, was that women took part in the services, collecting the offering and standing at the door to bless the congregation (yes, even the men). Concluding that most of the priests were sorcerers, de Lancre suspected them even of celebrating the sabbat in the sacred precincts.[21]

The most prestigious witch hunter by far, King James VI of Scotland and James I of England, published a treatise that had considerable impact. James began to suspect in 1590 that a coven of witches at North Berwick was plotting his death and the overthrow of the Scottish throne.[22] Impelled by fear not only of sorcery but of treason also, James interrogated the accused himself, being especially vicious to Agnes Sampson and Barbara Napier. Referring to Eve's seduction by the snake, he explained that all women are more easily entrapped by the devil than men. In his treatise he insisted that all witches deserved death by fire—all ages, all ranks, even "bairns" (children). Introducing the concepts of demonic pact and sabbat into Scotland, he in effect launched the witchcraze there,[23] a persecution that eventually took the lives of over a thousand persons, about 85 percent of them women.

In contrast to all these men from the establishment, young Matthew Hopkins of Essex County, England, was a nobody, a consumptive clerk who apparently took on witch hunting for a confusion of reasons: to earn money, to gain power, possibly even to serve the public.[24] Hopkins was wildly successful, hanging more witches in a two-year period than were hanged in England normally in two decades. Over two hundred persons, mostly women, were accused and seventy-one put to death in Essex and surrounding counties. Getting around the English prohibition against torture, Hopkins walked or ducked his victims until they confessed. He stressed practices new to English witchcraft, the pact with the devil and sex with the devil, and he made much of the English custom of searching for the devil's mark, or teat, on the bodies of the accused. Hopkins was rigorous about the search and obviously took part in it himself, for he argued, "If a w. plead the markes found are Emerods [sic], if I finde them on the bottome of the back-bone, shall I assent w/ him, knowing they are not neere that veine, and so others by child-bearing, when it may be they are in the contrary part?"[25] With a flair for words, he asserted that Satan called the witches "my delicate firebrand-darlings." With a flair for the dramatic, he used ventriloquism to simulate possession and sent a spy to infiltrate a coven.[26] Hopkins died at twenty-five, but he had made his mark.

The source with which historians have usually begun, the polemical works of the demonologists and their opponents, the skeptics, are actually the last that we should turn to. The intellectuals who wrote them had attended few trials and had little firsthand experience of the villagers among whom the charges originated; they are the farthest removed from the victims, their life situations, the foul prisons in which they lived and died. Still, these scholars were influential among the magistrates, judges, and clergy who carried out the witch hunt, and their work must be considered.

Foremost among the demonologists was the imminent French jurist Jean Bodin (d. 1596). Best known for his treatise on political theory, the *République,*[27] Bodin also wrote on philosophy of history, monetary theory, and comparative religions. That he also published one of the most influential guides to witch hunting, the *Démonomanie des sorciers,*[28] has long puzzled admirers of Bodin. Basing his work closely on the *Malleus,* he updated it for use in secular courts.[29] Although he had only slight experience of witch trials, Bodin organized the definitive description of the threat that witches posed to Christian civilization and the definitive guide to what to do about it. As E. William Monter observed, Bodin virtually created a new literary genre and set out arguments that all future writers on witchcraft had either to copy or refute.[30]

And extreme arguments they were. Bodin believed that witches promised to Satan babies still in the womb, ate human flesh, drank human blood, had intercourse with the devil, sacrificed their own children to Satan. Asserting that no punishment was cruel enough, he advocated torture, especially for children and delicate persons, and advocated encouraging children to give evidence against parents.[31] Believing the death penalty was warranted even if normal evidence was lacking, he concluded that it was better to kill innocent persons than to allow a witch to live. As for women, he knew them to be stronger and healthier than men and believed their vengeance knew no limit; he feared them accordingly. Claiming that he had known a few wise men but never a wise woman,[32] Bodin confirmed that the female sex was a potential threat to society.

Other scholarly studies that became well known at the height of the witchcraze include the works of the Jesuit Martin Del Rio, who advocated killing witches, even if they had done no harm, because of their loyalty to the devil,[33] and the Italian priest Guazzo, who gathered the opinions of over 250 authors on the dangers of demonic witchcraft.[34] The picture that emerges from this summary of the leading prosecutors and theorists of witchcraft is of privileged men of sophisticated mind who nonetheless believed in the power of magic, believed in and greatly feared the devil, assumed that women were weak-minded, treacherous, and vulnerable to Satan's power—and who transferred their fear of the devil onto the most vulnerable element in their society, women, mostly poor and mostly old, and punished them without mercy.

But there had always been doubters. From as early as 1489, immediately after the publication of the *Malleus*, the Swiss lawyer Ulric Molitor denied that witches cause illness or impotence, fly through the air to the sabbat, or are impregnated by the devil; he assumed that these phenomena occur only in dreams. Yet Molitor *believed in witches*, feared them, and advocated punishing them for their belief in the devil.[35]

The German physician Johann Weyer also believed in witches and the devil (as did virtually all sixteenth-century persons) but held, as Molitor had, that the devil merely deceives people into thinking that they have his power.[36] And who are the most credulous and vulnerable victims? Women, who are more given to melancholy and malice than are men. Though Weyer's arguments sufficiently threatened the belief in witchcraft to inspire Bodin's work in rebuttal, they did nothing to deflect the hostility toward women as witches that was building throughout the sixteenth century.

The most interesting challenger of witch beliefs was a Kentish gentleman farmer, Reginald Scot.[37] Scot applied his skeptical, pragmatic, Protestant mind to the issues raised by Nider, the *Malleus*, and especially Bodin. Although he believed in the devil, he thought of him only as a spirit, as one who could not preside over a sabbat or have sex. Scot's basic point was that it is God's power that is omnipotent, not the devil's, and that Christian faith therefore demands a skeptical stance toward witchcraft.[38]

Known for his experimental approach to farming, he applied the same standards of observation to witch phenomena. As for the claim that witches boil infants, Scot declared, "This is untrue, incredible, and impossible." That they eat children and men, he replied, "No one in France or England has seen this," and "if they should [eat humans] I believe it would poison them."[39]

Although Scot continued to believe that there were witches, he rejected most of their traditional attributes: nightwalking, flying, carnal copulation, transformation into animals, attendance at the sabbat. His attitude toward the accused women was sympathetic, yet his description of them was condescending: "poore, sullen, superstitious, and papists; or such as knowe no religion; in whose drousie mind the divell hath goten a fine seat. . . . Doting, scolds, mad, divelish."[40] Yet despite perpetuating this negative image of the village hag, still he pointed out that these women did nothing to warrant punishment, and he blamed their convictions on zealous judges gripped by a fear of the devil: "If a poore old woman, supposed to be a witch, be by the civill or canon lawe convented; I doubt, some canon will be found in force, not onlie to give scope to the tormentor, but also the hangman, to exercise their offices upon her."[41] Bemoaning that, given the extreme misogyny of some writers, "neither can anie [honest woman] avoid being a witch, except shee locke her selfe up in a chamber,"[42] Scot showed up the woman-hatred at the heart of the trials.

Scot's skepticism went further than any other commentator's. He saw that in order to give up one's fear of the devil's evil magic one must give up magic entirely; there would be no more miracles, prophecies, oracles. Though affirming biblical miracles, he acknowledged that the miraculous no longer broke through in his time: "Let us settle and acquiet our faith in Christ, and beleeving all his wonderous works, let us reject these old wives fables, as lieng vanities: whereof you may find in the golden legend, M[alleus] Mal[eficarum] and specialle in Bodin miraculous stuffe. . . . Which are of more credit with manie bewitched people, than the true miracles of Christ himselfe." These words anticipate a turning point in the Western mind; they look ahead to the time when belief in the devil (and, therefore, in witches) would no longer claim people's minds. But Scot's common sense and his courage in letting go old beliefs was ahead of his time. A century would pass before European society would begin to give up its belief in magic. The worst of the persecutions lay ahead; tens of thousands of executions would occur before a general sentiment against witch belief prevailed.

Other theoreticians of witchcraft whom I consulted follow:

Ady, Thomas. *A Candle in the Dark*. London, 1656.

Bekker, Balthasar. *De Betoverde Weerld*. Amsterdam, 1693. *The World Turned Upside Down*. Translated by Elizabeth Harris. London, 1700.

Binsfeld, Peter. *Tractatus de confessionibus maleficorum et sagarum*. Trier: Henry Bock, n.d.

Bovet, Richard. *Pandaemonium.* London, 1684; Aldington: Hand & Flower Press, 1951.

Bromhall, Thomas. *A Treatise of Specters.* London, 1658.

Ciruelo, Pedro. *Reprobación de hechicerias. Reproval of all Superstitions and Forms of Witchcraft.* Translated by E. Maio and D'Orsay Pearson. C. 1530; Rutherford, NJ: Fairleigh Dickinson University Press, 1977.

Daugis, M. *Traité sur la Magie, le sortilege, les possessions, obsessions, et malefices. . . Avec une Méthode s[acu]re et facile pour les discerner.* Paris: Pierre Prault, 1732.

Filmer, Sir Robert. *Advertisement to the Jurymen of England Touching Witches.* London, 1563.

Gaule, John. *Select Cases of Conscience Touching Witches and Witchcraft.* London: R. Clutterbuck, 1646; 1966.

Gifford, George. *Dialogue Concerning Witches and Witchcraft.* London, 1603, 1842.

Hopkins, Matthew. *The Discovery of Witches.* 1647. Edited by Montague Summers. London, 1928.

Hutchinson, Bishop Francis. *Historical Essay Concerning Witchcraft, and Two Sermons.* London, 1720.

James I. *Daemonologie.* 1597. London: Bodley Head, 1924.

Michaëlis, Sébastien. *Discours des esprits en tant qu'il est de besoin pour entendre la matière difficile des sorciers.* Lyon, 1614. *A Pneumology or Discourse of Spirits.* Translated by W. B. London, 1615.

Perkins, William. "The Good Witch Must also Die" (1608). In John Chandos, ed., *In God's Name: Examples of Preaching in England 1534–1662.* New York: Bobbs-Merrill, 1971.

Wodrow, Robert. *Analecta: Materials for a History of Remarkable Providence, mostly relating to Scotch Ministers and Christians.* 4 vols. Edinburgh: Maitland Club, 1843.

Appendix B

Numbers Chart

	Accused				Executed			
	TOTAL	F	M	% F	TOTAL	F	M	% F
Pre-1500[1]	705	502	203	71%	490+	348	142	71%
Holy Roman Empire								
S.W. Germany[2]	4,208			82%	1,280	1,050	238	82%
TOTALS					3,229	2,647	582	82%
Bavaria[3]					2,000+			
Mecklenburg[4]								
Trier					1,000+			
Nassau					400+			
Westphalia					800+			
Eichstätt					274+			
Walbeck & Schaumburg					200+			
Lippe					430			
Kurmainz					1,000			
Bamberg & Würzburg					1,602			
Fulda					700			
Saarland[5]	439	316	123	72%	almost all			
Bohemia[6]					c. 1,000			
Austria[7]					c. 1,500			
Alsace[8]					5,000+			
Lorraine[9]	4,000+	3,000+	1,000+	74%	3,000+	2,400+		80%
Franche-Comté[10]	202	153	49	76%				

	Accused				Executed			
	TOTAL	F	M	% F	TOTAL	F	M	% F
Montbéliard[11]	72	62	10	86%	55+			
Vaud[12]	107	62	45	58%	90			
Solothurn[13]	137	111	26	82%				
Basel[14]	190	181	9	95%				
Fribourg[15]	162	103	59	64%				
Geneva[16]	477	334	83	70%	141			
Neuchâtel[17]	341	259	59	81%	214			
Zurich & Lucerne[18]	725				328			
Dept. Nord[19]	277	211	49	82%				
Toul[20]	67	53	14	79%				
Luxembourg[21]	547	417	130	78%	355	268	87	79%
Namur[22]	366	337	29	92%	144			
Netherlands[23]	889	711	182	80%	238	222	16	93%
(Holy Roman Empire overall)[2]	c. 100,000+				c. 50,000+			
France								
Inclusive[25]	10,000+				5,000+			
Labourd[26]	600				80			
Ardennes[27]	40	(legal)			c. 300	(illegal)		
Rethelois[28]	7,760							
Champagne[29] (1587)					50+	(illegal)		
Appeals to Paris Parlement[30]	1,123				115			
British Isles								
Essex[31]	313	290	23	92%	74			
Home Counties[32]	558+	499	59	89%	121+	112+	9	92%
England overall:[33]	2,000				c. 1,000			
Scotland[34]	3,069	2,352	409	76%	1,337+			
Ireland[35]								
Channel Isles[36]	124	(Guernsey)						
	144	(Total)		66				

	Accused				Executed			
	TOTAL	F	M	% F	TOTAL	F	M	% F
(New England)[37]	334	267		c. 78%	35	28	7	80%
Scandinavia[38]								
Norway[39]	c. 1,400			c.350				
Sweden[40]	c. 740			85%	200+			
Finland[41]	710+	325	316	50%	115+			
Denmark[42]	c. 2,000				c. 1,000			
(overall)	5,000				1,500–1,800			
Estonia[43]	205	77	116	37%	65	29	26	44%
Poland[44]					c. 15,000+			
Russia[45]								
Appeals to Moscow	99	40	59	40%	10+			
Balkans[46]								
Hungary	c. 1,600	c. 1,440	c. 160	90%	c. 472	434	38	91%
Transylvania, Wallachia, Moldavia			c. 50					
Italy								
Venice[47]	1,041			78%				
Friuli[48]	777	391	386	50%				
Sicily[49]	375+					0		
Spain								
Logroño[50]	c. 1,813				6	6		
Castile[51]	456	324	132	71%				
Catalonia					45			
Aragon[52]	159	90	69	57%				
Navarre					50			
(overall)[53]	3,687							

Notes

Prologue

1. These statistics come from the National Coalition Against Sexual Assault and the National Crime Survey of 1989.

2. Carole J. Sheffield, "Sexual Terrorism: The Social Control of Women," 186.

On wife-beating, see Susan B. Thistlethwaite, "Every Two Minutes: Battered Women and Feminist Interpretation": "All day long, every day, women are verbally intimidated, battered, injured, and killed by the men they live with. . . . All women live with male violence" (p. 302). See also Lenore E. Walker, *The Battered Woman*, passim.

On rape, see Susan Brownmiller, *Against Our Will: Men, Women, and Rape:* "Murder, assault, rape, and robbery are the Big Four of violent crimes, and rape is the fastest-rising. The volume of rapes has increased 62% over a five-year period (since 1968) as compared with a 45% rise for the other criminal acts" (pp. 190–91). Sheffield brings these figures up to date: in 1984 over 84,000 rapes were reported, an increase of 50 percent over 1975 (p. 183).

On wife-murder: Although unable to find a study of wife-murder in the United States, I include it, based on the alarming number of reports in U. S. newspapers I have read in the seven years that I have worked on this book. I illustrate it here with examples from India.

3. *New York Times*, front page, July 24, 1991.

4. Fifth International Interdisciplinary Congress on Women, *Program*, San Jose, Costa Rica, February 1993.

5. This section is based on *In Search of Answers: Indian Women's Voices from Manushi*, edited by Madhu Kishwar and Ruth Vanita, chapter 3, "Violence Against Women." This is a compilation of articles from the first five years of the publication *Manushi*.

6. Govind Kelkar and Dev Nathan, *Gender and Tribe: Women, Land and Forests in Jharkhand* (New Delhi: Kali for Women, 1991), chapter 7, "Women, Witches and Land Rights." Barat Desai, "Witch Doctor Battered Her to Death," *Indian Express*, November 27, 1992. Shahnaz Anklesaria Aiyar, "Land Feuds Behind 'Witch' Killing," *Indian Express*, February 22, 1990. N. K. Singh, "Hunting for Witches," *India Today*, December 15, 1992. My thanks to Corinne Scott for this material.

7. Kelkar and Nathan, *Gender and Tribe*, 101.

8. Daniel Maguire, "Visit to an Abortion Clinic," *National Catholic Reporter*, October 5, 1984.

9. Caroline Blackwood, *On the Perimeter* (New York: Penguin Books, 1985), 1–8.

10. Starhawk, "The Heritage of Salem," *Common Boundary*, July–August 1992, 17–20, quote on p. 17.

Introduction

1. Gerhard Schormann, *Der Spiegel* 43 (1984): 117.

2. For a critical discussion of the literature, see Anne L. Barstow, "On Studying Witchcraft as Women's History: A Historiography of the European Witch Persecutions"; H. C. Erik Midelfort, "Recent Witch Hunting Research" and "Witchcraft, Magic, and the Occult," in *Reformation Europe: A Guide to Research*, edited by Steven Ozment (St. Louis: Center for Reformation Research, 1982), and "Recent Witch Hunting Research"; E. William Monter, "The Historiography of European Witchcraft: Progress and Prospects"; and David D. Hall, "Witchcraft and the Limits of Interpretation: Essay Review."

3. Julio Caro Baroja, *The World of the Witches*, 254–57.

4. H. R. Trevor-Roper, "The European Witch-Craze of the Sixteenth and Seventeenth Centuries," first published in *Encounter*, May and June 1967, then in his *Religion, Reformation, and Social Change* (London, 1967), 90–192; reprinted in *The European Witch-Craze of the Sixteenth and Seventeenth Centuries, and Other Essays*, 90–192, esp. 126–28, 176–78, and 190–92.

5. L'Estrange Ewen's first analysis of the English Home Counties trials, for example, provided plenty of information about misogyny in the courts, but he did not mention women as a category at all. Four years later, however, while publishing further trial documentation, he briefly stated his thoughts about the victims:

> That many of the condemned women, although innocent of witchcraft, were really undesirable neighbours cannot be doubted. Mental institutes not being features of the social life, numbers of melancholics were at large, others again, mentally sound, ranked as thieves, cozeners, whores, blasphemers, blackmailers, abortionists, perhaps even poisoners. Mentally degraded, they allowed vermin and domestic animals to suck or lick their blood, although many of such recorded practices can have been nothing more than misunderstanding or hallucination. . . . At heart they were murderers, and morally as guilty as cut-throat or poisoner. But their confessions are not greatly to be relied upon, obtained as they were by deceit and

duress, and, it may be supposed, sometimes coloured by vanity. (*Witchcraft and Demonianism*, 68.)

6. Alan Macfarlane, *Witchcraft in Tudor and Stuart England*, 160; Keith Thomas, *Religion and the Decline of Magic*, 568–69.

7. H. C. Erik Midelfort, *Witch Hunting in Southwestern Germany, 1562–1684: The Social and Intellectual Foundations*, 184 (emphasis added), cf. 86–90, 183–84.

8. Although the earliest German studies pointed out the importance of the victims' gender (Wilhelm Soldan and Heinrich Heppe, *Geschichte der Hexenprozesse* [Munich, 1912]; and Joseph Hansen, *Zauberwahn, Inquisition und Hexenprozesse* [Munich, 1900]), none of the German studies that came later followed up on this point until the 1977 publication of *Aus der Zeit der Verzweiflung*, edited by Gabriele Becker, S. Bovenschen, H. Brackert, S. Brauner (Frankfurt: Suhrkamp, 1977).

9. Émile Brouette, "La sorcellerie dans le Comté de Namur au début de l'époque moderne (1509–1646)," 354–55. "*Si l'on déclare qu'on peut être antiféministe sans nécessairement brûler les sorcières, il faut bien reconnaître qu'il n'y a théologiquement qu'un pas entre le mépris de la femme et l'affirmation que celle-ci est l'intermédiare entre l'homme et la diable.*"

10. Pierre Villette, *La sorcellerie et sa répression dans le Nord de la France*, 148–49.

11. Robert Muchembled, *La sorcière au village*, 148–49, and "The Witches of the Cambrésis: The Acculturation of the World in the Sixteenth and Seventeenth Centuries."

12. H. C. Erik Midelfort, "Heartland of the Witchcraze: Central and Northern Europe," esp. 28, 30.

13. Jeffrey B. Russell, *Witchcraft in the Middle Ages*, 78–81, 145–46, 183, 201–02, and esp. 279–84.

14. Jeffrey B. Russell, *A History of Witchcraft: Sorcerers, Heretics, and Pagans*, 118. An example of Russell's confusion about women's roles in history: having admitted that the idealization of woman in the cult of the Virgin Mary had in fact "created the shadow image of the hag," Russell nevertheless laments the current decline of Mary's cult, which he sees as a step backward for Christianity.

15. Carlo Ginzburg, *The Night Battles: Witchcraft and Agrarian Cults in the Sixteenth and Seventeenth Centuries*, 1966, translated by J. Tedeschi and A. Tedeschi (Baltimore: Johns Hopkins Press, 1983).

16. Joseph Klaits, *Servants of Satan: The Age of the Witch Hunts*, chapter 3, pp. 48–75 and 94–103.

17. Joseph Klaits, comments at the American Historical Association panel "Witches as Poisoners," New York City, December 28, 1985.

18. Brian P. Levack, *The Witch-Hunt in Early Modern Europe*, chapter 5, esp. pp. 124–39.

19. E. William Monter, *Witchcraft in France and Switzerland: The Borderlands During the Reformation*, 118–24, 136–41. See also Monter's article "Pedestal and Stake: Courtly Love and Witchcraft."

20. Monter, *Witchcraft in France and Switzerland*, 196–98.

21. Christina Larner, *Enemies of God: The Witch-hunt in Scotland*, chapter 8, and pp. 51–52, 197. See also Larner's essay "Witchcraft Past and Present," 79–91, esp. 84–88.

22. Larner, *Enemies of God*, 92, 197; "Witchcraft Past and Present," 85–87.

23. Andrea Dworkin, *Woman Hating: A Radical Look at Sexuality* (New York: Dutton, 1974); Mary Daly, *Gyn/Ecology: The Metaethics of Radical Feminism* (Boston: Beacon Press, 1978). See also Barbara Ehrenreich and Dierdre English, *Witches, Midwives and Nurses: A History of Women Healers* (New York: Feminist Press, 1973).

24. Demos, *Entertaining Satan*. See also his "Underlying Themes in the Witchcraft of Seventeenth-Century New England."

25. Carol Karlsen, *The Devil in the Shape of A Woman: Witchcraft in Colonial New England*. Note how greed for a widow's property fed witchcraft accusations in both seventeenth-century New England and present-day tribal India (see the Prologue).

26. For notice of the many other studies that ignore or minimize the issue of gender, see my comments in footnotes in chapters 2, 3, and 4.

27. Marianne Hester, *Lewd Women and Wicked Witches: A Study of the Dynamics of Male Domination*.

28. Hester, *Lewd Women and Wicked Witches*, 200.

29. *Women and Work in Preindustrial Europe*, edited by Barbara A. Hanawalt, and *Women and Work in Pre-Industrial England*, edited by Lindsey Charles and Lorna Duffin.

30. Some of this discussion appeared first in the *World History Bulletin* (Spring/Summer 1988): Anne L. Barstow, "Women, Sexuality, and Oppression: The European Witchcraft Persecutions."

31. This discussion owes its genesis to Joan W. Scott's article "Gender: A Useful Category of Historical Analysis," and her collection of essays, *Gender and the Politics of History* (New York: Columbia Univ. Press, 1988). The quotation is from the article, p. 1069, emphasis mine.

32. Scott, "Gender: A Useful Category," 1067.

33. Carroll Smith-Rosenberg, *Disorderly Conduct: Visions of Gender in Victorian America*, 38.

34. Smith-Rosenberg, *Disorderly Conduct*, 19.

35. Phyllis Trible, *Texts of Terror: Literary-Feminist Readings of Biblical Narratives* (Philadelphia: Fortress Press, 1984).

Chapter 1: Why Women?

1. Joan Peterson of Wapping (London) was on trial because she had refused to give evidence against a woman whom she believed to be innocent of witchcraft; having tried unsuccessfully to use her to give false evidence, her accusers were now trying to get rid of

her. C. L'Estrange Ewen, ed., *Witch Hunting and Witch Trials: Indictments for Witchcraft from the Records of 1,373 Assizes Held for the Home Circuit, 1559–1736,* 272–76.

2. David Hall, *Witch-Hunting in Seventeenth-Century New England,* 216–17; John Demos, "Underlying Themes in the Witchcraft of Seventeenth-Century New England," 1323, based on *Massachusetts Archives,* vol. 135, 3, 13.

3. Lois Banner, "A Reply to 'Culture et Pouvoir' from the Perspective of United States Women's History"; she exempts Susan Brownmiller and Jean Elshtain from this proscription, for their works on rape and war.

4. Reginald Scot, *The Discoverie of Witchcraft* (London, 1584; reprint 1930; New York: Dover Publications, 1972). Scot did not believe in witchcraft, because it "attributeth to a witch, such divine power, as dulie and onelie apperteineth unto GOD" (p. 7). Scot's Reformation theology of the majesty of God combined with a budding interest in scientific farming to overcome the credulity that he had at first shared with contemporaries about aspects of magic. See Leland Estes, "Reginald Scot and his *Discoverie of Witchcraft:* Religion and Science in the Opposition to the European Witch Craze."

5. Henri Boguet, *Discours des sorciers* (Paris, 1602; 2d ed., Lyon, 1608), *An Examen of Witches,* translated by E. A. Ashwin, edited by M. Summers (Bungay: J. Rodker, 1929), xxvii; Nicolas Remy, *Demonolatrie* (1595), *Demonolatry,* translated by E. A. Ashwin (London, 1930; Secaucus, NJ: University Books, 1974), 109.

6. The account, taken from the Fugger Newsletter, is printed in *European Witchcraft,* edited by E. William Monter, 75–81.

7. Edward Bever gave the suspected witches a role in their victimization when he suggested that "some old women . . . defiantly or compliantly adopted the very attitudes and behaviors for which they were vilified, and hallucinated the fantastic experiences concocted by their enemies." In "Old Age and Witchcraft in Early Modern Europe," 179.

8. Edward Bever, investigating why older women predominated as victims of witchcraft accusations, concluded that an old woman might feel guilt, might have "perceived her own evil thoughts as the work of the Devil, and fabricated stories . . . to bring her confession regarding real misdeeds into line with the expectations of her examiners." In "Old Age and Witchcraft," 169.

9. This overall portrait of a woman singled out as a witch is confirmed from trial records across Europe: for example, from northern France (Robert Muchembled, *Popular Culture,* 254–60); from England (Keith Thomas, *Religion and the Decline of Magic,* 519–23); from Scotland (Christina Larner, *Enemies of God: The Witch-Hunt in Scotland,* chapter 8); from Spain (Gustav Henningsen, *The Witches' Advocate: Basque Witchcraft and the Spanish Inquisition,* chapter 2); from the Jura (Monter, *Witchcraft in France and Switzerland: The Borderlands During the Reformation,* chapter 5); from Germany (H. C. Erik Midelfort, *Witch Hunting in Southwestern Germany, 1562–1684: The Social and Intellectual Foundations,* 178–90).

10. Sir Matthew Hale, *A Tryal of Witches, at the Assizes Held at Bury St. Edmunds on March 10, 1664* (1682; London, 1838).

11. Joseph Glanvill (d. 1680), *Sadducismus Triumphatus* 4th ed. (London, 1726); Bishop Francis Hutchinson, *Essay and Two Sermons* (London, 1720).

12. Rossell H. Robbins, *Encyclopedia of Witchcraft and Demonology*, 16–17. Robbins's work, though generally useful for reference, was written before the recent spate of archival studies and therefore lacks the fuller statistics that we work from today.

13. Andrea Dworkin, *Woman Hating*, chapter 7, "Gynocide: The Witches." See also Mary Daly, *Gyn/Ecology: The Metaethics of Radical Feminism*, 208, where she claims "that hundreds of thousands—probably millions—of women were executed."

14. Gunnar Heinsohn and Otto Steiger, "Warum wurden Hexen verbrannt?" *Der Spiegel* 43 (1984): 111–28.

15. Voltaire, "Bouc," *Dictionnaire philosophique*. Voltaire refers to the victims as *"prétendues sorcières."* Bodin, *De la démonomanie des sorciers* (Paris: 1587); Boguet, *An Examen of Witches*, xxxiii–iv.

16. Joan Ringelheim, "Women and the Holocaust: Taking Numbers into Account," a paper presented to the Women in Culture and Society Seminar, Columbia University, January 1986; and "Women and the Holocaust: A Reconsideration of Research." Ringelheim found that more Jewish women than men were deported to concentration camps, and more were killed in the camps.

17. Brian P. Levack, *The Witch-Hunt in Early Modern Europe*, 19–22.

18. Larner, *Enemies of God*, 118.

19. Nicolas Remy, *Demonolatry*, 163. Monter reports six deaths by suicide in prison during the Genevan witch hunt *(Witchcraft in France and Switzerland)*, 49. A sampling of other prison suicides: in Italy in 1528, Bellezza Orsini (Margaret King, *Women of the Renaissance*, 154), and the attempted suicide of N. N. in Eichstätt, Bavaria, 1637 (see chapter 2).

20. Richard Kieckhefer, *European Witch Trials: Their Foundations in Popular and Learned Culture*, 26.

21. Kieckhefer, *European Witch Trials*, 24, 55. The Alsatian material comes from an unpublished manuscript by Bertha Merritt in the Rare Book Room at the Cornell University Library, 588 pages of trial transcripts from the Vallée de la Bruche, 1607–74: the widow Nicolle was found *"sur le lit gisante, tort le col, meurtrissures, disjonctions."*

22. Alfred Soman, "The Parlement of Paris and the Great Witch Hunt (1565–1640)," see 42–43; and "Witch Lynching at Juniville." For Scotland, Larner commented that there are "enough references to executions whose cases never reached the central authorities to raise queries about the proportion of dubiously legal to official executions, and about the validity of any figures and projections for the total numbers of witches tried and executed." Christine Larner, Christopher Lee, and Hugh McLachlan. *A Source Book of Scottish Witchcraft*, vi.

23. Levack's figures on execution rates yield an average of 47 percent of those accused, a percentage that he considers too low (Levack, *The Witch-Hunt*, 19–21).

24. Robin Briggs concluded that ". . . a reputation for witchcraft was almost impossible to lose." In "Witchcraft and Popular Mentality in Lorraine, 1580–1630," *Occult and Scientific Mentalities in the Renaissance*, ed. Brian Vickers (Cambridge: Cambridge University Press, 1984), 346.

25. Henningsen, *The Witches' Advocate*, 291–92.

26. Alan Macfarlane, *Witchcraft in Tudor and Stuart England*, 158–61. Monter, *Witchcraft in France and Switzerland*, 119–20.

27. If the chief researcher of Essex witchcraft, Alan Macfarlane, had seen the centrality of gender to some of his insights, such as why better-off villagers accused poorer women, he could have explained the high rate of female victims in Essex County. Since writing this suggestion, I have seen Marianne Hester's work on the Essex trials, chapter 8 in *Lewd Women and Wicked Witches: A Study of the Dynamics of Male Domination*. Hester concluded that women caught in specifically female types of poverty and perceived as sexually deviant were most likely to fall under witch accusations.

28. Monter, *Witchcraft in France and Switzerland*, 151–57, gives the information but does not make the connection. Causing hailstorms or other tempests was a frequent charge against witches on the continent (not in England or Scotland). These accusations provided a scapegoat for the damage done to crops by bad weather.

29. Macfarlane, *Witchcraft in Tudor and Stuart England*, 160; Kieckhefer, *European Witch Trials*, 145; Russell Zguta, "Witchcraft Trials in Seventeenth-Century Russia," 1189; Larner, *Enemies of God*, 197.

30. Rossell Hope Robbins, Introduction to *Catalogue of the Witchcraft Collection in Cornell University Library*, xxxiv; H. C. Erik Midelfort, "Heartland of the Witchcraze: Central and Northern Europe," esp. 28.

31. Monter, *Witchcraft in France and Switzerland*, 120; Angel Gari Lacruz, "Variedad de competencias en el delito de brujeria (1600–1650) en Aragon," 326. The procedures used in witch trials originated in the inquisitional courts of the Roman Catholic church during the twelfth and thirteenth centuries as part of the church's campaign against heretics. By the sixteenth century secular courts had adopted these extreme procedures, and as these courts took over jurisdiction for cases of witchcraft they applied these inquisitional procedures to them. But the church did not lose concern over witchcraft. It often initiated charges and advised secular courts in how to proceed against alleged witches. For a detailed discussion, see chapter 2.

32. Midelfort, *Witch Hunting in Southwestern Germany*, 95; Larner, *Enemies of God*, 94. Monter observed that in the Jura male witches were numerous in areas where witchcraft was thought of as heresy (heretics having been mostly male), in *Witchcraft in France and Switzerland*, 118–20.

33. Pierre Villette, *La Sorcellerie et sa repression dans le Nord de la France*, 188–89.

34. Robert Muchembled, *La sorcière au village*, 24.

35. Remy, *Demonalatry*, xxii.

36. Ewen, *Witch Hunting and Witch Trials,* passim.

37. J. A. Sharpe, *Crime in Early Modern England: 1550–1750,* 109.

38. Already in 1584 Scot described these dynamics; see *Discoverie of Witchcraft,* 5. The syndrome has been analyzed by Keith Thomas, *Religion and the Decline of Magic,* chapter 17.

39. Muchembled, *La sorcière au village,* 195–200; Larner, *Enemies of God,* 89–97; Hans Eyvind Naess, "Norway: The Criminological Context," 372–77.

40. Robert Muchembled, "The Witches of the Cambrésis: The Acculturation of the World in the Sixteenth and Seventeenth Centuries." John Webster, *The Displaying of Supposed Witchcraft* (London, 1677), 82, quoted in Thomas, *Religion and the Decline of Magic,* 561, n. 4. Sharpe, *Crime in Early Modern England,* remarks of crime in general that "the impression is of regulative laws being imposed upon the poorer members of village society by the richer. . . . Crime is to a large extent defined by groups in power" (pp. 86, 169).

41. Midelfort, *Witch Hunting in Southwestern Germany,* 187. He notes teachers, merchants, magistrates, and their wives.

42. When convicted of witchcraft themselves, the poor Pappenheimer family named the wives of a mayor, a wealthy innkeeper, and a farmer. Two years after the Pappenheimers were executed, charges against these women were dropped: "There were vehement protests against their arrest on the part of relatives, respected citizens, friends in high places" (Michael Kunze, *Highroad to the Stake,* 414).

43. See Anne Kibbey, "Mutations of the Supernatural: Witchcraft, Remarkable Providences, and the Power of Puritan Men," 125–48, esp. 147. Kibbey argues that at Salem several of the accusations were made against the wives of newly successful men by a family that was being squeezed out: "In a society where the experiences of wives and children, indeed their very lives, were mere signs of an adult male's own personal success or failure, where the identity of family dependents was a mere extension of their father/husband, conflicts between women could easily be exploited to express conflicts between the men with/by whom they were identified." Clive Holmes's material from England concurs. He found that a number of charges of sorcery by wives were covers for family feuds of their men (paper presented at the Berkshire Conference on Women's History, Wellesley College, 1988).

44. Scot, *Discoverie of Witchcraft,* 4.

45. Larner, *Enemies of God,* 97, 125; Muchembled, "Sorcières du Cambrésis," 155.

46. Muchembled, *La sorcière au Village,* 168 ff.

47. Carol Karlsen, *The Devil in the Shape of a Woman: Witchcraft in Colonial New England,* 64: they clustered mainly in the forty to sixty age range.

48. Monter, *Witchcraft in France and Switzerland,* 122–24. Genevan witches had a median age of sixty; the typical Scottish witch was middle-aged (Larner, *Enemies of God,* 98); Essex witches were likely to be between fifty and seventy (Macfarlane, *Witchcraft in Tudor and Stuart England,* 161); in Sweden, most were older married women (Ankarloo, chapter 11).

49. Sharpe, *Crime in Early Modern England,* 88. Sharpe observes the connection between formal cursing and witchcraft, in which the harmful efficacy of words delivered rit-

ualistically was widely feared, and concludes, "Scolding, like witchcraft, was one of the distinctive offences of the early modern period."

50. John Demos, *Entertaining Satan: Witchcraft and the Culture of Early Modern England.*

51. Ralph Houlbrooke, *The English Family: 1450–1700* (London: Longman, 1984), chapter 5; Jean-Louis Flandrin, *Families in Former Times: Kinship, Household, and Sexuality;* M. Mitterauer and R. Sieder, *The European Family: Patriarchy to Partnership from the Middle Ages to the Present* (Oxford: Basil Blackwell, 1982).

52. Barbara G. Walker, *The Crone: Woman of Age, Wisdom, and Power,* 137–38.

53. Scot, *Discoverie of Witchcraft,* 46, based on Heinrich Kramer and James Sprenger, *Malleus Maleficarum* 1486, translated by Montague Summers (London, 1928; New York: Dover Publications, 1971), 51; Ewen, *Witch Hunting and Witch Trials,* 283.

54. Walker, *The Crone,* 132, 137; Bever, "Old Age and Witchcraft in Early Modern Europe."

55. Laurel Kendall, *Shamans, Housewives, and Other Restless Spirits: Women in Korean Ritual Life.*

Chapter 2: The Structure of a Witch Hunt

1. Gustav Henningsen, *The Witches' Advocate,* "Epilogue," 389.

2. Bruce Lenman and Geoffrey Parker, "The State, the Community, and the Criminal Law in Early Modern Europe."

3. Lenman and Parker, "The State, the Community, and the Criminal Law," 23.

4. Christine Larner, *Enemies of God: The Witch-Hunt in Scotland,* 193–94.

5. This section is based on the research of Hans De Waardt, "At Bottom a Family Affair: Feuds and Witchcraft in Nijkerk in 1550." De Waardt develops the chapter around the accuser, Jochum Bos, not around Neele. Though this entire volume is valuable as an introduction to Dutch witchcraft, it follows the assumption that "witch-hunting is not the same as woman-hunting" (p. 33), despite the fact that it confirms that from 90 percent to 95 percent of those punished for witchcraft in the Netherlands were women.

6. At any rate, the husband believed that Neele's father-in-law disapproved of the friendship, and for some reason this carried weight with him. Perhaps Neele's father-in-law disapproved of Luyt, or maybe this patriarch of the family did not like Neele's spending time in "frivolous" friendship. In any case, the two men put an end to the women's close companionship.

7. Cunning men and witches were natural enemies, professional rivals, as it were. There is evidence from many parts of Europe that male magicians were quick to call female diviners and healers "witches." In the Netherlands, where most of the cunning persons and "witch doctors" were male, this rivalry set up a hostile dynamic of men against women.

8. A well-known physician and skeptic about witch trials, Johan Wier, observed one of Geertgen's fits after she was brought to court at Arnhem, and concluded that though the girl did not actually vomit hard objects, still the devil deceived her and everyone into thinking that she did. In *De Praestigiis Daemonum*, IV, cap. iii, f. 90–91, in *Opera Omnia* (Amsterdam, 1660). Though Wier did not believe that most of the accused in witch hunts were in fact witches, still he believed firmly in the devil. Noted by De Waardt, "At Bottom a Family Affair," 148, n. 1.

9. Twenty persons had been bewitched. Of those whose sex is known, ten were women and five were men; apparently women were more susceptible to this illness. As De Waardt observes, women were both blamed for and more susceptible to bewitchment, were both perpetrators and victims.

Ten of the twenty bewitched were under seventeen years of age, whereas all the accused witches except Neele were middle-aged (De Waardt, "At Bottom a Family Affair," 137). This age split of young accusers and older victims occurred in many witch hunts in all parts of Europe and in New England.

10. Other forms of healing and protection that the villages turned to were exorcism with holy water and Scripture, potions, having one's urine studied, and placing words of Scripture under one's butter churn. One priest claimed that he had driven out evil spirits from another cleric, except for three that got away because they could fly. De Waardt, "At Bottom a Family Affair," 138.

11. De Waardt, "At Bottom a Family Affair," 146.

12. Many alleged witches were hounded for years. We saw that Walpurga Hausmänin believed she had been seduced by the devil thirty-one years before she was brought to trial, and that she was accused of maleficium going back ten or twelve years. A particularly egregious example was the case of Eunice Cole in New England, who was pursued by the courts from 1656 to 1680, much of which time she spent in prison; although she was allowed to die a natural death (if her extreme poverty and isolation can be called natural), she was buried with a stake through her body to exorcize its evil. See Carol Karlsen, *The Devil in the Shape of a Woman: Witchcraft in Colonial New England*, pp. 52–57.

13. Wallace Notestein, *A History of Witchcraft in England*, 101–04. King James I, while king of Scotland, had written a tract (*Demonology*, 1597) refuting Reginald Scot's skepticism about witches. A true believer until late in his life, James personally intervened in the trial of the North Berwick witches, accused of trying to kill him.

14. Günther Lottes, "Popular Culture and the Early Modern State in Sixteenth-Century Germany."

15. R. I. Moore, *The Formation of a Persecuting Society: Power and Deviance in Western Europe, 950–1250*, passim.

16. Susanne Burghartz, "No Justice for Women? Delinquency in Zurich in the Later Middle Ages."

17. Carol Z. Wiener, "Sex Roles and Crime in Late Elizabethan Hertfordshire," 39.

18. Wiener, "Sex Roles and Crime."

19. Wiener, "Sex Roles and Crime"; Burghartz, "No Justice for Women?" passim.

20. Larner, *Enemies of God*, 3–4, 100–102; P. C. Hoffer and N. E. H. Hull, *Murdering Mothers: Infanticide in England and New England, 1558–1803* (New York: New York Univ. Press, 1981).

21. Larner, *Enemies of God*, 51: "It was necessary to pass a special act in 1591 in order to allow [women's] testimony in witchcraft cases."

22. Larner, *Enemies of God*, 181.

23. Thomas Potts, *The Wonderfull Discoverie of Witches in the countie of Lancaster*, 1613, edited by James Crossley (London: Chetham Society, 1845). Potts, clerk of the court at the trial, here provided the most detailed account of any English witch trial.

24. Familiars were believed to be demonic animals; they fed from a witch's body and encouraged or aided her in doing evil. Cats, dogs, and toads were frequent familiars.

25. The record of the later 1633 trial stated that Jennet Device had a half-brother William Device, who could have been Elizabeth's illegitimate child or John Device's child from another marriage. See Peel and Southern, *The Trials of the Lancashire Witches*, 45, 97.

26. The two novelists are William H. Ainsworth, *The Lancashire Witches* (1848) and Robert Neill, *Mist Over Pendle* (1951).

27. The largest number hanged had been at St. Osyth, Essex, in 1582, when between thirteen and eighteen persons were put to death (Notestein, *History of Witchcraft in England*, 388).

28. In witchcraft cases, the willingness of courts to accept evidence of children was remarkable. In the Basque areas of Spain and France, in Scotland (see chapter 5), Sweden, Germany, Salem in New England, and in Franche-Comté, major witch hunts rested on the charges of children. An early and notorious case occurred in Franche-Comté, where the judge Boguet began his career as a witch hunter in 1598 on the testimony of an eight-year-old girl. Although he quoted the maxim that the devil is interested only in those past puberty, still, he condemned young children, believing that once possessed no one could struggle free of the devil's hold. But he also valued children's words, as when young Loyse Maillat claimed she had been bewitched by a woman who happened to walk by Loyse's window. Boguet tortured the woman until she named many accomplices, thereby launching Boguet on his career (Boguet, *An Examen of Witches*, 234, chapters 1–5).

29. A young woman, Grace Sowerbutts, of nearby Salmesbury, had accused three women of tormenting her for the past several years. Although she brought three men as witnesses, the court found no grounds for a witchcraft charge. At this point the women pressed her: who had put her up to these lies? Upon examination she admitted that a Catholic priest had done so. Though the court was able to see through this set of charges in Sowerbutts's case, it went for the "death by bewitchment" stories in the major trial.

30. Another example of class prejudice occurred in the trial at Warboys, Lincolnshire, in 1593. See "The most strange and admirable discoverie of the three witches of Warboys," 1593, described in Richard Boulton's *Complete History of Magic*, 1715, 1:49–152. A young girl from the prominent Throckmorton family, suffering from an illness, cried out against

a poor, aged neighbor, Alice Samuel, who happened to drop by her house. Her parents ignored this, but when the doctor asked if witchcraft was suspected and when four more of their daughters fell ill and seven servants as well, Mr. and Mrs. Throckmorton allowed Mother Samuel to be brought before the children, who promptly fell into fits. Old Mrs. Samuel was thereafter kept at the Throckmorton home in semi-imprisonment.

One day Lady Cromwell, wife of the richest commoner in England, called, and encountering Mrs. Samuel, accused her of witchcraft. The reply ("Madam, why do you use me thus? I never did you any harm, as yet") was held against her, and when Lady Cromwell sickened and died, the case against Mother Samuel took shape. After a year of living with the afflicted girls, during which they became possessed on sight of her and desisted on cue, she became convinced that she *was* a witch, and confessed, even naming her familiars, three chickens, Pluck, Catch, and White. By this time the Cromwells had implicated her aged husband and grown daughter as well, and all three were brought to trial and condemned. After their hangings, Lord Henry Cromwell seized their goods.

31. Peel, *Trial of the Lancashire Witches*, 94–99.

32. Notestein, *History of Witchcraft in England*, 146–56.

33. Bernard Hamilton, *The Medieval Inquisition*. Henry Kamen's work on the Spanish Inquisition reminds us, however, that some inquisitional processes were different from others. The priest Francisco Pena, for example, maintained that the Spanish Inquisition's main goal was not to save souls but "to achieve the public good and put fear into others." In Kamen, *Inquisition and Society in Spain in the Sixteenth and Seventeenth Centuries*, chapter 9, quote from p. 161.

34. Henry C. Lea, *Torture.*

35. This passage is based on Henry C. Lea, *Materials Toward a History of Witchcraft*, vol. 3, 1129–30, 1135, 1137–40.

36. Rossell Hope Robbins, *The Encyclopedia of Witchcraft and Demonology*, 148–156. Of this trial, Robbins wrote that "the procedure follows every approved cliche of witchdom. . . . For any reader who wants to understand [the persecution of] witchcraft, this record gives a very clear introduction." The report was written down during the trial by the official court scribe.

37. Lea, 1130, 1137–40. Anna's husband stood by her, sending her a letter in which he affirmed her innocence. Her priest also tried to help her, reporting to the court that she maintained that her confession was extorted by torture and the persons she had named were innocent; the court responded by torturing her all the more.

38. Lea, *Materials*, 1143–48; Midelfort, *Witch Hunting in Southwestern Germany 1562–1684: The Social and Intellectual Foundations*, 126–31.

39. The Rat was made up of representatives from the guilds and the merchants, with the two priests of the town as ex-officio.

40. The following month (January 1630) a mentally defective man was sent to Offenburg for trial and was executed (Lea, *Materials*, 1159). But no more of Offenburg's own were condemned as witches.

41. In 1627 "Brenn Catherin was admonished to confess by the priest, but she still insists on her innocence" (Midelfort, *Witch Hunting in Southwestern Germany,* 128); however, Lea believed that when priests intervened, it was usually on behalf of the accused. In 1629, priests asked for pay because they had to labor with many executions (Lea, *Materials,* 1157).

Chapter 3: Witchcraze in the Central Regions

1. Richard S. Dunn, *The Age of Religious Wars: 1559–1715,* 8–9.

2. For example, on central government: Ephraim Mizruchi, "Compulsory Apprenticeship and Education: The Quintessence of Control" (England, post-1562), in Mizruchi, *Regulating Society: Beguines, Bohemians, and Other Marginals;* Joseph Klaits, *Servants of Satan: The Age of the Witch Hunts,* on German governmental intervention, 137–47.

On religion: John Bossy, "The Counter-Reformation and the People of Catholic Europe," 51–70; Brian Levack, *The Witch-Hunt in Early Modern Europe,* 96–102; Robert Muchembled, "The Witches of the Cambrésis: The Acculturation of the World in the Sixteenth and Seventeenth Centuries," 259–67; Klaits, *Servants of Satan,* 59–65.

3. H. C. Erik Midelfort, "Heartland of the Witchcraze: Central and Northern Europe." The Holy Roman Empire was made up of three hundred separate political units, covering what is now Germany, Switzerland, Austria, the Low Countries, and parts of France, Poland, Czechoslovakia, and Italy; loosely controlled, they could not be disciplined when witch hunts broke out. Within Germany, the heaviest prosecutions took place in the southwest, the northern duchy of Mecklenburg, and the ecclesiastical duchies of Trier and Fulda. The larger, politically more coherent duchies of the north and east, along with Bavaria, also hunted witches but were able to limit the number of victims (Gerhard Schormann, *Hexenprozesse in Deutschland).*

4. H. C. Erik Midelfort, *Witch Hunting in Southwestern Germany, 1562–1684: The Social and Intellectual Foundations,* 179. Lea concluded, "It was especially in the territories of the prince-bishops of Germany that the persecution was the cruelest" *(Materials Toward a History of Witchcraft,* 1131).

5. Midelfort, "Heartland of the Witchcraze," 28.

6. Midelfort, *Witch Hunting in Southwestern Germany,* chapter 6 and p. 182.

7. Stuart Clark, "Protestant Demonology: Sin, Superstition, and Society," in *Early Modern European Witchcraft: Centres and Peripheries,* edited by Bengt Ankarloo and Gustav Henningsen, 45–82; Midelfort, *Witch Hunting in Southwestern Germany,* 36–56.

8. Günther Lottes, "Popular Culture and the Early Modern State in Sixteenth-Century Germany," 179.

9. Sigrid Brauner, "Martin Luther on Witchcraft: A True Reformer?"; Jane D. Douglass, "Women and the Continental Reformation," in *Religion and Sexism,* edited by Rosemary Ruether (New York: Simon & Schuster), 1974. For a revisionist view, see Allison Coudert, "The Myth of the Improved Status of Protestant Women: The Case of the

Witchcraze," in *The Politics of Gender in Early Modern Europe,* edited by Jean R. Brink, Allison P. Coudert, and Maryanne C. Horowitz, 61–89.

10. Elaine Camerlynck, "Féminité et sorcellerie chez les théoriciens de la démonologie a la fin du Moyen Age: Etude du 'Malleus Maleficarum.'"

11. Despite the old canard about Luther's having been fathered by the devil! (Schormann, *Hexenprozesse in Deutschland,* 159). On the subject of "blaming" a type of belief for witchcraft persecutions, note David Hall's conclusion: "The fact that witch-hunting flourished in very different religious cultures should make us wary of imputing great significance to any one set of beliefs." "Witchcraft and the Limits of Interpretation," 273.

12. Klaits, *Servants of Satan,* chapter 3.

13. Midelfort, *Witch Hunting in Southwestern Germany,* 22–24.

14. Further parallels: the devil's mark as baptism, the pact as confirmation, surrender to the demon rather than Christ, even the magical sabbat journey to worship the Great Devil as a parallel to the mystic's ascent to the highest heaven to see the face of God.

15. Richard Kieckhefer, *Repression of Heresy in Medieval German,* 107.

16. Heinrich Kramer and James Sprenger, *Malleus Maleficarum* (1486), translated by Montague Summers (London, 1928; New York: Dover Publications, 1971). The quotation is from p. 47. Though these ideas were not original to Kramer and Sprenger, they were brought together by them in a useful handbook that gave clear instructions about how to identify and convict a witch. With papal backing, the *Malleus* had a long, influential history, going through twenty-nine editions in its first two hundred years (see appendix A).

17. Kieckhefer, *Repression of Heresy in Medieval Germany,* 105–6.

18. Midelfort, *Witch Hunting in Southwestern Germany,* 93–94.

19. Poliakov, Leon. *A History of Antisemitism.*

20. Two authors make this point with illustrations from Spain, but it applies equally to northern Europe: H. R. Trevor-Roper, *The European Witch-Craze of the Sixteenth and Seventeenth Centuries, and Other Essays,* 110–15 (referring only to "witches," not to women); Harriet Goldberg, "Two Parallel Medieval Commonplaces: Antifeminism and Antisemitism in the Hispanic Literary Tradition."

21. Joshua Trachtenberg, *The Devil and the Jews: The Medieval Conception of the Jew and Its Relation to Modern Anti-Semitism,* chapter 4 and p. 122.

22. Guibert of Nogent, *Self and Society in Medieval France: the Memoirs of Abbot Guibert of Nogent,* edited and translated by J. F. Benson (New York, 1970).

23. Goldberg, "Two Parallel Medieval Commonplaces," 90.

24. Lea, *Materials,* 1253.

25. Poliakov, *History of Antisemitism.*

26. Trevor-Roper, *European Witch-Craze.* See also Klaits, *Servants of Satan,* 19: "Charges that early in the period (1100–1700) were directed against heretics, homosexuals, Jews, and magicians were later applied in modified form to people labelled as witches."

E. William Monter also confirms the scapegoating cycle from Jews to witches, by 1550, and then back to Jews by 1750, in *Ritual, Myth, and Magic in Early Modern Europe* (Athens: Ohio Univ. Press, 1984).

27. Lottes, "Popular Culture and the Early Modern State"; David Warren Sabean, *Power in the Blood: Popular Culture and Village Discourse in Early Modern Germany* (Cambridge: Cambridge Univ. Press, 1984), introduction.

28. Robin Briggs, "Witchcraft and Popular Mentality in Lorraine, 1580–1630," 341. For Alsace, see Henri Hiegel, *Le Bailliage d'Allemagne de 1600 à 1632* (Sarreguemines, 1961); and Bertha Merritt, unpublished manuscript on trials in the Vallée de la Bruche (Andrew Dickson White Collection, Cornell University). None of these authors makes a gender analysis.

29. Remy, *Demonolatry*, 92–94, 109, 103, 146–61; the quote is from p. 90.

30. Remy, *Demonolatry*, 4, 82–83, 43–66. Étienne Delcambre's superb study of witchcraft in Lorraine, *Le Concept de la sorcellerie dans le duché de Lorraine* (3 vols.) collects much evidence to support Remy's connection of sexuality and the sabbat: "*le Diable lorrain oublié donc parfois qu'il est pur esprit et s'avère un authentique Don Juan*" ("the Lorraine Devil forgets sometimes that he is pure spirit and proves to be an authentic Don Juan") (vol. 1, p. 72). Belief in the devil's role in maleficium was pervasive, freely confessed by the accused, avidly proclaimed by Remy and his judges. Lorrainers' descriptions of receiving the mark of the devil are unsurpassed in the literature of witchcraft, replete with descriptions of Satan's brutality.

31. E. William Monter, *Witchcraft in France and Switzerland: The Borderlands During the Reformation*, chapter 3, esp. 83.

32. Boguet, *An Examen of Witches*, 234.

33. Boguet, *Examen of Witches*, 131, 233, 234.

34. Boguet, *Examen of Witches*, 29, 28, 141, 88.

35. Monter, *Witchcraft in France and Switzerland*, 72–74.

36. Marie-Sylvie Dupont-Bouchat et al., *Prophètes et sorciers dans les pays-Bas, XVIe-XVIIIe siècle*, part 1, "Repression de la sorcellerie dans le duché de Luxembourg aux XVIe et XVIIe siècles" ("Repression of sorcery in the duchy of Luxembourg in the sixteenth and seventeenth centuries"), 138.

37. Martin Del Rio, *Disquisitionum Magicarum libri sex* (Louvain, 1599); French translation by A. Duchesne, *Les controversies et recherches magiques de Martin Del Rio* (Paris, 1611); Peter Binsfeld, *Tractatus de confessionibus maleficorum et sagarum* (Trier: Henry Bock, n.d.). Binsfeld, who inspired the mass killings at Trier, stressed the use of repeated torture and secret agents.

38. Dupont-Bouchat, *Prophètes et sorciers*, 137–38.

39. Dupont-Bouchat, *Prophètes et sorciers*, 142–44. "*Sorcellerie et sexualité son intimement liées, que se soit dans l'esprit des inqusiteurs or dans le sadisme des juges et des bourreaux*" ("Sorcery and sexuality are intimately bound, whether it be in the mind of inquisitors or in the sadism of judges and torturers"), 142.

40. Bohdan Baranowski, *Procesy Czarownic w Polsce w XVII:XVIII wieku* (French résumé; Lodz, 1952).

41. Poland had in fact been known earlier as a beacon of tolerance, for while western Europe had been torn with religious wars in the sixteenth century, Poland had worked out a policy of religious pluralism. But wars with Sweden and Russia in the mid-seventeenth century devastated the country, leaving the royal government weakened. Thereafter there was no stopping the witch hunt, which thrived in the municipal courts where inquisitional procedures and the unrestrained use of torture ensured large numbers of victims. See Janusz Tazbir, *A State Without Stakes: Polish Religious Toleration in the Sixteenth and Seventeenth Centuries.*

42. Tazbir, *State Without Stakes,* chapter 12. As for the rural population, it lost its freedom in the sixteenth century. Serfdom, coming late to Poland, established itself there only as it ended in western Europe. As landowners began to encroach on free farmer's prerogatives, the peasants, unarmed and without political rights, got even by terrorizing their masters. They threatened overbearing lords with black magic, a tactic for which they paid with their lives at the stake (Baranowski, *Procesy Czarownic w Polsce,* 181). Lottes reports that they tried strikes, slowdowns, running away, lawsuits, and threats, but still ended up in the nobles' dungeons ("Popular Culture and the Early Modern State").

43. Monter, *Witchcraft in France and Switzerland,* 49, 105–6.

44. Monter, *Witchcraft in France and Switzerland,* 50, 52–56, 106–7. Protestant Swiss considered the devil's mark an important feature of the witch hunt, as did Protestants elsewhere; their stress on the pact that each individual agreed to with the devil made the mark, as physical proof of the pact, a sure sign of witchery. Yet this very emphasis on the individual's relationship with Satan worked against the concept of a mass conspiracy of witches. Further restraints were the refusal of judges to accept children's testimony and the legal, that is, limited, use of torture, making it possible for most women and about half the men accused to withstand torture and not confess (157–59).

45. In other ways, however, Swiss witchcraft was close in type to Germany's. Many trials grew out of panics, smaller than the German mass manias, to be sure, but major persecutions nonetheless. Like the German lands, Switzerland followed the Holy Roman Empire's "Carolina" code, utilizing torture to force suspects to name names, and it emphasized the sabbat, both factors that unfailingly produced large numbers of suspects.

46. E. William Monter, "La sodomie à l'époque moderne en Suisse romande."

47. Monter, *Witchcraft in France and Switzerland,* 119, 196–98 and n. 14, 141.

48. Seventy-year-old Aldegonde, who had voluntarily turned herself in—in order to clear her name of witchcraft—was strangled and burned.

49. Alfred Soman, "The Parlement of Paris and the Great Witch Hunt (1565–1640)."

50. John Bossy, "The Counter-Reformation and the People of Catholic Europe," 54.

51. Robert Muchembled, *La Sorcière au village,* 130–37.

52. Pierre Villette, *La sorcellerie et sa répression dans le Nord de la France,* 47 and chapter 2; Robert Muchembled, *Popular Culture and Elite Culture in France, 1400–1750,* 247–51.

53. Robert Muchembled, *La Sorcière au village*, 169–73, 195–200, 158–60; and "Witches of the Cambrésis," 262–68.

54. Robert Mandrou, *Magistrats et sorciers en France au XVIIe siècle.* Witch hunting in this region was begun by the church, however, specifically by inquisitors, who in 1459–60 in Arras seized a woman as a heresy suspect. What is important about the case is that she and her co-conspirators were charged with flying to a meeting with the devil, who was in human form, worshiping him by kissing his buttocks, sharing a feast, and having sex with one another. By adding the concept of a mass meeting, thus implying an organized group of witches, to folklore about the devil, these trials launched the idea of the "sabbat" on its spectacular career, a concept that produced the main "conspiracy" theories of witchcraft in the sixteenth century. See Norman Cohn, *Europe's Inner Demons: An Inquiry Inspired by the Great Witch Hunt*, chapters 1–3, 12.

55. Fifteen-year-old Marie de Marigrane, for example, said she had often seen the devil have intercourse with "une infinité de femmes," whom she named. Jeannette d'Abadie, sixteen years old, had seen men and women mix promiscuously, doing all that nature abhors—committing incest, the penitent coupling with the confessor. The teenagers assured de Lancre that the devil picked the loveliest women as they danced, preferring to have sex with married women rather than girls, and that the friends of Satan took singular pleasure in talking about the times he made love to them. Pierre de Lancre, *Tableau de L'Inconstance des Mauvais Anges et Demons* (Paris, 1613) (see appendix A). His description of the sabbat runs through books 2 and 3; these items are found on pp. 218–23.

56. Believing totally in magic, he published instructions on how to practice divination and perform countermagic (to counter a witch's maleficium): de Lancre, *L'Incrédulité et mescreance du Sortilège plainement convainçue* (Paris, 1622) (see appendix A). The harshness of his interrogations, six hundred tortured, and the number of his executions, eighty in four months, contrast sharply with the leniency of the Spanish inquisitors on the southern side of the Pyrenees. In his severity he is typical of French civil judges. He published his two books in order to criticize the leniency of the Spanish Inquisition, which banished rather than burned, and he believed fervently that civil justice, because of its harshness, could carry out God's work better than ecclesiastical courts: Margaret M. McGowan, "Pierre de Lancre's *Tableau de L'Inconstance des Mauvais Anges et Démons: The Sabbat Sensationalized*," 194.

57. I. M. Lewis, *Ecstatic Religion: An Anthropological Study of Spirit Possession and Shamanism;* Erika Bourguignon, *Possession.*

58. *Case Studies in Spirit Possession*, edited by Vincent Crapanzano and Vivien Garrison (New York, 1973); Alfred Métraux, *Voodoo in Haiti;* Karen Brown, *Mama Lola: A Voodoo Priestess in Brooklyn* (Berkeley: Univ. of California Press, 1991); Laurel Kendall, *Shamans, Housewives, and Other Restless Spirits: Women in Korean Ritual Life;* Felicitas D. Goodman, *How About Demons? Possession and Exorcism in the Modern World;* "Julia, the Diviner," in *Unspoken Worlds*, edited by Nancy Falk and Rita Gross (San Francisco: Harper & Row), 1980.

59. Anne L. Barstow, *Joan of Arc: Heretic, Mystic, Shaman*, chapters 4 and 5.

60. The first three were discussed by Jules Michelet, *La Sorcière* (English translation by A. Allinson, *Satanism and Witchcraft: A Study in Medieval Superstition).* For more on Aix, see Sebastien Michaëlis, *Histoire admirable de possession et conversion d'une penitente* (Paris, 1613), translated by W. B., *The Admirable Historie of the Possession and Conversion of a Penitent Woman* (London, 1613). On Loudun, see Aldous Huxley, *The Devils of Loudun.* On Louviers, see Madeleine Bavent, *Confessions* (1648; translated by M. Summers, 1933). On Lille, see Robert Mandrou, *Magistrats et sorciers en France au XVIIe siècle,* 209–10, and D. P. Walker, *Unclean Spirits: Possession and Exorcism in France and England in the Late Sixteenth and Early Seventeenth Centuries.*

61. Robert Mandrou, *Possession et sorcellerie au XVIIe siècle: Textes inédits,* 404–23.

62. I know of only one other positive and one probable case in which lesbianism and witchcraft charges were conflated; they will be discussed in chapter 7.

63. Étienne Delcambre and Jean Lhermitte, *Un Cas énigmatique de possession diabolique en Lorraine au XVIIe siècle: Elisabeth de Ranfaing, l'énergumène de Nancy, fondatrice de l'ordre de Refuge.*

64. Soman, "Parlement of Paris and the Great Witch Hunt."

65. A jurist, social theorist, political philosopher, and influential writer on the witchcraze, Bodin is difficult to place in European intellectual history. Tolerant to the point of concluding that there was truth in all the major religions, he yet wrote one of the most inflammatory treatises on witch hunting, advocating torture of children and the death sentence even if clear evidence was lacking, and concluding that no punishment was cruel enough, given the monstrous threat that witches posed to Christian civilization.

Chapter 4: Witch Hunts on the Periphery

1. Michael MacDonald, *Mystical Bedlam: Madness, Anxiety, and Healing in Seventeenth-Century England,* 107–8. Taken from the diary of Rev. Richard Napier, folk healer.

2. Keith Thomas, *Religion and the Decline of Magic,* chapter 17; Alan Macfarlane, *Witchcraft in Tudor and Stuart England,* chapters 10–16, esp. chapter 15.

3. The one large outbreak, when Matthew Hopkins terrorized Essex and the surrounding area, occurred during the Puritan Revolution while central authorities were occupied with more pressing matters. The peculiarities of English witch hunting reflect the local, rural character of the trials and the Protestant background: accusations of cursing and defamation were frequent, and searching the victim's bodies for the devil's mark or teat (implying the victim's individual relation with Satan) was important, providing jobs for numbers of professional prickers (Thomas, *Religion and the Decline of Magic,* 502–12).

4. Rossell Hope Robbins, *The Encyclopedia* of Witchcraft and Demonology, 530.

5. Alan Anderson and Raymond Gordon, "Witchcraft and the Status of Women—the Case of England."

6. From a large literature I will mention J. K. Swales and Hugh V. McLachlan, "Witchcraft and the Status of Women: A Comment"; Retha M. Warnicke, *Women of the English Renaissance and Reformation* (Westport, CT: Greenwood Press, 1983); Antonia Fraser, *The Weaker Vessel.*

7. Swales and McLachlan, "Witchcraft and the Status of Women."

8. Christina Larner, *Enemies of God: The Witch-Hunt in Scotland*, 63, 197, 71, 201. Larner believed that the Scots' Calvinism forced them to turn to belief in witchcraft. Believing that God punished sin with affliction, these Protestants looked for a way out of connecting their illnesses or bad luck with their sinfulness, and witch beliefs offered them an alternative. She added that their strong belief in the concept of covenant—that they were God's covenanted people—accounted for their concern over pacts or covenants with Satan and their extraordinary descriptions of sabbats, one of which will be analyzed below.

9. Larner, *Enemies of God*, 102.

10. Larner, *Enemies of God*, chapter 8, esp. pp. 92, 93, 102.

11. After this notorious formative case in the fourteenth century (Richard de Ledrede, bishop of Ossary, c. 1350, *A Contemporary Narrative of Proceedings Against Dame Alice Kyteler, for Sorcery in 1324* [London, 1843]), the Irish engaged in only sporadic, mild witch hunting, following the English model of individual trials for maleficium. Much more work needs to be done on Irish witchcraft; having a rich store of magical beliefs and practices, Ireland probably eventually developed an antiwitch culture. But the one book on the subject, St. John Seymour's *Irish Witchcraft and Demonology*, tells us little.

12. Seymour, *Irish Witchcraft and Demonology*. Some of the charges involved shape-shifting; see appendix C.

13. There was almost no witch hunting in the British colonies outside New England. There were *no* executions for witchcraft in Spanish or French America, an astonishing fact, given the widespread practice of magic among all three segments of the population, the indigenous people, African-Americans, and European-Americans. The presence of inquisitional courts (in Central and South America at least) made it likely that demonic theories of witchcraft would spread, yet there was no witch hunt. (For Brazil, see *O diablo e a terra de Santa Cruz* by Laura de Mello e Souza. My thanks to A. J. R. Russell-Wood for an English summary of this important first study of Brazilian witchcraft and popular religion.) There were trials, to be sure, but the heaviest penalties were lashings and assignment to the galleys. This clemency needs further study; for a beginning, see E. William Monter, *Ritual, Myth, and Magic in Early Modern Europe*, chapter 6.

14. John Demos, *Entertaining Satan: Witchcraft and the Culture of Early New England.*

15. Boyer and Nissenbaum, in *Salem Possessed: The Social Origins of Witchcraft*, show how rivalry for land divided the leading families and triggered witch accusations among them.

16. Marion L. Starkey, *The Devil in Massachusetts.*

17. Charles W. Upham, *Salem Witchcraft: With an Account of Salem Village* (1867).

18. Carol Karlsen, *The Devil in the Shape of a Woman: Witchcraft in Colonial New England.*

19. Karlsen's point is so important for understanding the economic bias against women in witchcraft cases that I have searched the European records for parallels. Finding few, I conclude that New England men were extraordinarily obsessed with property

ownership. I did find a particularly tragic parallel from Luxembourg: When Jean Kirstgen, owner of a comfortable fortune, was put to death for sorcery in 1607, all his possessions were confiscated by the archduke; his wife Isabeau had to go deeply in debt in order to buy back even part of their goods. Two years later *she* was declared a sorceress and was in turn executed; everything that she owned was taken by the state. Their deaths left six orphans, four very young, who were not only destitute but who had to live in fear that they would be killed also (Marie-Sylvie Dupont-Bouchat, et al., *Prophètes et sorciers dans les pays-Bas, XVIe–XVIIIe siècle,* 139–40). In this case it was not one woman but a well-to-do family that was singled out for destruction, but the motive and the method were the same: to gain wealth by means of witchcraft accusation.

20. Laurel Thatcher Ulrich, *Good Wives: Image and Reality in the Lives of Women in Northern New England,* 94–99.

21. George L. Haskins, *Law and Authority in Early Massachusetts: A Study in Tradition and Design,* 145–46, 124–25.

22. Thomas Bromhall, *A Treatise of Specters* (London, 1658). See also Demos, *Entertaining Satan,* 11–13.

23. Russell Zguta, "Witchcraft Trials in Seventeenth-Century Russia."

24. Norman Cohn argued there were *no* witch persecutions in Orthodox areas (*Europe's Inner Demons: An Inquiry Inspired by the Great Witch Hunt,* 253). His view is corrected by Zguta and by Gerhard Schormann, *Hexenprozesse in Deutschland,* 6: persecutions were few, but they did occur. The lack of a central papal authority to enforce a witch hunt has been argued as the reason for this mildness (Sigmund von Riezler, *Geschichte der Hexenprozesse in Bayern,* 51) but the absence of a witchcraze in Italy, the land most closely controlled by the papacy, belies this theory. In order to understand how the Orthodox lands avoided the witchcraze, more investigation needs to be made into the Orthodox church's beliefs regarding witchcraft, its relationship to the state, its attitudes toward women, and folk religion among its people.

25. Zguta, "Witchcraft Trials in Seventeenth-Century Russia," 1189, 1193, 1201. Old women may have been singled out for sacrifice because in a time of scarcity they were seen as unproductive, as expendable. But if so, why not old men too?

26. Eve Levin, *Sex and Society in the World of the Orthodox Slavs, 900–1700* (Ithaca: Cornell Univ. Press, 1989). The following section is based on Levin's book, which is an invaluable addition to women's history, the social history of the Slavs being seldom written about in a western European language.

27. Levin, *Sex and Society,* 237.

28. Zguta, "Witchcraft Trials in Seventeenth-Century Russia," 1206, based on George P. Fedotov, *The Russian Religious Mind: Kievan Christianity, the Tenth to the Thirteenth Centuries* (New York, 1960), chapters 1, 12.

29. Margaret A. Murray, *The Witch-Cult in Western Europe: A Study in Anthropology* and *The God of the Witches.*

30. Hans Eyvind Naess, "Norway: The Criminological Context," 377–78, see also 367–82.

31. Levack, 189–91.

32. J. C. V. Johansen, "Denmark: The Sociology of Accusations," 346, see also 339–66.

33. Grethe Jacobsen, "Nordic Women and the Reformation," in *Women in Reformation and Counter-Reformation Europe*, edited by Sherrin Marshall, 54.

34. Bengt Ankarloo, "Sweden: The Mass Burnings (1668–76)," in Ankarloo, *Early Modern European Witchcraft*, 310, see also 285–318.

35. Kirsten Hastrup, "Sorcerers and Paganism," 383–402. Hastrup agrees essentially with Katherine Morris, who concluded that, though Iceland was rich in beliefs about magic and had powerful sorceresses, it did not convert to Christianity until late, paganism remaining an important force there into early modern times. Whereas the Christian church in northern Europe, with its negative attitude toward female sexuality and its lack of distinction between sorcery and diabolism, turned the useful sorceress into the malevolent witch, bloodthirsty and cannibalistic, the Icelandic sorceress was able to remain active (Katherine Morris, *Sorceress or Witch? The Image of Gender in Medieval Iceland and Northern Europe)*.

36. Maia Madar, "Estonia I: Werewolves and Poisoners," 257–72.

37. Gabor Klaniczay, "Hungary: The Accusations and the Universe of Popular Magic," 219–56. The earlier work on Hungary by H. C. Lea (in *A History of the Inquisition in the Middle Ages*, vol. 3, 1251–73; 1887, reprint 1955) was based only on trial records and used a much smaller statistical base.

38. Anne L. Barstow, *Joan of Arc, Heretic, Mystic, Shaman*, chapters 4 and 5. On Marguerite Porete, see Anne L. Barstow's Introduction to *The Mirror for Simple Souls*, 2d ed. (New York: Crossroad, 1990).

39. Marijke Gijswijt-Hofstra and Willem Frijhoff, eds., *Witchcraft in the Netherlands: From the Fourteenth to the Twentieth Century*, translated by R. van der Wilden-Fall.

40. The following information by Marijke Gijswijt-Hofstra comes from chapter 1 of *Witchcraft in the Netherlands*.

41. As far as I know, the attitude and actions of Catholic churches have not been surveyed.

42. Jeffrey Burton Russell, *Witchcraft in the Middle Ages*, 211–14.

43. Richard Kieckhefer, *European Witch Trials: Their Foundations in Learned and Popular Culture*, 21, 115.

44. E. William Monter and John Tedeschi, "Toward a Statistical Profile of the Italian Inquisitions, Sixteenth to Eighteenth Centuries."

45. Fortunately, this treasure trove is being worked on. See "44,000 Cases of the Spanish Inquisition (1540–1700): Analysis of a Historical Data Bank," by Jaime Contreras

and Gustav Henningsen, in Henningsen and Tedeschi, eds., *The Inquisition in Early Modern Europe*, 100–129.

46. Hansen, *Quellen*, 310–12, and *Zauberwahn*, 500–501; H. R. Trevor-Roper, *The European Witch-Craze of the Sixteenth and Seventeenth Centuries, and Other Essays*, 135.

47. Geoffrey Parker, "Some Recent Work on the Inquisition in Spain and Italy," 530.

48. Gustav Henningsen, *The Witches' Advocate: Basque Witchcraft and the Spanish Inquisition:* Julio Caro Baroja, *The World of the Witches*, chapter 13.

49. Carlo Ginzburg, *The Night Battles: Witchcraft and Agrarian Cults in the Sixteenth and Seventeenth Centuries.*

50. Ginzburg mentions similar rites elsewhere in Europe, additional to those in Friuli, in *Night Battles*, 40–61. The longevity of this theme is remarkable. On April 1, 1983, in Nara, Japan, I witnessed a Shinto-Buddhist ritual called The Killing of Winter and the Chasing of Demons, complete with banishing the evil one with blazing torches. In addition, five current examples from Russia of annual Killing of Winter rituals have been reported by Alesander Milovsky; four of them involve "killing" a male or female figure in order to ensure good crops ("The Death of Winter," *Natural History*, January 1993, 34–39).

51. Ginzburg, *Night Battles*, 28–32, 40–42, 184 n. 73.

52. E. William Monter and John Tedeschi, "Toward a Statistical Profile of the Italian Inquisitions, Sixteenth to Eighteenth Centuries," esp. 133–36.

53. O'Neil, Mary R. "*Sacerdote ovvero strione:* Ecclesiastical and Superstitious Remedies in Sixteenth-Century Italy."

54. Monter and Tedeschi, "Toward a Statistical Profile," 135–36.

55. Henry Kamen, *The Spanish Inquisition; Inquisition and Society in Spain in the Sixteenth and Seventeenth Centuries.* Kamen's work contains no gender analysis. See also Gustav Henningsen, "The Archives and the Historiography of the Spanish Inquisition," in Henningsen and Tedeschi, eds., *The Inquisition in Early Modern Europe*, 54–78.

56. Kamen, *Inquisition and Society in Spain.* Although no one was killed for witchcraft by the Inquisition after Logroño (1614), many witches were hanged by secular courts in Aragon, and forty-five were put to death at Vic in Catalonia (p. 214).

57. Sara T. Nalle has shown how this "new puritanism" worked out in the diocese of Cuenca, in *God in La Mancha: Religious Reform and the People of Cuenca, 1500–1650* (Baltimore: Johns Hopkins Univ. Press, 1992).

58. Kamen, *Inquisition and Society in Spain*, 207–8; Parker, "Some Recent Work on the Inquisition in Spain and Italy."

59. Martin de Castanega, *Tratado de las Superstitiones y Hechicherias* (1529); Kamen, *Inquisition and Society in Spain*, 210 n. 41. William Christian's research confirms the bias against women seers and magic workers; see *Apparitions in Late Medieval and Renaissance Spain* (Princeton, NJ: Princeton Univ. Press, 1981), 196–98.

60. Trevor-Roper, *European Witch-Craze*, 110–11.

Chapter 5: Women and Work

1. *The Wonderful Discoverie of the Witch-crafts of Margaret and Phillip Flower, daughters of Joan Flower, by Beaver Castle, and executed at Lincolne, March 11, 1618,* n.a., London, 1619.

2. Of the many cases throughout Europe where a mother-daughter pair were executed, I will mention the English examples: 1593 at Warboys, Mother Samuel and daughter hanged (and in this case, her husband as well); Joanna Harrison and daughter, Hertford, 1606; a grandmother, mother, and daughter killed at Lancaster in 1612; Mother Sutton and Mary Sutton in Bedford, 1613; Elizabeth Clarke and her mother in Chelmesford, c. 1645; Mother and daughter Boram hanged at Bury St. Edmunds, 1655; and late in the chronology of English persecutions, four cases in which the accused were probably let off, including one case of a widow and her two daughters at Worcester, 1669.

3. Wallace Notestein, *A History of Witchcraft in England,* 134, n. 19.

4. J. A. Sharpe, in *Crime in Early Modern England: 1550–1750,* argues that there was a class bias in justice, even at the village level, where slightly wealthier villagers began to identify with national reforms, to turn against their very poor neighbors, and to criminalize them. We saw a similar sixteenth-century process in northern France and Norway (see chapters 3 and 4 in this book).

5. David Sabean, *Power in the Blood: Popular Culture and Village Discourse in Early Modern Germany,* 32, 56–58.

6. Carlo M. Cipolla, *Before the Industrial Revolution: European Society and Economy, 1000–1700;* Richard Dunn, *The Age of Religious Wars: 1559–1715,* 8–9.

7. For England, see Sharpe, *Crime in Early Modern England,* chapter 3. For France, see Alfred Soman, "Criminal Jurisprudence in Ancien-Regime France," in *Crime and Justice in Europe and Canada,* edited by L. Knafla (Montreal, 1980). For European crime, see *Crime and the Law,* edited by B. Lenman, G. Parker, and V. Gatrell (London, 1980); Michael Weisser, *Crime and Punishment in Early Modern Europe;* Alfred Soman, "Deviance and Criminal Justice in Western Europe, 1300–1800: An Essay in Structure." All these historians confirm a higher crime rate for late sixteenth- and early seventeenth-century Europe.

8. Keith Thomas, *Religion and the Decline of Magic,* chapters 6 and 7.

9. Myron P. Guttman, *Toward the Modern Economy: Early Industry in Europe, 1500–1800* (New York: Alfred Knopf, 1988) chapter 4; Geoffrey Parker and Lesley M. Smith, eds. *The General Crisis of the Seventeenth Century* (London: Routledge & Kegan Paul, 1978), introduction.

10. From an extensive literature that argues this point, these are some of the best, and most recent, works: Barbara A. Hanawalt, ed., *Women and Work in Preindustrial Europe;* Lindsey Charles and Lorna Duffin, eds., *Women and Work in Pre-Industrial England;* Judith M. Bennett, *Women in the Medieval English Countryside* (New York: Oxford Univ. Press, 1987); Martha C. Howell, *Women's Work, the Structure of Market Production, and*

Patriarchy in Late Medieval Cities of Northern Europe; Merry E. Wiesner, *Working Women in Renaissance Germany.*

11. Diane Willen, "Women in the Public Sphere in Early Modern England," in *Sixteenth Century Journal* 4 (1988): 559.

12. Statistics for remarriage vary from region to region, but all are low. Kathryn Reyerson, "Women in Business in Medieval Montpellier," in Hanawalt, ed., *Women and Work in Preindustrial Europe,* 137, reports 5 percent of known marriages were remarriages for women; Sue Wright, "'Churmaids, Huswyfes and Hucksters': The Employment of Women in Tudor and Stuart Salisbury," in Charles and Duffin, eds., *Women and Work in Pre-Industrial England,* 111, records that "a third of the women bereaved between 1570 and 1599 remarried."

13. Maryanne Kowaleski, "Women's Work in a Market Town: Exeter in the Late Fourteenth Century," in Hanawalt, ed., *Women and Work in Preindustrial Europe,* 155–57.

14. Barbara Hanawalt has given a positive view of the economic side of medieval marriages in "Women's Contribution to the Home Economy," chapter 9 in her book *The Ties That Bound: Peasant Families in Medieval England.*

15. Natalie Z. Davis, "Women in the Crafts in Sixteenth-Century Lyon"; Michael Roberts, "'Words They Are Women, and Deeds They Are Men,'" in Charles and Duffin, eds., *Women and Work in Pre-Industrial England,* 122–80.

16. Martha C. Howell, "Women, the Family Economy, and the Structures of Market Production in Cities of Northern Europe During the Late Middle Ages," in Hanawalt, ed., *Women and Work in Preindustrial Europe,* 204, 211–14

17. Davis, "Women in the Crafts," 183.

18. Wright, "Churmaids, Huswyfes and Hucksters," 106.

19. Bennett, *Women in the Medieval English Countryside,* 127.

20. Heidi Hartmann, "Capitalism, Patriarchy, and Job Segregation by Sex," 137–69, esp. 168.

21. The same process is found in the Third World throughout the twentieth century, with equally harsh results, especially on women. See Esther Boserup, *Women's Role in Economic Development* (London: Allen & Unwin, 1970).

22. Thomas, *Religion and the Decline of Magic,* chapter 17.

23. Paul Boyer and Stephen Nissenbaum, *Salem Possessed: The Social Origins of Witchcraft,* chapters 5 and 6.

24. Carol Karlsen, *The Devil in the Shape of a Woman: Witchcraft in Colonial New England,* 84–89. For some of the documents in the case, see David Hall, *Witch-Hunting in Seventeenth-Century New England: A Documentary History,* 170–84.

25. Boyer and Nissenbaum, *Salem Possessed,* 180–81.

26. England: J. A. Sharpe, *Crime in Early Modern England,* 201. Scotland: Christina Larner, *Enemies of God: The Witch-Hunt in Scotland,* 57, 193–94, 198. Germany: Sabean, *Power in the Blood,* conclusion; and Lottes, "Popular Culture and the Early Modern State

in Sixteenth-Century Germany"; and Michael Kunze, *Highroad to the Stake: A Tale of Witchcraft*, 170–72. France: Robert Muchembled, *Popular Culture and Elite Culture in France, 1400–1750*, chapter 5 and conclusion. Spain: Contreras and Henningsen, "Forty-four Thousand Cases of the Spanish Inquisition," in Gustav Henningsen and John Tedeschi, eds., *The Inquisition in Early Modern Europe: Studies on Sources and Methods*, 115; and Geoffrey Parker, "Some Recent Work on the Inquisition in Spain and Italy," 520. Luxembourg: Marie-Sylvie Dupont-Boucher et al., *Prophètes et sorciers dans les pays-Bas, XVIe–XVIIIe siècle*, 86 ff. Venice and Naples: Monter and Tedeschi, "Toward a Statistical Profile of the Italian Inquisitions, Sixteenth to Eighteenth Centuries," 131–32.

27. Howell, "Women, the Family, and Market Production," 215. Liliane Mottu-Weber reports a similar trend in Geneva: see "Les Femmes dans la vie économique de Geneve, XVI–XVII siècles."

28. Jean H. Quataert, "The Shaping of Women's Work in Manufacturing: Guilds, Households, and the State in Central Europe, 1648–1870," 1124.

29. Kay E. Lacey, "Women and Work in Fourteenth and Fifteenth Century London," in Charles and Duffin, eds., *Women and Work in Pre-Industrial England*, 24–82.

30. Merry E. Wiesner, "Women's Defense of Their Public Role," in Mary Beth Rose, ed., *Women in the Middle Ages and Renaissance: Literary and Historical Perspectives*, 1–27, esp. 3–8.

31. Kunze, *Highroad to the Stake.*

32. Bruce Lenman and Geoffrey Parker, "The State, the Community, and the Criminal Law in Early Modern Europe," 37.

Chapter 6: From Healers into Witches

1. The phrase is Cynthia Nelson's, in "Public and Private Politics: The Middle Eastern World," see p. 556. There is widespread evidence in preindustrial societies for women's asserting power through control of magic, access to the supernatural, experiencing possession, and so on. See, for example, Lewis, *Ecstatic Religion: An Anthropological Study of Spirit Possession and Shamanism;* Karen McCarthy Brown, *Mama Lola: A Vodou Priestess in Brooklyn* (Berkeley: Univ. of California Press, 1991); Vincent Crapanzano and Vivian Garrison, eds., *Case Studies in Spirit Possession* (New York: John Wiley, 1977).

2. Nicolas Remy, *Demonolatrie*, 1595, English translation by E. A. Ashwin, *Demonolatry*, hereafter referred to as Remy. This passage is found on p. 155, where Remy laments that witches disguise their work by performing it in a Christian setting. He warns the reader to be alert to the pagan elements a witch uses, such as silence, measurements, fire, and excrement.

3. Carlo Ginzburg, *The Night Battles: Witchcraft and Agrarian Cults in the Sixteenth and Seventeenth Centuries*, 81, taken from the Archivio della Curia Arcivescouvile, Udine, S. Uffizio, 'Ab anno 1612 usque ad annum 1620 incl. N. 743 usque ad 916 incl. trial #850.

4. Edward J. Kealey, *Medieval Medicus: A Social History of Anglo-Norman Medicine;* Monica Green, "Women's Medical Practice and Health Care in Medieval Europe."

5. Keith Thomas, *Religion and the Decline of Magic*, sections on "Magic" and "Witchcraft."

6. Richard Burton, *Anatomy of Melancholy*, II.i.1 (1621); quoted in Thomas, *Religion and the Decline of Magic*, 177.

7. This is a problem in the otherwise excellent discussion by Leland Estes, "The Medical Origins of the European Witch Craze: A Hypothesis." My research into records Europe-wide indicates that (1) very few licensed or official midwives were accused, protected as they were by municipal governments, (2) few sorceresses were accused, but (3) many healers/magic-workers were; I agree with Richard Horsley's conclusion that "some, but not many of the victims . . . were sorceresses, and that a large number of the victims were wise women (and men) i.e., healers and diviners" in "Who Were the Witches? The Social Roles of the Accused in the European Witch Trials," 700.

8. Chadwick Hansen, *Witchcraft at Salem* (New York: Mentor Books, 1970), 22.

9. Boguet, *An Examen of Witches*, 75–79. See appendix A.

10. Mary O'Neil, "Magical Healing, Love Magic and the Inquisition in Sixteenth-Century Italy."

11. Richard Kieckhefer, *European Witch Trials: Their Foundations in Popular and Learned Culture*, 12.

12. D. P. Walker, *Spiritual and Demonic Magic from Ficino to Campanella* (London: Scolar Press, 1958), 205–7.

13. Wayne Shumaker, *The Occult Sciences in the Renaissance: A Study of Intellectual Patterns* (Berkeley: Univ. of California Press, 1972), 54.

14. Michael MacDonald, *Mystical Bedlam: Madness, Anxiety and Healing in Seventeenth-Century England*, 26, 107, 211.

15. George Sinclair, *Satan's Invisible World Discovered* (Edinburgh, 1685, 1871), 126. So firm was Sinclair's belief in demonic magic that he maintained that without it, "farewell all religion, all faith, all hope of a life to come." The inverse of this belief was Roger Hutchinson's "If there be a God . . . verily there is a Devil also" *(The Works of Roger Hutchinson*, edited by J. Bruce [Cambridge, 1842], 140–41).

16. O'Neil, Mary R. "Sacerdote ovvero strione. Ecclesiastical and Superstitious Remedies in Sixteenth-Century Italy," 68–69.

17. Eliane Camerlynck, "Féminité et sorcellerie chez les théoriciens de la démonologie a la fin du Moyen Age: Etude du 'Malleus Maleficarum,'" *Renaissance and Reformation* 7 (1983): 13–25.

18. Gunnar Heinsohn and Otto Steiger. "The Elimination of Medieval Birth Control and the Witch Trials of Modern Times." Eliane Camerlynck points out how the fear of midwives' demographic power influenced the authors of the *Malleus Maleficarum* to write their diatribe against them (see earlier note).

19. *Malleus Maleficarum*, 66, 140–41. See also Boguet, *An Examen of Witches*, 88–89. See appendix A.

20. Jane B. Donovan, *Women and Men Midwives: Medicine, Morality, and Misogyny in Early America*, chapter 1.

21. *Malleus Maleficarum*, 114–22. Renate Blumenfeld-Kosinski confirms that it was the midwife's control over sexuality and emergency baptism that made priests attack them. See *Not of Woman Born: Representations of Caesarian Birth in Medieval and Renaissance Culture.*

22. Arthur E. Imhoff, "From the Old Mortality Pattern to the New: A Radical Change from the Sixteenth to the Twentieth Century," 13: "In analyzing social networks of traditional peasant societies, therefore, we will no longer be surprised to find that, even after marriage, men and women were still primarily members of two distinct 'societies'—the male and the female—and stayed in close contact with their old friends and neighbors who were of the same sex and about the same age." There is ample proof of this in Emmanuel Le Roy Ladurie's *Montaillou: The Promised Land of Error* (New York: Random House, 1979), and Martine Segalen's *Love and Power in the Peasant Family.*

23. Green, "Women's Medical Practice," passim. Green does not take cognizance of the economic factor in premodern health care, that doctors were available only to townspeople and only to the better-off segment there.

24. Clary is an antispasmodic, hyssop is used with purgatives, lily is anti-inflammatory, parsley has diuretic properties, spearmint oil is an antispasmodic, pellitory root is used in dentifrices, and sage is still used to reduce sprains and swellings and for sore or ulcerated throats and bleeding gums. See Anne L. Barstow, "Women as Healers, Women as Witches."

25. Barbara Ehrenreich and Dierdre English, *Witches, Midwives, and Nurses: A History of Women Healers*, 14; Muriel J. Hughes, *Women Healers in Medieval Life and Literature*, 86–89.

26. Thomas, *Religion and the Decline of Magic*, 179, 188.

27. David Sabean, *Power in the Blood: Popular Culture and Village Discourse in Early Modern Germany* (Cambridge, 1984), chapter 6.

28. Thomas, *Religion and the Decline of Magic*, 188.

29. Le Roy Ladurie, *Montaillou*, 172–73. Based on records of an inquisition in southwestern France in 1320, Le Roy Ladurie's study is rich in material on peasant beliefs about magic, the Cathar heresy, and Christianity. Concluding, "Specifically Christian piety was always the attribute of an elite in the Middle Ages" (p. 305), Ladurie shows the remarkable degree of pagan folk practice still maintained in Christian Europe.

30. Lucy Mair, *Witchcraft*, chapter 4.

31. Ginzburg, *Night Battles*, 78.

32. Christina Larner, *Enemies of God: The Witch-hunt in Scotland*, 141–42.

33. Ginzburg, *The Night Battles*, 73. Other connections between demonism and ovens: The *Malleus* (102) recorded that a witch "named Walpurgis was notorious for her power of preserving silence (when interrogated) and used to teach other women how to achieve a like quality of silence by cooking their first-born sons in an *oven*"; and in New

York City in 1980 a mother placed her baby son in a hot oven in order to drive out demons. The child died and the mother was arrested (*New York Times*, January 3, 1980).

34. Thomas, *Religion and the Decline of Magic*, chapter 7, esp. 189.

35. Thomas, *Religion and the Decline of Magic*, 207: "They cherish the dramatic side of magical healing, the ritual acting-out of sickness, and the symbolic treatment of disease in its social context."

36. Larner concluded that in Scotland the healer "represented power at the most basic local level" *(Enemies of God*, 139).

37. George Gifford, *Dialogue Concerning Witches and Witchcraft*, 1603 (London, 1842).

38. Thomas, *Religion and the Decline of Magic*, 183, 251.

39. Ginzburg, *Night Battles*, 81; C. L'Estrange Ewen, *Witchcraft and Demonianism*, 37.

40. Ginzburg, *Night Battles*, 114, 129.

41. Remy, 150; Thomas, *Religion and the Decline of Magic*, 272.

42. At Modena in northern Italy in 1499 a woman testified that she "who knows how to heal knows how to destroy" (Ginzburg, *Night Battles*, 78). At Zurich in 1487 a woman was tried by the municipal court for diabolism, sorcery, *and curing* (Henry C. Lea, *Materials Toward a History of Witchcraft*, I.256). For Scotland, Larner observed, the healer's power "is two-edged . . . she can be dangerous" *(Enemies of God*, 138–39). See also Monter, *Witchcraft in France and Switzerland: The Borderlands During the Reformation*, 184–85.

43. Muchembled, *La Sorcière au village*, 56–59.

44. In January 1980 I attended a New Year's purification party in Port-au-Prince, Haiti, that centered around a bath of herbs; the purpose was to become clear with oneself about one's tasks for the coming year; the mood was quiet, reflective. Gathering on the patio of a well-known *mambo*, the participants all wore an item of red, a scarf or blouse. Under the guidance of a *houngan*, we shredded aromatic leaves into a tub of water, while singing songs in praise of Papa Legba, the vodoun spirit of the crossroads and of beginnings, in this case, of the New Year. A bowl of flaming liquid floated in the tub; we scooped the flames out with our hands and rubbed them on our faces and arms. As an outsider to the religion, I was then asked to leave, so I was not able to take part in the immersion ceremony.

For an analysis of another vodoun ceremony involving the bath of leaves, this time held on Christmas Eve and in a different mood, see Erika Bourguignon, *Possession* (San Francisco: Chandler and Sharp, 1976), 18–24.

45. Jeffrey Burton Russell, *Witchcraft in the Middle Ages* (Secaucus, NJ: Citadel Press, 1972), 211–14, based on Ettore Verga, "Intorno a due inediti documenti di stregoneria milanese del secolo XIV," *Rendiconti del Reale Istituto Lombardo di scienze e lettere*, series 2, vol. 32 (1899).

46. Kieckhefer, *European Witch Trials*, 21–22.

47. Stephen Wessley, "The Thirteenth-Century Guglielmites: Salvation Through Women," 289–303. Cf. the much later Anglo-American sect, the Shakers, led by Mother Ann Lee, whom they believed to be the female incarnation of God.

48. Russell, *Witchcraft in the Middle Ages* 211–14; Kieckhefer, *European Witch Trials*, 22.

49. Carlo Ginzburg, *Clues, Myths, and the Historical Method*, chapter 1.

50. In regard to Chiara, Ginzburg observes that "witchcraft can be considered a weapon of both offense and defense in the social struggle" *(Clues*, 5). To this, I would add that mysticism has both uses as well, and that here Chiara was cleverly calling on both: yes, she cast spells and, yes, she had mystical visions. It was a bold attempt to legitimize her sorcery with an overlay of Christian piety.

51. A similar process can be traced in Joan of Arc's trial before an inquisitional court, when the judges asked if she saw, touched, or smelled the "voices" that guided her, with intent to prove that they came not from God, as Joan averred, but from the devil (a not-so-subtle example: "Is there anything between their crowns and hair?"—meaning horns). See Anne L. Barstow, *Joan of Arc: Heretic, Mystic, Shaman*, chapter 4.

52. This pattern of forced confession followed by recantation appears in hundreds of trial records where torture was applied. For a trial almost identical to Chiara's in this respect, see my account of the trial of N. N. at Eichstätt in 1637 in chapter 2.

53. Monter, *Witchcraft in France and Switzerland*, 110–11 and n. 37.

54. George F. Black, *Some Unpublished Scottish Witchcraft Trials*, 4–10; Ginzburg, *Night Battles*, 53.

55. Larner, *Enemies of God*, 125–33.

56. Thomas, *Religion and the Decline of Magic*, 523.

57. Sabean, *Power in the Blood*, chapter 3.

58. Other examples of persons who drew a charge of witchcraft upon themselves by repeatedly talking about (boasting about) witches were Elizabeth Godman of New Haven and John Godfrey, a Massachusetts wanderer. Elizabeth's case was like Catherina's in that she caused chickens to die and no one wanted to speak to her; she differed in being a widow with an estate of two hundred pounds, yet she had to beg because the politically powerful man in whose home she lived, Samuel Goodyear, had borrowed most of it. John Godfrey spoke of witches to many persons and described sealing a pact with the devil; he was accused of being in two towns simultaneously. (See Hall, *Witch-hunting in Seventeenth-Century New England: A Documentary History*, 61–67 and 115–33; Karlsen, *The Devil in the Shape of a Woman: Witchcraft in Colonial New England*, 297 n. 6; and Demos, *Entertaining Satan*, chapter 2.)

59. Sabean, *Power in the Blood*, 109.

60. Remy, 112.

61. Remy, 146–48.

62. Remy, 147.

63. *A History of the Witches of Renfrewshire*, 76–79, 104, 110, 131, 151–52, 175. Including "A True Narrative of the Sufferings and Relief of a Young Girle," first published in 1698. See appendix A.

64. Robert Woodrow, *Analecta: Materials for a History of Remarkable Providence, Mostly Relating to Scotch Ministers and Christians*, 4 vols. (Edinburgh: Maitland Club, 1843), vol. 3, xxvii–xxxi.

65. Edward Fairfax, *Daemonologia: A Discourse on Witchcraft as It Was Acted in the Family of Mr. Edward Fairfax of Fuyston, Yorkshire, in 1621*; Sir Matthew Hale, *A Tryal of Witches, at the Assizes Held at Bury St. Edmunds on March 10, 1664*; Thomas Potts, *The Wonderfull Discoverie of Witches in the County of Lancaster*, vi–vii; *The Records of Salem Witchcraft Copied from Original Documents*, edited by W. E. Woodward, 1864–65 (New York: Da Capo Press, 1969).

Out of the vast secondary material on Salem, the following relate especially to the topic of the bewitched girls: Marion Starkey, *The Devil in Massachusetts*; Demos, *Entertaining Satan*; and Karlsen, *Devil in the Shape of a Woman*, chapter 7.

66. *History of the Witches of Renfrewshire*, 161.

67. Margaret's final words were recorded by a witness to the executions, Robert Wodrow, in *Analecta*, vol 3, xxviii–xxix.

68. *A History of the Witches of Renfrewshire*, 151–52.

69. Heinsohn and Steiger, "The Elimination of Medieval Birth Control." Étienne Delcambre, *Le Concept de la sorcellerie dans le duché de Lorraine*, I.139 ff.

70. Kieckhefer, *European Witch Trials*, 56, and Russell, *Witchcraft in the Middle Ages*, 260–61; Ginzburg, *Night Battles*, 81; Thomas, *Religion and the Decline of Magic*, 266, 191.

71. Ginzburg, *Night Battles*, 64, 15.

72. Thomas, *Religion and the Decline of Magic*, 267.

73. Russell, *Witchcraft in the Middle Ages*, 280–83. Russell points out that the church's exclusion of women from the priesthood forced spiritually gifted women to seek leadership roles where they could find them—in heretical groups and the practice of witchcraft.

74. On the right of Quaker women to preach and witness in public, see Elaine C. Huber, "A Woman Must Not Speak: Quaker Women in the English Left Wing," *Women of Spirit*, edited by Rosemary Ruether and Eleanor McLaughlin (New York: Simon & Schuster, 1979).

75. *A History of the Witches of Renfrewshire* (see appendix A); Sébastien Michaelis, *Histoire admirable de possession et conversion d'une penitente*, 7 (see appendix A); D. P. Walker, *Unclean Spirits: Possession and Exorcism in France and England in the Late Sixteenth and Early Seventeenth Centuries*, 23–27.

76. William Perkins, "The Good Witch Must Also Die," printed in *A Discourse of the Damned Art of Witchcraft* (Cambridge, 1608), reprinted in John Chandos, ed., *In God's Name: Examples of Preaching in England, 1534–1662*, 129–35. Emphasis mine.

77. Scot, *Discoverie*, 174 (see appendix A).

Chapter 7: Controlling Women's Bodies

1. John Demos, *Entertaining Satan: Witchcraft and the Culture of Early New England*, 180.

2. David D. Hall, *Witch-hunting in Seventeenth-Century New England: A Documentary History*, 21–23; Demos, *Entertaining Satan*, 180; Carol Karlsen, *The Devil in the Shape of a Woman: Witchcraft in Colonial New England*, 20–21, 116, 128–29.

3. Matthew Hopkins, *The Discovery of Witches*, 4.

4. Christina Larner, *Enemies of God: The Witch-hunt in Scotland*, 110–12; pricking was also practiced in Protestant Jura (Monter, *Witchcraft in France and Switzerland*, 159).

5. Ralph Gardiner, *England's Grievance Discovered in Relation to the Coal Trade*, 107; quoted in C. L'Estrange Ewen, *Witch Hunting and Witch Trials: Indictments for Witchcraft from the Records of 1,373 Assizes Held for the Home Circuit, 1559–1736*, 62–63.

6. Ewen, *Witch Hunting and Witch Trials.* That justice was finally done in this case does not lessen its ability to signify the thousands of cases in which innocent women were first terrorized and then put to death. On a second examination this woman was released, and the pricker himself was eventually hanged, but not before he had sent 220 women to their deaths, having earned twenty shillings for each conviction.

7. Sixteenth-century artists used female nudity to signify the same negative qualities as court officers did. Margaret R. Miles writes that "in the representation of woman as sensual, sinful, or threatening, whether in images of Eve, Susanna, grotesque figures, or witches, the primary pictorial device by which the problem of 'woman'—for men—is signalled is female nakedness" (*Carnal Knowing: Female Nakedness and Religious Meaning in the Christian West*, 120).

8. Lois W. Banner, "A Reply to 'Culture et Pouvoir' from the Perspective of United States Women's History," 104. Reflecting on the past twenty years of women's history, Banner observes that "we may have too much overlooked the realm of male power. By not precisely naming its full dimensions, we may have too easily allowed patriarchy to engage in that disappearing act at which it has been so adept."

9. Robert Muchembled, *Popular Culture and Elite Culture in France, 1400–1750*, 250.

10. Robert Muchembled, *La Sorcière au village*, 91; J. Français, *L'Église et la sorcellerie—suivi des documents officiels*, 144.

11. Remy, *Demonolatry*, 166; H. C. Erik Midelfort, *Witch-hunting in Southwestern Germany, 1562–1684: The Social and Intellectual Foundations*, 107–8.

12. Muchembled, *Popular Culture*, 264.

13. Gilbert Geis, "Lord Hale, Witches, and Rape." Geis points out that the same man, Matthew Hale, presided over a witch trial that condemned two women to death (at Lowestoft, 1662) and wrote the basic legal strictures on rape that are still followed in English law. The reply to Geis's article by Hugh McLachlan and J. K. Swales, in the same journal,

denies, in effect, that the witch hunts were gender-specific and argues that rape is difficult to prove. The latter point may be granted, given the bias against women in sex-related cases, but to claim that witch hunts were not woman hunting is to deny the most obvious fact about them.

14. George Lincoln Burr, ed. *Narratives of the Witchcraft Cases, 1648–1706*, 325; noted in Joseph Klaits, *Servants of Satan: The Age of the Witch Hunts*, 73.

15. Aldous Huxley, *The Devils of Loudun;* Étienne Delcambre and Jean Lhermitte, *Un Cas énigmatique de possession diabolique en Lorraine au XVIIe s.: Elisabeth de Ranfaing, l'énergumène de Nancy, fondatrice de l'ordre du Refuge;* Marie-Sylvie Dupont-Bouchat, *Prophètes et sorcières dans les pays-Bas, XVIe–XVIIIe siècle*, 142.

16. Susan Brownmiller, *Against Our Will: Men, Women, and Rape*, 91.

17. At Fribourg, Lausanne, and Ajore in Switzerland, men were arrested on charges of sodomy and witchcraft (Monter, *Witchcraft in France and Switzerland*, 135–36); Thieran Chaudan confessed that for thirty years he had been a witch, made hail, turned himself into a wolf and a fox, committed incest, and performed sodomy with his animals (pp. 156–57). Bestiality figured in Luxembourg witch trials, where three men were burned to death for sorcery and having sex with animals (Dupont-Bouchat, *Prophètes et sorcières*, 142 and n. 35).

18. Merry Wiesner, "Early Modern Midwifery: A Case Study."

19. Ewen, *Witch Hunting and Witch Trials*, 36; Dupont-Bouchat, *Prophètes et sorcières*, 142–43; Karlsen, *Devil in the Shape of a Woman*, 242.

20. Hall, *Witch-Hunting in Seventeenth-Century New England*, 28.

21. In "Warum wurden Hexen verbrannt?" two German sociologists, Gunnar Heinsohn and Otto Steiger, argue that the main cause of the witch hunts was an attack, by the church and the nobility, on midwives, because of their knowledge of birth control and abortion. The church's hostility was based on its antisexual values, whereas the nobility were concerned about how the precipitous population decline at the end of the Middle Ages weakened the work force. The former argument is valid, but the thesis about the nobles doesn't fit: by the time the witch hunt broke out (1560s) Europe's population already had risen and was in fact being controlled by enforced late marriage.

The quoted material is found on p. 123.

22. Alison Legrand: Alfred Soman, "The Parlement of Paris and the Great Witch Hunt (1565–1640)," esp. p. 38. Jehanne de Monchecourt: Muchembled, "Sorcières du Cambrèsis: L'Acculturation du monde rural aux XVIe et XVIIe siècles," 188. Elizabeth Lowys: Ewen, *Witch Hunting and Witch Trials*, 33.

23. Children as witches: Pierre Villcte, *La Sorcellerie et sa répression dans le Nord de la France*, 47, 188; Julio Caro Baroja, *The World of the Witches* (Basque), 174; Midelfort, *Witchhunting in Southwestern Germany*, 179; Monter, *Witchcraft in France and Switzerland*, 128–29; Michael Kunze, *Highroad to the Stake: A Tale of Witchcraft*, passim; Karlsen, *Devil in the Shape of a Woman*, 3, 64.

Children as accusers: Midelfort, *Witchhunting in Southwestern Germany*, 145, 160 (as young as three); Chadwick Hansen, *Witchcraft at Salem* (New York, 1969), chapters 2 and

3; Boguet, *An Examen of Witches* (see appendix A); Wallace Notestein, *History of Witchcraft in England*, 140–45, 47–51; *A History of the Witches of Renfrewshire*, passim (see appendix A).

24. Soman, "The Parlement of Paris," 34.

25. Edward Peters, *The Magician, the Witch, and the Law*, 152.

26. Matteuccia of Todi: Richard Kieckhefer, *European Witch Trials: Their Foundations in Popular and Learned Culture*, 73–74.

27. Classic descriptions of the sabbat (see appendix A for the first four): Remy, *Demonolatry*, 50–51; de Lancre, *Tableau de l'inconstance des mauvais anges et démons* (Paris, 1612), 65–168, 193–234; J. Anderson, *Confessions of the Forfar Witches* (Edinburgh, 1661); *A History of the Witches of Renfrewshire* (Paisley, 1877); David Webster, ed., *A Collection of Rare and Curious Tracts* (Edinburgh: 1820); Midelfort, *Witchhunting in Southwestern Germany*, 106; Villette, *La Sorcellerie et sa répression*, 80–81. Gustav Henningsen gives a detailed description of the Basque *aquelarre* in *The Witches' Advocate: Basque Witchcraft and the Spanish Inquisition*, 71–93; Kunze retells at length the German woman Anna Pappenheimer's recollection of a *Hexentanze*, in *Highroad to the Stake*, 274–80.

How the devil copulates: Remy, 14, 90–91; Larner, *Enemies of God*, 148–49. Women as amorous: Muchembled, *La sorcière au village*, 113.

28. *Malleus Maleficarum*, 47, 58–61 (see appendix A).

29. Pierre de Lancre, *L'Incrédulité et mescreance du sortilège plainement convaincre* (1622): *"Le pacte et convention qu'elle avoit fait avec le Diable, escrite en sang de menstrues et si horribles qu'on avait horreur de la regarder"* ("The pact and covenant that she had made with the Devil, written in menstrual blood and so horrible that it was horrifying to look at") (see appendix A). At Forfar, Scotland, Helen Guthrie confessed she had learned witchcraft from one Joannet Galloway, who gave her three bloody papers as proof of her initiation (Joseph Anderson, "The Confessions of the Forfar Witches").

30. Patricia Crawford, "Attitudes to Menstruation in Seventeenth-Century England."

31. *Aristotle's Complete and Experienc'd Midwife* (London, 1697), 96 (referred to by Crawford, 49).

32. Larner, *Enemies of God*, 93.

33. Kathryn Gravdal, "Camouflaging Rape: The Rhetoric of Sexual Violence in the Medieval Pastourelle," *Romanic Review* 76 (1985): 361–73. Gravdal notes that the history of rape in the Middle Ages has not been written. A beginning has been made, however; see John Marshall Carter, *Rape in Medieval England: An Historical and Sociological Study* (Lanham, MD: University Press of America, 1985).

34. Martine Segalen, *Love and Power in the Peasant Family*, 126–27. She quotes Sara Matthews-Grieco on this subject: "French sixteenth-century society considered the woman to be dangerous; she threatened society through her sexuality, through her association with nature and with the animal world and through her leanings towards evil."

35. Charles Carlton, "The Widow's Tale: Male Myths and Female Reality in Sixteenth- and Seventeenth-Century England," *Albion* 10.2 (1978): 127. Carlton found that

men stereotyped widows as "a figure, at best, of fun, at worst, ridicule, who was highly sexed . . . much courted, especially by virile young men."

36. Carlton, "The Widow's Tale," 126.

37. Barbara G. Walker, *The Crone: Woman of Age, Wisdom, and Power,* 141.

38. Antonia Fraser, *The Weaker Vessel,* 113.

39. *A True and Impartial Relation of the Informations Against Three Witches, viz. Temperance Lloyd, Mary Trembles, and Susanna Edwards . . . at Exon, Aug. 14, 1682* (London, 1682).

40. This point sheds light on the reaction to the current women's movement, namely, the antiwoman backlash observed in the United States since the early 1980s: the high rate of rape, wife beating, and wife murder, and the violence of part of the antiabortion movement. If the early modern witch hunts and the current backlash are interpreted together, they document the ability of patriarchal societies to punish women for asserting themselves sexually and claiming control of their own bodies.

41. Boguet, *An Examen of Witches,* 31 (see appendix A).

42. Suzanne Gaudry: Muchembled, *La Sorcière au village,* 113–14.

43. In comments ranging from the *Malleus*' "[female] insatiable carnal lust" to Boguet's "[the devil] knows that women love carnal pleasure," witch hunters reiterated the commonly held early modern view that women were highly sexed.

44. *The Witches of Renfrewshire,* 98–99; Remy, *Demonolatry,* 93–94. See appendix A.

45. I have found two references to male homosexuality combined with charges of sorcery. The first involved the devil and a male partner: in the Basque country, Martin Vizcar became a witch as a child; once he grew up, the devil seduced him, making him hemorrhage. When his wife asked him why he bled, he told her he had grazed his leg. Henningsen, *The Witches' Advocate,* 154.

The second is Monter's account of eight men arrested at Fribourg for witchcraft and sodomy (*Witchcraft in France and Switzerland,* 135–36), but this is ambiguous because the term *sodomy* was also used to cover the crime of bestiality.

46. The ecstatic fits of the laywoman Elisabeth de Ranfaing were similar, as was her charge that her doctor had bewitched her. He too was put to death; see Étienne Delcambre and Jean Lhermitte, *Un Cas énigmatique de possession diabolique.*

47. Robert Mandrou, *Magistrats et sorciers en France au XVIIe siècle,* 404–23.

48. Judith C. Brown, *Immodest Acts: The Life of a Lesbian Nun in Renaissance Italy.*

49. Brown, *Immodest Acts,* 133–34 and 165 n. 5. Lesbianism is doubly obscured in historical writings, first by the paucity of references to it (Europeans apparently did not define it as a discrete subject until the late nineteenth century) and, second, by the way current writers ignore it. Brown, who concludes that "[lesbianism] does not yet have a history" (p. 174), has made a beginning with this careful study of Benedetta Carlini.

50. Marianne Hester, *Lewd Women and Wicked Witches: A Study of the Dynamics of*

Male Domination, 182–83. Hester concluded, "In the final analysis the case of Elizabeth Bennet probably tells us that a woman who was a lesbian was accused of witchcraft."

51. *The Witches of Renfrewshire,* 104, 110, 151–52, 175 (see appendix A); Soman, "The Parlement of Paris," 40–41.

52. Remy, *Demonolatry,* 93–94; Barbara Rosen, ed., *Witchcraft,* 43.

53. Only in England in the 1600s was a near-majority (48 percent) of the accusers female (Clive Holmes, paper presented at the Berkshire Conference on Women's History, 1987), and those women were often acting on behalf of their men, who were the chief organizers of the accusations and trials.

54. Muchembled, *La Sorcière au village,* 124; Soman, "The Parlement of Paris," does not mention gender.

55. Christina Larner, "Witchcraft Past and Present," 85.

56. Larner, *Enemies of God,* 3–4, 51–52.

57. David Hall, *Worlds of Wonder, Days of Judgment.* See pp. 178–96 for a discussion of public execution as ritual in New England.

58. Kunze, *Highroad to the Stake.* The following account comes mainly from pp. 406–15. See also Wolfgang Behringer, *Hexenverfolgung in Bayern,* 242–45.

59. Kunze, *Highroad to the Stake,* 31.

60. Kunze, *Highroad to the Stake,* 407.

61. Sigmund von Riezler, *Geschichte der Hexenprozesse in Bayern* (Stuttgart, 1896, 1983). Behringer reported that the result of the Pappenheimer trial and the others it triggered was extraordinary. The trials were noted in woodcuts, newspapers, chronicles, and poems. One chronicler included these executions among the most significant events in his world chronicle (Behringer, *Hexenverfolgung in Bayern,* 242).

62. Von Riezler, *Geschichte der Hexenprozesse,* 266.

Chapter 8: Keeping Women in Their Place

1. Bonnie Anderson and Judith Zinsser, *A History of Their Own: Women in Europe,* vol. 1, xxii.

2. Anderson and Zinsser, *A History of Their Own,* 172.

3. I concur with Edward Bever, who also asked why the stereotype of woman changed "completely" from the 1500s to the 1800s. Bever concluded that "certainly there were many forces during the intervening centuries contributing to the changing status . . . but the witch hunts, protracted, brutal, and pervasive, would seem to have been a primary cause" ("Old Age and Witchcraft in Early Modern Europe," 180).

4. The acquittal rate in Scotland was high enough that an accused Scotswoman might have some hope of going free (Christina Larner, *Enemies of God: The Witch-hunt in*

Scotland, 63). On the Continent, because the accused was considered guilty by virtue of being charged, few were exonerated; banishment or death was their fate.

5. In commenting on the sexual harassment of women today, Carole Sheffield wrote, "In an era when women are indeed exercising hard-won options in areas such as employment, childbearing, and politics, they often seem to be limited in simpler choices—whether to go to the movies alone, where to walk or jog, whether to answer the door or telephone. . . . To the extent that women's personal freedom is still restricted and denied, we can continue to speak of oppression." In "Sexual Terrorism: The Social Control of Women."

6. Sheffield, "Sexual Terrorism," 171.

7. Macfarlane complains (in *Witchcraft in Tudor and Stuart England,* 84) that the one brief description he gives was "the most unusual feature" of the sixteenth-century pamphlet he worked from. I have found that many studies of witch hunts contain little or no material on what happened at the scaffold or stake, and absolutely no mention of the crowd's reaction.

8. Tom F. Driver, *The Magic of Ritual: Our Need for Liberating Rites That Transform Our Lives and Our Communities,* chapter 5. Though Driver conceives of ritual mainly in a positive, transformative sense, he notes that, like magic, its morality is determined by the practitioner.

9. Mutilating a woman's breasts occurs as an extreme form of torture in other contexts. During the conquest of the Americas, for example, some Spanish soldiers cut off the breasts of recalcitrant Native American women (Tzvetan Todorov, *The Conquest of America: The Question of the Other,* 111–15). In present-day Guatemala, human rights activist Rigoberta Menchu describes how an army soldier slit a woman's breasts as he killed her (she had refused sexual advances), in *I, Rigoberta Menchu: An Indian Woman in Guatemala* (New York: Verso Press, 1984). In Argentina, the Junta that kidnapped, tortured, and killed over twelve thousand students and workers in the late 1970s applied electric shock and cigarette butts to women's breasts; guards bit women's breasts, in one case biting off the nipple; see Frank Graziano, *Divine Violence: Spectacle, Psychosexuality, and Radical Christianity in the Argentine "Dirty War"* (Boulder, CO: Westview Press, 1992), 38–39, 155.

10. Graziano, *Divine Violence.*

11. Though these ideas are discussed throughout Graziano's book, the following pages are especially pertinent: 8, 107–26. Graziano provides no gender analysis. An article that does reflect on gender, politics, and torture in Argentina is Ximena Bunster, "Surviving Beyond Fear: Women and Torture in Latin America," in *Surviving Beyond Fear: Women, Children and Human Rights in Latin America,* Marjorie Agosin, ed. (Fredonia, NY: White Pine Press, 1993). Unfortunately, it was published too late to be used in this discussion.

12. Graziano observed of the Argentine Junta that, by projecting victimization onto a surrogate (political prisoners), it avowed the truth of "ritual violence [torture] as the efficacious means of remedying some social deficiency" *(Divine Violence,* 199).

13. Driver, *Magic of Ritual,* 97–98, working from Henri Hubert and Marc Mauss, *Sacrifice: Its Nature and Function* (1899; London: Cohen and West, 1964).

14. René Girard, *The Scapegoat.* Girard's thesis is that the ultimate scapegoat, Christ, brought a potential end to violence in history, except that the church could not live up to the gift it was thus presented with. I find the "except" too large to deal with. Important as Girard's massive analysis of violence is, it does not answer the problem of human destructiveness in history. Violence, even the violence of the Cross, breeds violence. And witch killings created more hatred and fear in European communities, not less.

15. Peggy Reeves Sanday, *Divine Hunger: Cannibalism as a Cultural System,* 149.

16. David Brion Davis observes that "Europeans of all nations continually expressed horror at the Amerindians' sadism, sodomy, idolatry, and cannibalism, but they hardly needed tutoring, as the later cantos of Dante's *Inferno* vividly show, in any conceivable sin" *(Slavery and Human Progress,* 70).

17. Sanday, *Divine Hunger,* 149.

18. Europeans sometimes gave cannibalism an erotic twist. One of the earliest European depictions of the New World showed "a cannibalistic feast in combination with open lovemaking, complete with parts of dismembered bodies dangling from trees—a kind of orgy for all appetites" (Graziano, *Divine Violence,* 176). The word *cannibal* came into European languages through Columbus's transcription of the Arawakan word *caniba* or *cariba.*

19. Macfarlane, *Witchcraft in Tudor and Stuart England,* chapters 15 and 16. Robert Muchembled, "The Witches of the Cambrésis: The Acculturation of the World in the Sixteenth and Seventeenth Centuries."

20. H. C. Erik Midelfort, *Witch Hunting in Southwestern Germany, 1562–1684: The Social and Intellectual Foundations,* 154.

21. Nazife Bashar, "Rape in England between 1550 and 1700," 40. Bashar gathered these statistics from the Assize records of England and the Quarter Sessions of the five home counties and Yorkshire. Observing that sixteenth- and seventeenth-century legal authorities and laws give the impression that rape was taken seriously, Bashar notes that the trial records contradict that.

22. Bridget Hill, *Eighteenth Century Women: An Anthology* (London: George Allen & Unwin, 1984), 255–56.

23. Jane Abray, "Feminism in the French Revolution," *American Historical Review* 80 (1975): 43–62.

24. Olympe de Gouges, "Declaration of the Rights of Woman and Citizen," in *European Women,* edited by E. Riemer and J. Fout (New York: Schocken Books, 1980), 62–67; de Gouges died on the guillotine in 1793. In England, Mary Wollstonecraft, *A Vindication of the Rights of Women,* 1792 (New York: Norton, 1967).

25. Judith Walkowitz, "The Maiden Tribute of Modern Babylon" (prostitution in late nineteenth-century London), paper presented to the Seminar on Women in Society and Culture, Columbia University.

26. Davis, *Slavery and Human Progress,* 27–30.

27. Anderson and Zinsser, *A History of Their Own,* vol. 1, 358–59: "In southern France, Italy, Spain, and Portugal from the fourteenth to sixteenth centuries, the young servant might find that she worked side by side with a girl bought and enslaved."

28. Orlando Patterson, *Slavery and Social Death* (Cambridge: Harvard University Press, 1982), chapter 1.

29. Lynn White, Jr., "Death and the Devil," 26. See also Levack's discussion of how these unprecedented changes encouraged witch hunting (*The Witch-hunt in Early Modern Europe,* 139–42).

30. So wrote the Portuguese civil servant Duarte Pacheco in about 1508; quoted in Ronald Sanders, *Lost Tribes and Promised Lands: The Origins of American Racism,* 120.

31. Davis, *Slavery and Human Progress,* 334 n. 114. Though Philip Curtin's estimate of 11.5 million has been revised upward by some scholars, it remains the baseline. Whatever exact numbers are used, the transfer of slaves from Africa to the Americas remains the largest forced movement of people in history.

32. Todorov, *Conquest of America,* 133: "If the word genocide has ever been applied to a situation with some accuracy, this is here the case. . . . None of the great massacres of the twentieth century can be compared to this hecatomb."

33. Sanders, *Lost Tribes and Promised Lands.*

34. This fifteenth-century change in the concept of race parallels the sixteenth-century revision in the attitude toward menstrual blood. In both, a *condition,* neutral and inevitable, is turned into a characteristic of a group, pejorative and potentially evil. This personalizing of difference made these groups, blacks and women, more alien and thus easier to persecute.

35. Sanders, *Lost Tribes and Promised Lands,* 147.

36. Todorov, *Conquest of America,* 48, 150–54, Columbus's quote is from p. 48; Todorov's from p. 146.

37. I use the Spanish conquest as my example because it was the first, thus fitting in closest to the beginning of the witch hunts back home, not because it was necessarily more severe. Given the enormity of the destruction carried out against Amerindian civilization by all European colonizers, I find debates over "who was worse" beside the point. There were some cultural differences between northern and southern European conquerors, but none were "better." Genocide is genocide.

38. Todorov, *Conquest of America,* 111, 115, 141, 179. Las Casas had been an eyewitness to the sword-testing murders. Later, he came over entirely to the Indians' side, freeing his Indian slaves (but not his Africans) and even defending their non-Christian practices.

39. *The Letters of Amerigo Vespucci,* edited and translated by Clements R. Markham, this passage retranslated by Ronald Sanders, *Lost Tribes and Promised Lands,* 103.

40. Sanders, *Lost Tribes and Promised Lands,* 105.

41. Todorov, *Conquest of America,* 50.

42. Todorov, *Conquest of America*, 143–45.

43. Richard Horsely, "Who Were the Witches? The Social Roles of the Accused in the European Witchcraft Trials," 719.

44. Todorov, *Conquest of America*, 145.

45. The causes for the cessation of witch hunting are almost as complex as are its beginnings, ranging from a repulsion against demonic possession (for France, see Mandrou) to a diversion from witch belief to belief in vampires (in Hungary, see Klaniczay). Though it is clear that Europeans' *belief in* witchcraft has not died to this day (see Jeanne Favret-Saada, *Deadly Words: Witchcraft in the Bocage*), people's willingness to kill others for magical acts or devil worship virtually ended in the eighteenth century. For a brief discussion of two influential doubters, see pp. 397–400.

Epilogue

1. Information from Jeanne Audrey Powers. In light of the protest, the mayor backed down, canceled the "tourist attraction," and declared the tower to be a memorial to those who had been killed there.

Appendix A

1. W. G. Soldan's *Geschichte der Hexenprozesse* (Stuttgart, 1843; 2d ed. 1879; 3d ed. Soldan-Heppe, 1911). Hansen, *Zauberwahn, Inquisition Und Hexen prozess in Mittelalter* (Munich, 1900) and *Quellen und Untersuchungen zur geschichte des hexenwahns. . .* (Bonn, 1901); Henry C. Lea, *Materials Toward a History of Witchcraft;* William Woods, *A Casebook of Witchcraft: Reports, Depositions, Confessions, Trials, and Executions for Witchcraft During Three Hundred Years.*

2. Richard Kieckhefer, *European Witch Trials: Their Foundations in Popular and Learned Culture*, 108–45; Christine Larner, Christopher Lee, and Hugh McLachlan, *A Source Book of Scottish Witchcraft.* Two useful regional studies of trials that include transcripts are George F. Black, *Some Unpublished Scottish Witchcraft Trials*, and C. L'Estrange Ewen, ed., *Witch Hunting and Witch Trials: Indictments for Witchcraft from the Records of 1,373 Assizes Held for the Home Circuit, 1559–1736.*

3. David Hall, *Witch-hunting in Seventeenth-Century New England: A Documentary History. The Salem Witchcraft Papers: Verbatim Transcripts of the Legal Documents*, edited by Boyer and Nissenbaum.

4. Alan C. Kors and Edward Peters, *Witchcraft in Europe, 1100–1700*, and E. William Monter, ed., *European Witchcraft.*

5. Guido Bader, *Hexenprozesse in der Schweiz* (Affoltern, 1945). I know of only a few regional works published prior to 1945, of which only one will be used in this work, Ewen, ed., *Witch Hunting and Witch Trials.*

6. Germany: Gerhard Schormann, *Hexenprozesse in Deutschland.*

Basque lands: Julio Caro Baroja, *The World of the Witches,* parts 3 and 4; Gustav Henningsen, *The Witches' Advocate: Basque Witchcraft and the Spanish Inquisition.*

Friuli: Carlo Ginzburg, *Night Battles.* Luxembourg: Marie-Sylvie Dupont-Bouchat et al., *Prophètes et sorciers dans les pays-Bas, XVIe–XVIIIe siècle,* part 1.

Alsace: Henri Hiegel, *Le Bailliage d'Allemagne de 1600 à 1632.* Lorraine: Étienne Delcambre, *Le Concept de la sorcellerie dans le duché de Lorraine.*

Northern France: Emile Brouette, "La Sorcellerie dans le Comté de Namur au début de l'époque moderne (1509–1646)"; Pierre Villette, *La Sorcellerie et sa répression dans le Nord de la France;* Robert Muchembled, *La Sorcière au village,* and "The Witches of the Cambrésis: The Acculturation of the World in the Sixteenth and Seventeenth Centuries."

Jura: E. William Monter, *Witchcraft in France and Switzerland: The Borderlands During the Reformation.*

Franche-Comté: Francis Bavoux, *La Sorcellerie au pays de Quingey,* and *Hantises et diableries dans la terre abbatiale de Luxeuil d'un procès d'Inquisition, 1529 . . . et 1628–30,* and *La Sorcellerie en Franche-Comté.*

Scotland: Christina Larner, *Enemies of God: The Witch-hunt in Scotland.*

English Home Counties: Ewen, *Witch-hunting and Witch Trials.*

Essex: Alan Macfarlane, *Witchcraft in Tudor and Stuart England.*

Sweden: Bengt Ankarloo, *Trolldomsprocesserna i Sverige* (Stockholm, 1971).

Poland: Bohdan Baranowski, *Procesy Czarownic w Polsce w XVII:XVIII wieku.*

Russia: Russell Zguta, "Witchcraft Trials in Seventeenth-Century Russia."

Finland, Hungary, Estonia, Sweden, Denmark, Norway, Iceland, and Portugal: Bengt Ankarloo and Gustav Henningsen, eds., *Early Modern European Witchcraft: Centres and Peripheries.*

The Netherlands: Marijke Gijswijt-Hofstra and Willem Frijhoff, eds., *Witchcraft in the Netherlands from the Fourteenth to the Twentieth Century.*

7. Edward Fairfax (d. 1635), *Daemonologia: A Discourse on Witchcraft as It Was Acted in the Family of Mr. Edward Fairfax of Fuyston, Yorkshire, in 1621* (Harrogate: Ackrill Publishers, 1882).

8. Rossell Hope Robbins, Introduction to *Catalogue of the Witchcraft Collection in Cornell University Library.*

9. Thomas Bromhall, *A Treatise of Specters* (London, 1658). The title page of the copy in the Houghton Library, Harvard University, has the notation: "This volume belonged to Increase Mather."

10. See Kieckhefer's discussion, *European Witch Trials,* 23, 30 ff.

11. Heinrich Kramer and James Sprenger, *Malleus Maleficarum* 1486, translated by Montague Summers (London, 1928; New York: Dover Publications, 1971), 41–48. The tirade against women's sexual powers extends from 41–66 and permeates other parts of the document's 275 pages, esp. 109–22, 140–44, 227–30. Part 3 offers instruction in how to arrest, try, torture, and execute a witch.

12. For example, Francesco-Maria Guazzo's *Compendium Maleficarum* (Milan, 1608), translated by M. Summers, 1929 (Secaucus, NJ: University Books, 1974).

13. Pope Innocent VIII, "Summis desiderantes affectibus," 1484, translated by M. Summers, *Malleus Maleficarum*, xliii–xlv.

14. Nicolas Remy, *Demonolatrie*, 1595; translated by E. A. Ashwin, *Demonolatry* (London, 1930; Secaucus, NJ: University Books, 1974).

15. Remy, 163. I computed the gender figure from his records. See appendix B.

16. Henri Boguet, *Discours des sorciers* (Paris, 1602; 2d ed., Lyon, 1608); *An Examen of Witches*, translated by A. E. Ashwin, edited by M. Summers (Bungay: J. Rodker, 1929), 29.

17. Monter, *Witchcraft in France and Switzerland*, 71.

18. Pierre de Lancre, *Tableau de l'inconstance des mauvais anges et demons* (Paris, 1612), 560; Margaret M. McGowan, "Pierre de Lancre's *Tableau de L'inconstance des mauvais anges et demons:* The Sabbat Sensationalized," in Anglo, ed., *The Damned Art*.

19. Pierre de Lancre, *L'Incrédulité et mescreance du sortilege plainement convaincue* (Paris, 1622), 627; cf. Martin Del Rio, *Disquisitionum magicarum libri sex* (Louvain, 1599–1600), translated by André du Chesae, *Les Controverses et recherches magiques* (Paris, 1611), 526–28.

20. Had he read the inquisitional records for the village of Montaillou c. 1300, he would have known precisely what they were doing, for there the mistress of the priest confessed that he made a bed for the two of them behind the altar. Emmanuel Le Roy Ladurie, *Montaillou: The Promised Land of Error* (New York: Random House, 1979).

21. De Lancre, *Tableau*, 55–57. He appeared to fear the sensual lethargy of this southern region: the women entered the church in "*le matin à l'obscur, et sur le midi, qui est l'heure du silence des Eglises, et sur le soir, lorsque l'Esprit tenebreux commence à tirer les rideaux pour faire esvanouir la clarité*" ("morning before dawn, and at noon, which is the hour of silence in church, and at night, while the dark Spirit starts to draw the curtains to make the light disappear."

22. James I, *Daemonologie* (1597; London: Bodley Head, 1924).

23. Stuart Clark, "King James's *Daemonologie:* Witchcraft and Kingship," 157. Clark corrects Kittredge's estimate of James's innocence in this affair: (George Lyman Kittredge, "English Witchcraft and James I").

24. Matthew Hopkins, *The Discovery of Witches* (London, 1647; 1928, Introduction by M. Summers). Alan Macfarlane claims the latter motives *(Witchcraft in Tudor and Stuart England*, XX); Richard Deacon, *(Matthew Hopkins: Witch Finder General*, 65), the former. As for his greed, Hopkins did refuse to seek out witches in a town until he had been promised a fee.

25. Hopkins, *Discovery of Witches*, 4.

26. Deacon, *Matthew Hopkins*, 120, 174.

27. *Six livres de la République* (1576), in which Bodin argued that the republic had the unlimited power to make law, but that the sovereign must respect the fundamental laws of France and private property and the family.

28. Paris, 1580, with nine French editions by 1604, three Latin editions, and one Italian. See E. William Monter, "Inflation and Witchcraft: The Case of Jean Bodin," 376 n. 22.

29. Monter, "Inflation and Witchcraft," 386–87.

30. Monter, "Inflation and Witchcraft," 384, 387.

31. Bodin, *Démonomanie des sorciers* (Lyon, 1593), 509, 515 ff.

32. Bodin, *Démonomanie*, 418: *"Car le naturel des femmes impotet brusle d'un appetit de vengeance incroyable, et ne peut tenir sa langue, si elle a puissance de nuire"* ("For the nature of women burns with an incredible appetite for vengeance, and cannot hold its tongue, if it has the power to harm"), and book 2, chapter 3.

33. Del Rio, *Disquisitionum magicarum libri sex*, 738.

34. Guazzo, *Compendium Maleficarum.*

35. Ulric Molitor, *De lamiis et phitonicis mulieribus* (Cologne, 1489); translation, *Des Sorcières et des devineresses.*

36. Weyer, Johann. *De praestigüs daemonum.* Basel, 1563. Translation: *Witches, Devils, and Doctors in the Renaissance.* George Mora and Benjamin Kohl, eds., John Shea, trans. (Bingamptom, NY: Medieval and Renaissance Texts and Studies, 1991).

37. Reginald Scot, *The Discoverie of Witchcraft* (London, 1584, 1930; New York: Dover Publications, 1972).

38. Scot, *Discoverie of Witchcraft*, 41, 34.

39. Scot, *Discoverie of Witchcraft*, 18–19.

40. Scot, *Discoverie of Witchcraft*, 4–5.

41. Scot, *Discoverie of Witchcraft*, 10.

42. Scot, *Discoverie of Witchcraft*, 158.

Appendix B

1. Kieckhefer, *European Witch Trials*, 6.

2. Midelfort, *Witch Hunting*, 180–81. The first line refers to large hunts only.

3. Von Riezler, *Geschichte der Hexenprozesse*, 241–42.

4. Schormann, *Hexenprozesse in Deutschland*, 66–71. The following nine estimates are taken from Schormann.

5. Monter, *Witchcraft in France and Switzerland*, 49, 120–21.

6. Levack, *Witch-Hunt*, 179.

7. Levack, *Witch-Hunt*, 179.

8. Hiegel, *Le Bailliage d'Allemagne de 1600 à 1632*, chapter 4; J. Français, *L'église et la sorcellerie*, 112 n. 1.

9. Briggs, "Witchcraft and Popular Mentality in Lorraine, 1580–1630," 338, 343; Levack, *Witch-Hunt*, 180.

10. Monter, *Witchcraft in France and Switzerland*, 120–21.

11. Monter, *Witchcraft in France and Switzerland*, 120–21.

12. Monter, *Witchcraft in France and Switzerland*, 120–21, 105.

13. Monter, *Witchcraft in France and Switzerland*, 120–21.

14. Monter, *Witchcraft in France and Switzerland*, 119.

15. Monter, *Witchcraft in France and Switzerland*, 49.

16. Monter, *Witchcraft in France and Switzerland*, 105.

17. Monter, *Witchcraft in France and Switzerland*, 105, 119.

18. Monter, *Witchcraft in France and Switzerland*, 49.

19. Monter, *Witchcraft in France and Switzerland*, 49, 120.

20. Levack, *Witch-Hunt*, 124.

21. Dupont-Bouchat et al., *Prophètes et sorciers dans les pays-Bas, XVIe–XVIIIe siècle*, 138.

22. Brouette, "La Sorcellerie dans le Comté de Namur," 138.

23. My thanks to Prof. Joke Spaans of the University of Leiden for this information. These statistics do not include much current research.

24. Schormann, *Hexenprozesse in Deutschland*, 71. In 1935, the Nazi official Heinrich Himmler collected over thirty thousand cases of trials for witchcraft, most from Germany. As many were group trials, the total for individuals tried must be higher (Schormann, *Hexenprozesse in Deutschland*, 8–15).

25. Levack, *Witch-Hunt*, 181.

26. Henningsen, *Witches' Advocate*, 23–25 and 480–481

27. Soman, "The Parlement of Paris," 40.

28. Soman, "Witch Lynching at Juniville," 10–11.

29. Soman, "Witch Lynching at Juniville," 10–11.

30. Soman, "The Parlement of Paris."

31. Macfarlane, *Witchcraft in Tudor and Stuart England*, 160.

32. Ewen, *Witch Hunting and Witch Trials*.

33. Levack, *Witch-Hunt*, 182.

34. Larner, Lee, and McLachlan, *A Source Book of Scottish Witchcraft*.

35. No statistical work has been done on Irish witchcraft.

36. Pitts, *Witchcraft and Devil Lore in the Channel Islands*, 28–32.

37. Karlsen, *Devil in the Shape of a Woman*, 48–49.

38. Levack, *Witch-Hunt*, for the overall estimate: 20, 187–94.

39. Naess, "Norway," 372.

40. Ankarloo and Henningsen, 310–11.

41. Heikkinen and Kervinen, in Ankerloo and Henningsen, 321.

42. Henningsen, in Johansen,"Denmark," 345 n. 16.

43. Madar, "Estonia," 267.

44. Baranowski, *Procesy Czarownic w Polsce w XVII:XVIII wieku*, 180.

45. Zguta, "Witchcraft Trials in Seventeenth-Century Russia."

46. Klaniczay, "Hungary," 222–23; Lea, *History of the Inquisition*, vol. 3, 1259, 1264–65, 1271–73, 1282.

47. Monter, *Witchcraft in France and Switzerland*, 120.

48. Monter and Tedeschi, "Toward a Statistical Profile," 135, 144.

49. Monter and Tedeschi, "Toward a Statistical Profile"; Contreras and Henningsen, in Henningsen and Tedeschi, 114; Henningsen, "'The Ladies from Outside': An Archaic Pattern of the Witches' Sabbath" (Sicily), in Ankarloo and Henningsen.

50. Henningsen, *Witches' Advocate.*

51. Monter, *Witchcraft in France and Switzerland*, 119, 121.

52. Levack, *Witch-Hunt*, 124.

53. Parker, "Some Recent Work," 529. This figure is only for inquisitional courts; for persons punished by secular courts, see Kamen, *Inquisition and Society in Spain*, 210–15.

Bibliography

For sixteenth- and seventeenth-century works, see Appendix A.

Accati, Luisa. "Lo spirito della fornicazione: virtu dell'anima e virtu del corpo in Friuli, Fra '600 e '700." *Quaderni Storici* 14.2 (May–August 1979): 644–72.

Anderson, Alan, and Gordon, Raymond. "Witchcraft and the Status of Women—the Case of England." *British Journal of Sociology* 29.2 (June 1978).

Anderson, Bonnie, and Judith Zinsser. *A History of Their Own: Women in Europe.* 2 vols. New York: Harper & Row, 1988.

Anglo, Sydney, ed. *The Damned Art: Essays in the Literature of Witchcraft.* London: Routledge, Kegan Paul, 1977.

Ankarloo, Bengt, and Gustav Henningsen, eds. *Early Modern European Witchcraft: Centres and Peripheries.* Oxford: Clarendon Press, 1990.

Ariès, Philippe. *Centuries of Childhood: A Social History of Family Life.* Translated by R. Baldick. New York: Knopf, 1965.

Bak, Janos, and Gerhard Benecke, eds. *Religion and Rural Revolt.* Manchester: Manchester Univ. Press, 1984.

Banner, Lois W. "A Reply to 'Culture et Pouvoir' from the Perspective of United States Women's History." *Journal of Women's History* 1.1 (Spring 1989): 101–7.

Baranowski, Bohdan. *Procesy Czarownic w Polsce w XVII:XVIII wieku* (French résumé). Lodz, 1952.

Barstow, Anne Llewellyn. *Joan of Arc: Heretic, Mystic, Shaman.* Lewiston, NY: Edwin Mellen Press, 1986.

———. "On Studying Witchcraft as Women's History: A Historiography of the European Witch Persecutions." *Journal of Feminist Studies in Religion* 4 (Fall 1988).

———. "Women as Healers, Women as Witches." *Old Westbury Review* 2 (1986): 121–33.

———. "Women, Sexuality, and Oppression: The European Witchcraft Persecutions." *World History Bulletin* (Spring–Summer 1988).

Baschwitz, Kurt. *Hexen und Hexenprozesse: Die Geschichte eines Massenwahns.* Munich, 1963.

Bashar, Nazife. "Rape in England between 1550 and 1700." In *The Sexual Dynamics of History,* edited by London Feminist History Group. London: Pluto Press, 1983.

Bavoux, Francis. "Les Caractères originaux de la sorcellerie au Pays de Montbéliard." *Mémoires de la Société pour l'Histoire du Droit. . .* 20 (1958–59): 89–105.

———. *Hantises et diableries dans la terre abbatiale de Luxeuil d'un procès d'Inquisition, 1529. . . et 1628–30.* Monaco: Éditions du Rocher, 1956.

———. *La Sorcellerie au pays de Quingey.* Besançon: Éditions Servir, 1947.

———. *La Sorcellerie en Franche-Comté.* Monaco: Éditions du Rocher, 1954.

Becker, Gabriele, et al., eds. *Aus der Zeit der Verzweiflung zur Genese und Aktualität des Hexenbildes.* Frankfurt: Suhrkamp Verlag, 1977.

Behringer, Wolfgang. *Hexenverfolgung in Bayern: Volksmagie, Glaubenseifer und Staatsräson in der frühen neuzeit.* Munich: Oldenbourg, 1987.

Ben-Yehuda, Nachman. *Deviance and Moral Boundaries: Witchcraft, the Occult, Science Fiction, Deviant Sciences and Scientists.* Chicago: Univ. of Chicago Press, 1985.

———. "The European Witch Craze of the Fourteenth to Seventeenth Centuries: A Sociologist's Perspective." *American Journal of Sociology* 86 (1980).

Benedek, Thomas G. "The Changing Relationship Between Midwives and Physicians During the Renaissance." *Bulletin of the History of Medicine* 51 (1977): 550–64.

Bever, Edward. "Old Age and Witchcraft in Early Modern Europe." In *Old Age in Preindustrial Society,* edited by Peter N. Stearns. New York: Holmes & Meier, 1983.

Black, G. F. *Calendar of Cases of Witchcraft in Scotland, 1510–1727.* New York, 1938.

———. *Some Unpublished Scottish Witchcraft Trials.* New York: New York Public Library, 1941.

Blumenfeld-Kosinski, Renate. *Not of Woman Born: Representations of Caesarian Birth in Medieval and Renaissance Culture.* Ithaca, NY: Cornell Univ. Press, 1989.

Bordo, Susan. "The Cartesian Masculinization of Thought." *Signs* 11.3 (Spring 1986): 439–56.

Bossy, John. "The Counter-Reformation and the People of Catholic Europe." *Past and Present* 47 (May 1970).

Bourguignon, Erika. *Possession.* San Francisco: Chandler and Sharp, 1976.

Bovenschen, Sylvia. "The Contemporary Witch, the Historical Witch, and the Witch Myth." *New German Critique* 15 (Fall 1978): 83–119.

Boyer, Paul, and Stephen Nissenbaum. *Salem Possessed: The Social Origins of Witchcraft.* Cambridge: Harvard Univ. Press, 1974.

Boyer, Paul, and Stephen Nissenbaum, eds. *The Salem Witchcraft Papers: Verbatim Transcripts of the Legal Documents. . . .* 3 vols. New York: Da Capo Press, 1977.

Brann, Noel L. "The Conflict Between Reason and Magic in Seventeenth-Century England: A Case Study of the Vaughan-More Debate." *Huntington Library Quarterly* 43.2 (Spring 1980): 103–26.

———. "The Shift from Mystical to Magical Theology in the Abbot Trithemius (1462–1516)." *Studies in Medieval Culture* 11 (Western Michigan University, The Medieval Institute): 147–59.

Brauner, Sigrid. "Martin Luther on Witchcraft: A True Reformer?" In *The Politics of Gender in Early Modern Europe*, edited by Jean R. Brink, Allison P. Coudert, and Maryanne C. Horowitz. Vol XII of *Sixteenth Century Essays and Studies.*

Brewer, J., and J. Styles, eds. *An Ungovernable People: The English and Their Law in the Seventeenth and Eighteenth Centuries.* London: Hutchinson, 1980.

Briggs, Robin. *Communities of Belief: Cultural and Social Tension in Early Modern France.* Oxford: Clarendon Press, 1989.

———. "Witchcraft and Popular Mentality in Lorraine, 1580–1630." In *Occult and Scientific Mentalities in the Renaissance*, edited by Brian Vickers. Cambridge: Cambridge Univ. Press, 1984.

Brouette, Emile. "La Sorcellerie dans le Comté de Namur au début de l'époque moderne (1509–1646)." *Annales de la Société archeologique de Namur* 47 (1953–54): 360–420.

Brown, Judith C. *Immodest Acts: The Life of a Lesbian Nun in Renaissance Italy.* New York: Oxford Univ. Press, 1986.

Brownmiller, Susan. *Against Our Will: Men, Women, and Rape.* New York: Bantam Books, 1976.

Burghartz, Susanne. "No Justice for Women? Delinquency in Zurich in the Later Middle Ages." Paper presented to the Seventh Berkshire Conference on the History of Women, Wellesley College, 1987.

Burr, George Lincoln, ed. *Narratives of the Witchcraft Cases, 1648–1706.* New York, 1914; New York: Barnes & Noble, 1946, 1975.

Burstein, Sona Rosa. "Demonology and Medicine in the Sixteenth and Seventeenth Centuries." *Folklore* (1955): 16–33.

Camerlynck, Eliane. "Féminité et sorcellerie chez les théoriciens de la démonologie à la fin du Moyen Age: Étude du 'Malleus Maleficarum.'" *Renaissance and Reformation* 7 (1983): 13–25.

Carnochan, W. B. "Witch-Hunting and Belief in 1751: The Case of Thomas Colley and Ruth Osborne." *Journal of Social History* 4.4 (Summer 1971).

Caro Baroja, Julio. *The World of the Witches.* Translated by O. Glendinning. Chicago: Univ. of Chicago Press, 1965.

Chandos, John, ed. *In God's Name: Examples of Preaching in England, 1534–1662.* New York: Bobbs Merrill, 1971.

Charles, Lindsey, and Lorna Duffin, eds. *Women and Work in Pre-Industrial England.* London: Croom Helm, 1985.

Chesler, Phyllis. *Mothers on Trial: The Battle for Children and Custody.* New York: McGraw-Hill, 1986.

———. *Women and Madness.* New York: Avon, 1973.

Cipolla, Carlo M. *Before the Industrial Revolution: European Society and Economy, 1000–1700.* New York: W. W. Norton, 1976.

———. *The Economic History of World Population.* Hammondsworth: Penguin Books, 1978.

———. *Faith, Reason, and the Plague in Seventeenth-Century Tuscany.* Translated by M. Kittel. Ithaca, NY: Cornell Univ. Press, 1979.

Clark, Alice. *Working Life of Women in the Seventeenth Century.* London, 1919; London: Routledge and Kegan Paul, 1982.

Clark, Stuart. "Inversion, Misrule, and the Meaning of Witchcraft." *Past and Present* 87 (1980): 98–127.

———. "King James's *Daemonologie:* Witchcraft and Kingship." In Anglo, ed., *The Damned Art.*

Cockburn, J. S., ed. *Crime in England: 1550–1800.* London: Methuen, 1977.

Cohn, Norman. *Europe's Inner Demons: An Inquiry Inspired by the Great Witch Hunt.* New York: New American Library, 1975.

Cornell University Libraries. *Catalogue of the Witchcraft Collection.* Millwood, NY: KTO Press, 1977.

Coudert, Allison P. "The Myth of the Improved Status of Protestant Women: The Case of the Witchcraze." *The Politics of Gender in Early Modern Europe,* edited by Jean R. Brink, Allison P. Coudert, and Maryanne C. Horowitz. Vol. XII in *Sixteenth Century Essays and Studies,* 61–89.

Crawford, Patricia. "Attitudes to Menstruation in Seventeenth-Century England." *Past and Present* 91 (May 1981): 47–73.

Currie, Elliott P. "The Control of Witchcraft in Renaissance Europe." In *The Social Organization of Law,* edited by Donald Black and Maureen Mileski. New York: Academic Press, 1973.

Daly, Mary. *Gyn/Ecology: The Metaethics of Radical Feminism.* Boston: Beacon Press, 1978.

Darnton, Robert. *The Great Cat Massacre and Other Episodes in French Cultural History.* New York: Basic Books, 1984.

Dauphin, Cecile, et al. "Women's Culture and Women's Power: An Attempt at Historiography." *Journal of Women's History* 1.1 (Spring 1989): 63–88.

Davis, David Brion. *Slavery and Human Progress.* New York: Oxford Univ. Press, 1984.

Davis, Natalie Zemon. *The Return of Martin Guerre.* Cambridge: Harvard Univ. Press, 1983.

———. *Society and Culture in Early Modern France: Eight Essays.* Stanford, CA: Stanford Univ. Press, 1975.

———. "Some Themes and Tasks in the Study of Popular Religion." In *The Pursuit of Holiness in Late Medieval and Renaissance Religion,* edited by Charles Trinkaus and Heiko Oberman. Leiden, 1974.

———. "Women in the Crafts in Sixteenth-Century Lyon." In Hanawalt, ed., *Women and Work.*

Deacon, Richard. *Matthew Hopkins: Witch Finder General.* London: Frederick Muller, 1976.

de Lauretis, Teresa. "Feminist Studies/Critical Studies: Issues, Terms, and Contexts." In *Feminist Studies/Critical Studies*, edited by Teresa de Lauretis. Bloomington: Indiana Univ. Press, 1986.

Delcambre, Étienne. *Le Concept de la sorcellerie dans le duché de Lorraine.* 3 vols. Nancy, 1948–51.

———. "Les Procès de sorcellerie en Lorraine: Psychologie des juges," *Revue d'histoire du droit* 21 (1953). *Tijdschrift voor Rechtsgeschiedenis* 21 (1954): 25–419.

———. "La Psychologie des inculpès lorrains de sorcellerie." *Revue historique de droit français et étranger* 4th series (1954): 383–404, 508–26.

Delcambre, Étienne, and Jean Lhermitte. *Un Cas énigmatique de possession diabolique en Lorraine au XVIIe s.: Elisabeth de Ranfaing, l'énergumène de Nancy, fondatrice de l'ordre du Refuge.* Nancy: Société d'archeologie Lorraine, 1955.

Delumeau, Jean. *La Peur en Occident, XIV–XVIII siècles.* Paris, 1978.

Demos, John. *Entertaining Satan: Witchcraft and the Culture of Early New England.* New York: Oxford Univ. Press, 1982.

———. *A Little Commonwealth: Family Life in Plymouth Colony.* New York, Oxford University Press, 1970.

———. "Underlying Themes in the Witchcraft of Seventeenth-Century New England." *American Historical Review* 75 (1970): 1311–26.

Denis, A. *La Sorcellerie à Toul aux XVIe et XVIIe siècles.* Toul, 1888.

De Waardt, Hans. "At Bottom a Family Affair: Feuds and Witchcraft in Nijkerk in 1550." In Gijswijt-Hofstra and Frijhoff, eds., *Witchcraft in the Netherlands from the Fourteenth to the Twentieth Century.*

Diefendorf, Barbara. "Prologue to a Massacre: Popular Unrest in Paris, 1557–1572." *American Historical Review* 90.5 (December 1985): 1067–91.

Donegan, Jane B. *Women and Men Midwives: Medicine, Morality, and Misogyny in Early America.* Westport, CT: Greenwood Press, 1978.

Driver, Tom F. *The Magic of Ritual: Our Need for Liberating Rites That Transform Our Lives and Our Communities.* San Francisco: Harper San Francisco, 1991.

Dunn, Richard S. *The Age of Religious Wars: 1559–1715.* 2d ed. New York: W. W. Norton, 1979.

Dupont-Bouchat, Marie-Sylvie, et al. *Prophètes et sorciers dans les pays-Bas, XVIe–XVIIIe siècle.* Paris: Hachette, 1978.

Dworkin, Andrea. *Intercourse.* New York: Free Press, 1987.

———. *Woman Hating: A Radical Look at Sexuality.* New York: Dutton, 1974.

Ehrenreich, Barbara, and Dierdre English. *Witches, Midwives, and Nurses: A History of Women Healers.* Old Westbury, NY: Feminist Press, 1973.

Eliade, Mircea. "Some Observations on European Witchcraft." In *Occultism. Witchcraft, and Cultural Fashions: Essays in Comparative Religions.* Chicago, 1976.

Elworthy, Frederick T. *The Evil Eye.* London, 1895; Secaucus, NJ: University Books, n.d.

Estes, Leland L. "The Medical Origins of the European Witch Craze: A Hypothesis." *Journal of Social History* 17 (1983): 271–84.

———. "Reginald Scot and His *Discoverie of Witchcraft:* Religion and Science in the Opposition to the European Witch Craze." *Church History* 52 (1983): 444–56.

Evans, R. J. W. *The Making of the Habsburg Monarchy: 1500–1700.* Oxford: Oxford Univ. Press, 1979.

Ewen, C. L'Estrange. *Witchcraft and Demonianism.* London: Heath, Cranton, 1933.

Ewen, C. L'Estrange, ed. *Witch Hunting and Witch Trials: Indictments for Witchcraft from the Records of 1,373 Assizes Held for the Home Circuit, 1559–1736.* New York: Dial Press, 1929.

Favret-Saada, Jeanne. *Deadly Words: Witchcraft in the Bocage.* Translated by Catherine Cullen. Cambridge: Cambridge Univ. Press, 1980.

Febvre, Lucien. "Sorcellerie, sottise ou révolution mentale?" *Annales: Economies, sociétiés, civilisations* 3 (1948): 9–15.

Flandrin, Jean-Louis. *Familles: Parenté, maison, sexualité dans l'ancienne société.* Paris, 1976. Translated as *Families in Former Times: Kinship, Household, and Sexuality.* Cambridge: Cambridge Univ. Press, 1979.

Fox-Genovese, Elizabeth. Essay review of *Women and Religion in America,* edited by Rosemary Ruether and Rosemary Keller, vols. 1 and 2. *Journal of the American Academy of Religion* 53.3 (1985): 471.

Francais, J. *L'Église et la sorcellerie—suivi des documents officiels,* Paris: Librairie Critique, 1910.

Fraser, Antonia. *The Weaker Vessel.* New York: Alfred A. Knopf, 1984.

Gage, Matilda Joslyn. *Woman, Church, and State.* 1893. 2d ed., New York: Arno Press, 1972.

Gari Lacruz, Angel. "Variedad de competencias en el delito de brujeria (1600–1650) en Aragon." In *Inquisicion espanola: nueva vision, nuevos horizontes,* edited by J. Perez Villanueva. Madrid, 1980.

Garrett, Clarke. "Witches and Cunning Folk in the Old Regime." In *The Wolf and the Lamb: Popular Culture in France from the Old Regime to the Twentieth Century,* edited by J. Beauroy et al. Stanford, CA: Stanford Univ. Press, 1976.

———. "Women and Witches: Patterns of Analysis." *Signs* 3 (1977): 461–70.

Geis, Gilbert. "Lord Hale, Witches, and Rape." *British Journal of Law and Society* 5 (1978): 26–44.

Gijswijt-Hofstra, Marijke, and Willem Frijhoff, eds. *Witchcraft in the Netherlands from the Fourteenth to the Twentieth Century.* Translated by R. van der Wilden-Fall. Rotterdam: Universitaire Pers, 1991.

Gillis, John R. *For Better, for Worse: British Marriages, 1600 to the Present.* New York: Oxford Univ. Press, 1985.

Ginzburg, Carlo. *The Cheese and the Worms: The Cosmos of a Sixteenth-Century Miller.* Translated by John Tedeschi and Anne Tedeschi. New York: Penguin Books, 1982.

———. *Clues, Myths, and the Historical Method.* Translated by J. Tedeschi. Baltimore: Johns Hopkins Univ. Press, 1989.

———. *Ecstasies: Deciphering the Witches' Sabbath.* Translated by R. Rosenthal. New York: Pantheon, 1991.

———. *The Night Battles: Witchcraft and Agrarian Cults in the Sixteenth and Seventeenth Centuries.* Translated by John Tedeschi and Anne Tedeschi. 1966; trans. New York: Penguin Books, 1983.

———. "The Witches' Sabbat: Popular Cult or Inquisitional Stereotype?" In Kaplan, ed., *Understanding Popular Culture.*

Girard, René. "Generative Scapegoating." In *Violent Origins: Ritual Killing and Cultural Formation,* edited by R. G. Hamerton-Kelly. Stanford, CA: Stanford Univ. Press, 1987.

———. *The Scapegoat.* Translated by Yvonne Freccero. Baltimore: Johns Hopkins Univ. Press, 1986.

———. *Violence and the Sacred.* Translated by Patrick Gregory. Baltimore: Johns Hopkins Univ. Press, 1977.

Godbeer, Richard. *The Devil's Dominion: Magic and Religion in Early New England.* Cambridge: Cambridge Univ. Press, 1992.

Goldberg, Harriet. "Two Parallel Medieval Commonplaces: Antifeminism and Antisemitism in the Hispanic Literary Tradition." In *Aspects of Jewish Culture in the Middle Ages,* edited by Paul E. Szarmach. Albany: State Univ. of New York Press, 1979.

Goodman, Felicitas D. *How About Demons? Possession and Exorcism in the Modern World.* Bloomington: Indiana Univ. Press, 1988.

Goubert, Pierre. *The French Peasantry in the Seventeenth Century.* Translated by I. Patterson. Cambridge: Cambridge Univ. Press, 1982.

Graziano, Frank. *Divine Violence: Spectacle, Psychosexuality, and Radical Christianity in the Argentine "Dirty War."* Boulder, CO: Westview Press, 1992.

Green, Monica. "Women's Medical Practice and Health Care in Medieval Europe." *Signs* 14.2 (Winter 1989): 434–73.

Griffin, Susan. *Woman and Nature: The Roaring Inside Her.* New York: Harper & Row, 1978.

Guilhem, Claire. "L'Inquisition et la dévaluation des discours féminins." In *L'Inquisition espagnole,* edited by Bartolomé Benassar. Paris: Librairie Hachette, 1979.

Hajnal, John. "*European Marriage Patterns in Perspective,*" *Population in History,* edited by D. Glass and D. Eversley. Chicago: Univ. of Chicago Press, 1965.

Hall, David D. "Witchcraft and the Limits of Interpretation: Essay Review." *The New England Quarterly* 54.2 (June 1985): 253–81.

———. *Witch-hunting in Seventeenth-Century New England: A Documentary History.* Boston: Northeastern Univ. Press, 1991.

———. *Worlds of Wonder, Days of Judgment.* New York: Knopf, 1989.

Hamilton, Bernard. *The Medieval Inquisition.* London, 1981.

Hanawalt, Barbara A. *The Ties That Bound: Peasant Families in Medieval England.* New York: Oxford Univ. Press, 1986.

Hanawalt, Barbara A., ed. *Women and Work in Preindustrial Europe.* Bloomington: Indiana Univ. Press, 1986.

Harner, Michael J. "The Role of Hallucinogenic Plants in European Witchcraft." In *Hallucinogens and Shamanism,* edited by Michael J. Harner. New York: Oxford Univ. Press, 1973.

Hartmann, Heidi. "Capitalism, Patriarchy, and Job Segregation by Sex." In *Women and the Workplace: The Implications of Occupational Segregation,* edited by Martha Blaxall and Barbara Reagan. Chicago: Univ. of Chicago Press, 1979.

Haskins, George Lee. *Law and Authority in Early Massachusetts: A Study in Tradition and Design.* Archon Books, 1968.

Hastrup, Kirsten. "Iceland: Sorcerers and Paganism." In Ankarloo and Henningsen, eds., *Early Modern European Witchcraft.*

———. "The Semantics of Biology: Virginity." In *Defining Females: The Nature of Women in Society,* edited by Shirley Ardener. New York: Wiley, 1978.

Heikkinen, Antero, and Timo Kervinen. "Finland: the Male Domination." In Ankarloo and Henningsen, eds., *Early Modern European Witchcraft.*

Heinsohn, Gunnar, and Otto Steiger. "The Elimination of Medieval Birth Control and the Witch Trials of Modern Times." *International Journal of Women's Studies* 5.3 (May-June 1982): 193–214.

———. "Warum wurden Hexen verbrannt?" *Der Spiegel* 43 (1984): 111–28.

Henningsen, Gustav. *European Witch-Persecution.* Copenhagen, 1973.

———. *The Witches' Advocate: Basque Witchcraft and the Spanish Inquisition.* Reno: Univ. of Nevada Press, 1980.

Henningsen, Gustav, and John Tedeschi, eds. *The Inquisition in Early Modern Europe: Studies on Sources and Methods.* De Kalb: Northern Illinois Univ. Press, 1986.

Herlihy, David. *Medieval Households.* Cambridge: Harvard Univ. Press, 1985.

Hester, Marianne. *Lewd Women and Wicked Witches: A Study of the Dynamics of Male Domination.* London: Routledge, 1992.

Hiegel, Henri. *Le Bailliage d'Allemagne de 1600 à 1632.* Sarreguemines, 1961.

Hole, Christina. *A Mirror of Witchcraft.* London: Chatto & Windus, 1957.

———. *Witchcraft in England.* London: Batsford, 1945.

Holmes, Clive. "Popular Culture? Witches, Magistrates, and Divines in Early Modern England." In Kaplan, ed., *Understanding Popular Culture.*

Horsley, Richard. "Who Were the Witches? The Social Roles of the Accused in the European Witchcraft Trials." *Journal of Interdisciplinary History* 9.4 (Spring 1979): 689–715.

Howell, Martha C. *Women's Work, the Structures of Market Production, and Patriarchy in Late Medieval Cities of Northern Europe.* Chicago: Univ. of Chicago Press, 1986.

———. "Women, the Family, and Market Production." In Hanawalt, ed., *Women and Work in Preindustrial Europe.*

Hughes, Muriel J. *Women Healers in Medieval Life and Literature.* Freeport, New York: Books for Libraries Press, 1943.

Hults, Linda C. "Baldung and the Witches of Freiburg: The Evidence of Images." *Journal of Interdisciplinary History* 18 (1987): 249–76.

Huxley, Aldous. *The Devils of Loudun.* New York: Harper & Row, 1952, 1971.

Hyatte, Reginald. *Laughter for the Devil: The Trials of Gilles de Rais of 1440.* Cranbury, NJ: Fairleigh Dickinson Univ. Press, 1982.

Imhoff, Arthur E. "From the Old Mortality Pattern to the New: A Radical Change from the Sixteenth to the Twentieth Century." *Bulletin of the History of Medicine* 59.1 (Spring 1985).

Jacobsen, Grethe. "Nordic Women and the Reformation." In Sherrin Marshall, ed., *Women in Reformation and Counter-Reformation Europe.* Bloomington: Indiana Univ. Press, 1989.

Johansen, Jens Christian V. "Denmark: The Sociology of Accusations." In Ankarloo and Henningsen, eds., *Early Modern European Witchcraft.*

Jong, Erika. *Witches.* New York: Harry Abrams, 1981.

Kakar, Sudhir. *Shamans, Mystics, and Doctors: A Psychological Inquiry into India and Its Healing Traditions.* New York: Alfred Knopf, 1982.

Kamen, Henry. *Inquisition and Society in Spain in the Sixteenth and Seventeenth Centuries.* Bloomington: Indiana Univ. Press, 1985.

———. *The Spanish Inquisition.* London: Weidenfeld and Nicholson, 1965.

Kanner, Barbara, ed. *The Women of England from Anglo-Saxon Times to the Present: Interpretive Bibliographical Essays.* Hamden: Archon Books, 1979.

Kaplan, Steven L., ed. *Understanding Popular Culture: Europe from the Middle Ages to the Nineteenth Century.* Berlin and New York: Mouton Publishers, 1984.

Karlsen, Carol. *The Devil in the Shape of a Woman: Witchcraft in Colonial New England.* New York: W. W. Norton, 1987.

Kealy, Edward J. *Medieval Medicus: A Social History of Anglo-Norman Medicine.* Baltimore: Johns Hopkins Univ. Press, 1981.

Kelly, Joan. *Women, History, and Theory.* Chicago: Univ. of Chicago Press, 1984.

Kendall, Laurel. *Shamans, Housewives, and Other Restless Spirits: Women in Korean Ritual Life.* Honolulu: Univ. of Hawaii Press, 1985.

Kibbey, Anne. "Mutations of the Supernatural: Witchcraft, Remarkable Providences, and the Power of Puritan Men." *American Quarterly* 34.2 (Summer 1982).

Kieckhefer, Richard. *European Witch Trials: Their Foundations in Popular and Learned Culture.* Berkeley: Univ. of California Press, 1976.

———. *Magic in the Middle Ages.* Cambridge: Cambridge Univ. Press, 1990.

———. *Repression of Heresy in Medieval Germany.* Philadelphia: Univ. of Pennsylvania Press, 1979.

King, Margaret L. *Women of the Renaissance.* Chicago: Univ. of Chicago Press, 1991.

Kinsman, Robert S., ed. *The Darker Vision of the Renaissance: Beyond the Fields of Reason.* Berkeley: Univ. of California Press, 1974.

Kishwar, Madhu, and Ruth Vanita, eds. *In Search of Answers: Indian Women's Voices from Manushi.* London: Zed Books, 1984.

Kittredge, George Lyman. "English Witchcraft and James I." In *Studies in the History of Religions Presented to C. H. Toy.* New York: Macmillan, 1912.

Klaits, Joseph. *Servants of Satan: The Age of the Witch Hunts.* Bloomington: Univ. of Indiana Press, 1985.

Klaniczay, Gabor. "Hungary: The Accusations and the Universe of Popular Magic." In Ankarloo and Henningsen, eds., *Early Modern European Witchcraft.*

———. *The Uses of Supernatural Power: The Transformation of Popular Religion in Medieval and Early-Modern Europe.* Translated by Susan Singerman, edited by Karen Margolis. Princeton, NJ: Princeton Univ. Press, 1990.

Koehler, Lyle. "The Case of the American Jezebels: Anne Hutchinson and Female Agitation During the Years of Antinomian Turmoil, 1636–1640." *William and Mary Quarterly* 31 (January 1974): 55–78.

Koestler, Arthur. *The Watershed: A Biography of Johannes Kepler.* Garden City, NY: Doubleday Anchor, 1960.

Kors, Alan C., and Edward Peters, eds. *Witchcraft in Europe. 1100–1700.* Philadelphia: Univ. of Pennsylvania Press, 1972.

Kowaleski, Maryanne. "Women's Work in a Market Town." In *Women and Work in Preindustrial Europe,* ed. Barbara Hanawalt. Bloomington: Indiana Univ. Press, 1986.

Kunze, Michael. *Highroad to the Stake: A Tale of Witchcraft.* Translated by W. Yuill. Chicago: Univ. of Chicago, 1987.

Langbein, John. *Prosecuting Crime in the Renaissance.* Cambridge: Cambridge Univ. Press, 1974.

Larner, Christina. *Enemies of God: The Witch-hunt in Scotland.* London: Chatto & Windus, 1981.

———. "Two Late Scottish Witchcraft Tracts: *Witch-Craft Proven* and *The Tryal of Witchcraft,*" In Anglo, ed., *The Damned Art.*

———. "Witchcraft Past and Present." In *Witchcraft and Religion: The Politics of Popular Belief,* edited by and Foreword by Alan Macfarlane. London: Basil Blackwell, 1984.

Larner, Christina, Christopher Lee, and Hugh McLachlan. *A Source Book of Scottish Witchcraft.* Glasgow: Univ. of Glasgow, 1977.

Lea, Henry C. *A History of the Inquisition of the Middle Ages.* 3 vols. New York: 1887; New York: Russell & Russell, 1955.

———. *Materials Toward a History of Witchcraft,* arranged and edited by Arthur C. Howland. 3 vols. Philadelphia: Univ. of Pennsylvania Press, 1939.

———. *Torture.* 1866. Philadelphia: Univ. of Pennsylvania Press, 1973.

Lenman, Bruce, and Geoffrey Parker. "The State, the Community, and the Criminal Law in Early Modern Europe." In *Crime and the Law,* edited by Lenman, Parker, and V. Gatrell. London, 1980.

Le Roy Ladurie, Emmanuel. *Jasmin's Witch.* Translated by B. Pearce. New York: George Braziller, 1987.

Levack, Brian P. *The Witch-Hunt in Early Modern Europe.* London and New York: Longman, 1987.

———. "Possession, Witchcraft, and the Clergy in Early Modern England." Unpublished paper.

Leventhal, Herbert. *In the Shadow of the Enlightenment: Occultism and Renaissance Science in Eighteenth-Century America.* New York: New York Univ. Press, 1976.

Lewis, I. M. *Ecstatic Religion: An Anthropological Study of Spirit Possession and Shamanism.* Baltimore: Penguin Books, 1971.

Lottes, Günther. "Popular Culture and the Early Modern State in Sixteenth-Century Germany." In Kaplan, ed., *Understanding Popular Culture.*

MacDonald, Michael. *Mystical Bedlam: Madness, Anxiety, and Healing in Seventeenth-Century England.* Cambridge: Cambridge Univ. Press, 1981.

Macfarlane, Alan. *Witchcraft in Tudor and Stuart England.* New York: Harper & Row, 1970.

Madar, Maia. "Estonia I: Werewolves and Poisoners." In Ankarloo and Henningsen, eds., *Early Modern European Witchcraft.*

Mair, Lucy. *Witchcraft.* New York: McGraw-Hill, 1969.

Mandrou, Robert. *Magistrats et sorciers en France au XVIIe siècle.* Paris: Libraire Plon, 1968.

———. *Possession et sorcellerie au XVIIe siècle: Textes inédits.* Paris: Fayard, 1979.

Martines, Lauro, ed. *Violence and Civil Disorder in Italian Cities, 1200–1500.* Berkeley: Univ. of California Press, 1972.

Marwick, Max, ed. *Witchcraft and Sorcery: Selected Readings.* 2d ed. Baltimore: Penguin Books, 1982.

Matelene, Carolyn. "Women as Witches." *International Journal of Women's Studies* 1.6 (1978): 573–87.

McGowan, Margaret M. "Pierre de Lancre's *Tableau de l'inconstance des mauvais anges et démons:* The Sabbat Sensationalized." In Anglo, ed., *The Damned Art.*

McLachlan, Hugh, and J. K. Swales. "Lord Hale, Witches, and Rape (a reply)." *British Journal of Law and Society* 5 (1978): 251–56.

———. "Witchcraft and Anti-feminism." *Scottish Journal of Sociology* 4.2 (May 1980): 141–65.

McLaren, Angus. *Reproductive Rituals: The Perception of Fertility in England from the Sixteenth to the Nineteenth Century.* London: Methuen, 1984.

Mello e Souza, Laura de. *O diablo e a terra de Santa Cruz.* Sao Paulo: Companhia as Letras, 1987.

Merchant, Carolyn. *The Death of Nature: Women, Ecology, and the Scientific Revolution.* 1980. With new preface, San Francisco: Harper & Row, 1990.

Merzbacher, Friedrich. *Die Hexenprozesse in Franken.* Munich: Verlag C. H. Beck, 1970.

Metraux, Alfred. *Voodoo in Haiti.* Translated by H. Charteris. New York: Schocken Books, 1972.

Michelet, Jules. *La Sorcière.* Paris, 1862. English translation by A. Allinson. *Satanism and Witchcraft: A Study in Medieval Superstition.* New York: Citadel Press, 1939.

Middleton, John, ed. *Magic, Witchcraft, and Curing.* Austin: Univ. of Texas Press, 1967, 1982.

Midelfort, H. C. Erik. "Heartland of the Witchcraze: Central and Northern Europe." *History Today,* February 1981, 27–31.

———. "Recent Witch Hunting Research." *The Papers of the Bibliographical Society of America* 62 (1968): 373–420.

———. "Were There Really Witches?" In *Transition and Revolution: Problems and Issues of European Renaissance and Reformation History,* edited by Robert M. Kingdon. Minneapolis: Burgess, 1974.

———. *Witch Hunting in Southwestern Germany, 1562–1684: The Social and Intellectual Foundations.* Stanford, CA: Stanford Univ. Press, 1972.

Miles, Margaret R. *Carnal Knowing: Female Nakedness and Religious Meaning in the Christian West.* Boston: Beacon Press, 1989.

Miller, Arthur. *The Crucible.* New York: Viking Penguin, 1976.

Mizruchi, Ephraim. *Regulating Society: Beguines, Bohemians, and Other Marginals.* Chicago: Univ. of Chicago Press, 1987.

Molitor, Ulric. *Des Sorcières et des devineresses.* Latin text, Cologne, 1489; French trans., Paris, 1926.

Monter, E. William. "French and Italian Witchcraft." *History Today* 30 (1980): 31–35.

———. "The Historiography of European Witchcraft: Progress and Prospects." *Journal of Interdisciplinary History* 2 (1972): 435–51.

———. "Inflation and Witchcraft: The Case of Jean Bodin." In *Action and Conviction in Early Modern Europe,* edited by T. K. Rabb and J. E. Seigel. Princeton, NJ: Princeton Univ. Press, 1969.

———. "Pedestal and Stake: Courtly Love and Witchcraft." In *Becoming Visible: Women in European History,* edited by R. Bridenthal and C. Koonz. Boston, 1977.

———. *Ritual, Myth, and Magic in Early Modern Europe.* Athens: Ohio Univ. Press, 1984.

———. "La sodomie à l'époque moderne en Suisse romande." *Annales* 29 (1974): 1023–33.

———. *Witchcraft in France and Switzerland: The Borderlands During the Reformation.* Ithaca, NY: Cornell Univ. Press, 1976.

———. "Women and the Italian Inquisitions." In Rose, ed., *Women in the Middle Ages and Renaissance.*

Monter, E. William, ed. *European Witchcraft.* New York: Random House, 1969.

Monter, E. William, and John Tedeschi. "Toward a Statistical Profile of the Italian Inquisitions, Sixteenth to Eighteenth Centuries." In Henningsen and Tedeschi, eds., *Inquisition in Early Modern Europe.*

Moore, R. I. *The Formation of a Persecuting Society: Power and Deviance in Western Europe, 950–1250.* Oxford: Basil Blackwell, 1987.

Morris, Katherine. *Sorceress or Witch? The Image of Gender in Medieval Iceland and Northern Europe.* Lanham, MD: University Press of America, 1991.

Mottu-Weber, Liliane. "Les femmes dans la vie économique de Genève." *Bulletin de la Société d'histoire et d'archéologique de Genève* 16 (1979): 381–401.

Muchembled, Robert. *Culture populaire et culture des élites dans La France moderne: XVe–XVIIIe siècles.* Paris: Flammerion, 1977. Translated by Lydia Cochrane. *Pop-*

ular Culture and Elite Culture in France, 1400–1750. Baton Rouge: Louisiana State Univ. Press, 1985.

———. *La Sorcière au village.* Paris: Éditions Juillard-Gallimard, 1979.

———. "Sorcières du Cambrèsis: L'Acculturation du monde rural aux XVIe et XVIIe siècles." In DuPont-Bouchat et al., eds., *Prophètes et sorciers dans les pays-Bas,* part 2.

———. "The Witches of the Cambrésis: The Acculturation of the World in the Sixteenth and Seventeenth Centuries." In *Religion and the People,* edited by James Obelkovich. Chapel Hill: Univ. of North Carolina Press, 1979.

Murray, Margaret. *The God of the Witches.* 2d ed. Oxford: Oxford Univ. Press, 1931, 1952.

———. *The Witch-Cult in Western Europe: A Study in Anthropology.* Oxford: Clarendon Press, 1921.

Naess, Hans Eyvind. "Norway: The Criminological Context." In Ankarloo and Henningsen, eds., *Early Modern European Witchcraft.*

Nelson, Cynthia. "Public and Private Politics: The Middle Eastern World." *American Ethnologist* 1 (1974): 551–63.

Notestein, Wallace. *A History of Witchcraft in England.* Washington, 1911; New York: Crowell, 1968.

Oesterreich, T. K. *Possession, Demoniacal and Other.* London, 1930.

O'Neil, Mary R. "Sacerdote ovvero strione: Ecclesiastical and Superstitious Remedies in Sixteenth-Century Italy." In Kaplan, ed., *Understanding Popular Culture.*

———. "Magical Healing, Love Magic and the Inquisition in Late Sixteenth-Century Modena," in Stephen Haliczer, *Inquisition and Society in Early Modern Europe* (Totowa: Barnes and Noble, 1987).

Parker, Geoffrey. "The European Witchcraze Revisited." *History Today* 30 (1980): 31–35.

———. "Some Recent Work on the Inquisition in Spain and Italy." *Journal of Modern History* 54.3 (Sept 1982): 519–32.

Parrinder, Geoffrey. *Witchcraft: European and African.* New York: Barnes & Noble, 1963. Also *Witchcraft.* Baltimore: Penguin, 1958.

Patterson, Orlando. *Slavery and Social Death.* Cambridge: Harvard Univ. Press, 1982.

Pearl, Jonathan. "Folklore and Religion in the Sixteenth and Seventeenth Centuries." *Studies in Religion* 5–6 (1975–76): 380–89.

———. "French Catholic Demonologists and Their Enemies in the Late Sixteenth and Early Seventeenth Centuries." *Church History* 52.4 (December 1983): 457–67.

Peel, Edgar, and Pat Southern. *The Trials of the Lancashire Witches: A Study of Seventeenth-Century Witchcraft,* 3d ed. Nelson, Lancashire: Hendon Publishing, 1985.

Peters, Edward. *The Magician, The Witch, and the Law.* Philadelphia: Univ. of Pennsylvania Press, 1978.

———. *Torture.* Basil Blackwell, 1985.

Pinchbeck, Ivy. *Women Workers and the Industrial Revolution 1750–1850.* 1930. London: Virago, 1981.

Pinto, Lucile B. "The Folk Practice of Gynecology and Obstetrics in the Middle Ages." *Bulletin of the History of Medicine* 47 (1973).

Pitts, John L. *Witchcraft and Devil Lore in the Channel Islands.* Guernsey, 1886.

Poliakov, Leon. *A History of Antisemitism.* 2 vols. New York: Schocken Books, 1974.

Quataert, Jean H. "The Shaping of Women's Work in Manufacturing: Guilds, Households, and the State in Central Europe, 1648–1870." *American Historical Review* 90.5 (December 1985): 1122–48.

Quinn, David Beers. *The Elizabethans and the Irish.* Ithaca, NY: Cornell Univ. Press, 1966.

Rich, Adrienne. *The Dream of a Common Language.* New York: Norton, 1978.

Riezler, Sigmund von. *Geschichte der Hexenprozesse in Bayern.* 1896. Stuttgart: Magnus-Verlag, 1983.

Ringelheim, Joan. "Women and the Holocaust: A Reconsideration of Research." *Signs* 10.4 (Summer 1985): 740–61.

Robbins, Rossell Hope. *The Encyclopedia of Witchcraft and Demonology.* New York: Dover Publications, 1981.

———. Preface and Introduction to *Catalogue of the Witchcraft Collection in Cornell University Library.* Millwood, NY: KTO Press, 1977.

Rose, Elliott. *A Razor for a Goat.* Toronto: Univ. of Toronto Press, 1962.

Rose, Mary Beth, ed. *Women in the Middle Ages and Renaissance: Literary and Historical Perspectives.* Syracuse, NY: Syracuse Univ. Press, 1986.

Rosen, Barbara, ed. *Witchcraft.* New York: Taplinger Publishing, 1972.

Rosen, George. "A Study of the Persecution of Witches in Europe as a Contribution to the Understanding of Mass Delusions and Psychic Epidemics." *Journal of Health and Human Behavior* 1 (1960): 200–11.

Ruether, Rosemary. *New Woman, New Earth: Sexist Ideologies and Human Liberation.* New York: Seabury, 1975.

Russell, Jeffrey Burton. *A History of Witchcraft: Sorcerers, Heretics, and Pagans.* London: Thames and Hudson, 1980.

———. *Lucifer: The Devil in the Middle Ages.* Ithaca, NY: Cornell Univ. Press, 1984.

———. *Witchcraft in the Middle Ages.* Secaucus, NJ: Citadel Press, 1972.

Russo, Mary. "Female Grotesques: Carnival and Theory." In de Lauretis, ed., *Feminist Studies.*

Sabean, David. *Power in the Blood: Popular Culture and Village Discourse in Early Modern Germany.* Cambridge: Cambridge Univ. Press, 1984.

Samaha, Joel. *Law and Order in Historical Perspective: The Case of Elizabethan Essex.* New York: Academic Press, 1974.

Sanday, Peggy Reeves. *Divine Hunger: Cannibalism as a Cultural System.* Cambridge: Cambridge Univ. Press, 1987.

Sanders, Ronald. *Lost Tribes and Promised Lands: The Origins of American Racism.* Boston: Little, Brown, 1978.

Scarre, Geoffrey. *Witchcraft and Magic in Sixteenth- and Seventeenth-Century Europe.* Atlantic Highlands: Humanities Press International, 1987.

Schormann, Gerhard. *Hexenprozesse in Deutschland.* Gottingen: Vandenhoeck & Ruprecht, 1981.

———. *Hexenprozesse in Nordwestdeutschland.* Hildersheim, 1977.

Scott, Joan W. "Gender: A Useful Category of Historical Analysis." *American Historical Review* 91.5 (December 1986): 1053–75.

———. *Gender and the Politics of History.* New York: Columbia Univ. Press, 1988.

Sebald, Hans. *Witchcraft: The Heritage of a Heresy.* New York: Elsevier, 1978.

Segalen, Martine. *Mari et femme dans la société paysanne.* Paris: Flammarion, 1980. Published as *Love and Power in the Peasant Family,* translated by Sarah Matthews. Chicago: Univ. of Chicago Press, 1983.

Seymour, St. John. *Irish Witchcraft and Demonology.* Dublin, 1913.

Sharpe, J. A. *Crime in Early Modern England: 1550–1750.* London: Longman, 1984.

———. "The History of Crime in Late Medieval and Early Modern England: A Review of the Field." *Social History* 7.2 (1982).

Sheffield, Carole. "Sexual Terrorism: The Social Control of Women." In *Analyzing Gender: A Handbook of Social Science Research,* edited by Beth Hess and Myra Ferree. Beverly Hills, CA: Sage Publications, 1987.

Shumaker, Wayne. *The Occult Sciences in the Renaissance: A Study of Intellectual Patterns.* Berkeley: Univ. of California Press, 1972.

Smith, Ginnie. "Thomas Tryon's Regimen for Women: Sectarian Health in the Seventeenth Century." In *The Sexual Dynamics of History,* edited by London Feminist History Group. London: Pluto Press, 1983.

Smith-Rosenberg, Carroll. *Disorderly Conduct: Visions of Gender in Victorian America.* New York: Knopf, 1985.

———. "Writing History: Language, Class, and Gender." In de Lauretis, ed., *Feminist Studies.*

Soman, Alfred. "Deviance and Criminal Justice in Western Europe, 1300–1800: An Essay in Structure." In *Criminal Justice. History: An International Annual,* London, 1980.

———. "The Parlement of Paris and the Great Witch Hunt (1565–1640)." *Sixteenth Century Journal* 9.2 (1978): 31–44.

———. "Witch Lynching at Juniville." *Natural History,* October 1986.

Starkey, Marion L. *The Devil in Massachusetts.* Garden City, NY: Doubleday, 1949, 1969.

Staub, Ervin. *The Roots of Evil: The Origins of Genocide and Other Group Violence.* New York: Cambridge Univ. Press, 1989.

Stone, Lawrence, *The Family, Sex and Marriage in England, 1500–1800.* New York: Harper & Row, 1977.

Summers, Montague. *The History of Witchcraft.* London, 1925; Secaucus, NJ: The Citadel Press, 1974.

———. *The Vampire: His Kith and Kin.* London, 1928. Reprint. New Hyde Park, NY: University Books, 1960.

Swales, J. K., and Hugh V. McLachlan. "Witchcraft and the Status of Women: A Comment." *British Journal of Sociology* 30.3 (September 1979): 349–58.

Tazbir, Janusz. *A State Without Stakes: Polish Religious Toleration in the Sixteenth and Seventeenth Centuries,* Translated by A. T. Jordan. Wydawniczy, 1967; Twayne Publishers, 1973.

Theilmann, John M. "Saintly Medicine and the Rise of Witchcraft." Paper presented at the Twenty-first International Congress of Medieval Studies, May 1986.

Thistlethwaite, Susan B. "Every Two Minutes: Battered Women and Feminist Interpretation." In *Weaving the Visions,* edited by Judith Plaskow and Carol Christ. New York: Harper & Row, 1989.

Thomas, Keith. *Religion and the Decline of Magic.* New York: Scribners, 1971.

Tilly, Charles. "Routine Conflicts and Peasant Rebellions in Seventeenth-Century France." In *Power and Protest in the Countryside,* edited by Robert P. Weller and Scott E. Guggenheim. Durham, NC: Duke Univ. Press, 1989.

Todorov, Tzvetan. *The Conquest of America: The Question of the Other.* New York: Harper & Row, 1984.

Trachtenberg, Joshua. *The Devil and the Jews: The Medieval Conception of the Jew and Its Relation to Modern Anti-Semitism.* 1943. Cleveland: World Publishing, 1961.

Trevor-Roper, H. R. *The European Witch-Craze of the Sixteenth and Seventeenth Centuries, and Other Essays.* New York: Harper Torchbooks, 1969.

Trible, Phyllis. *Texts of Terror: Literary-Feminist Readings of Biblical Narratives.* Philadelphia, PA: Fortress Press, 1984.

Ulrich, Laurel Thatcher. *Good Wives: Image and Reality in the Lives of Women in Northern New England, 1650–1750.* New York: Oxford Univ. Press, 1983.

Villette, Pierre. "La Sorcellerie dans le Nord de la France." *Mélanges de science religieuse,* 1956, 39–52, 129–56.

———. *La Sorcellerie et sa répression dans le Nord de la France.* Paris, La Pensée universelle, 1976.

Walker, Barbara G. *The Crone: Woman of Age, Wisdom, and Power.* New York: Harper & Row, 1985.

Walker, D. P. *Unclean Spirits: Possession and Exorcism in France and England in the Late Sixteenth and Early Seventeenth Centuries.* Philadelphia: Univ. of Pennsylvania Press, 1981.

Walker, Lenore E. *The Battered Woman.* New York: Harper & Row, 1979.

Walkowitz, Judith. "The Maiden Tribute of Modern Babylon." Paper presented to the Seminar on Women in Society and Culture, Columbia University.

Weisman, Richard. *Witchcraft, Magic, and Religion in Seventeenth-Century Massachusetts.* Amherst: Univ. of Massachusetts Press, 1984.

Weisser, Michael R. *Crime and Punishment in Early Modern Europe.* London: Hassocks, 1979.

———. *The Peasants of the Montes: The Roots of Rural Rebellion in Spain.* Chicago: Univ. of Chicago Press, 1976.

Wessley, Stephen. "The Thirteenth-Century Guglielmites: Salvation Through Women." In *Medieval Women,* edited by Derek Baker. Oxford: Basil Blackwell, 1978.

Wiener, Carol Z. "Sex Roles and Crime in Late Elizabethan Hertfordshire." *Journal of Social History* 8 (Summer 1975): 38–60.

Wiesner, Merry E. "Early Modern Midwifery: A Case Study." In Hanawalt, ed., *Women and Work.*

———. "Women's Defense of Their Public Role." In Rose, ed., *Women in the Middle Ages and Renaissance.*

———. *Working Women in Renaissance Germany.* New Brunswick, NJ: Rutgers Univ. Press, 1986.

Woods, William. *A Casebook of Witchcraft: Reports, Depositions, Confessions, Trials, and Executions for Witchcraft During a Period of Three Hundred Years.* New York: G. P. Putnam's Sons, 1974.

Wrightson, Keith. "Two Concepts of Order: Justices, Constables, and Jurymen in Seventeenth-Century England." In Brewer and Styles, eds., *An Ungovernable People.*

Wrightson, Keith, and David Levine. *Poverty and Piety in an English Village: Terling, 1525–1700.* New York: 1979.

Yates, Frances. *The Occult Philosophy in the Elizabethan Age.* London: Routledge and Kegan Paul, 1979.

Yoshioka, Barbara. "Woman as Witch and Preacher in Seventeenth-Century England." Unpublished dissertation, Union Theological Seminary, 1978.

Zguta, Russell. "Witchcraft Trials in Seventeenth-Century Russia." *American Historical Review* 82.5 (1977): 1187–1207.

Zilboorg, Gregory. *The Medical Man and the Witch During the Renaissance.* Baltimore: John Hopkins Univ. Press, 1935.

Index

Photo credit: Tom F. Driver

Anne Llewellyn Barstow is professor of history, retired, at the State University of New York at Old Westbury. She is the author of *Joan of Arc: Heretic, Mystic, Shaman* and *Married Priests and the Reforming Papacy*, as well as many articles.